Up the University

Up the University

Re-Creating Higher Education in America

ROBERT and JON SOLOMON

Addison-Wesley Publishing Company

Reading, Massachusetts · Menlo Park, California · New York
Don Mills, Ontario · Wokingham, England · Amsterdam · Bonn
Sydney · Singapore · Tokyo · Madrid · San Juan
Paris · Seoul · Milan · Mexico City · Taipei

Library of Congress Cataloging-in-Publication Data

Solomon, Robert C.
   Up the university : re-creating higher education in America / Robert C. and Jon Solomon.
       p. cm.
   Includes bibliographical references (p.) and index.
   ISBN 0-201-57719-4
   1. Education, Higher—United States—Aims and objectives.
   2. College teaching—United States. I. Solomon, Jon. II. Title.
LA227.4.S6 1993
378′.01′0973—dc20   92-24418
                                                           CIP

Jacket design by Richard Rossitor
Text design by Diane Levy
Set in 10½-point Stone Serif by DEKR Corporation, Woburn, MA

1 2 3 4 5 6 7 8 9-MA-9695949392
First printing, December 1992

For Kathy, Lois, and all the others
who continue to learn along with us

Contents

Preface

Falling enrollments, mounting financial pressures, diminishing public confidence, more non-traditional students and studies, pressure for new programs, questions about teaching methods and the value of the liberal arts. Our colleges are stationary, in danger of being left behind.

—From an Amherst College report on "the crisis in higher education"—*in 1827!*[1]

Quietly, and perhaps against its better judgment, the university has become the dominant social institution of American society.[2] Our colleges and universities provide the gateway to our much-celebrated upward social mobility, and half of America's graduates now go to college—a remarkable statistic that, more than any other, says something powerful about our commitment to democracy and higher education (whatever else one might say about either American democracy or higher education).[3]

The first thing to be said about the university is its enormous success. It is not a failure but one of the grandest and most promising experiments in the history of humanity. The attempt to provide "higher" education for so many people, five million students every year, is unprecedented in the history of the world. It is the success, not the failure, of the university that has created the current crisis in higher education.

But the university has become much more than just an educational institution. The university now runs the national (and international) "human resource" industry—testing, weeding out, assigning credentials to the leaders and professionals of tomorrow. It is the primary training and recruiting ground for many or most of America's athletes. It is also an entertainment center, playing host to the leading orchestras and musicians of the world, and serves as a forum for a bewildering menu of lectures, workshops, rallies, and gatherings. And of course, it is in our universities that most of the nation's military, industrial, and social research proceeds—a multibillion-dollar enterprise. The university, accordingly, has become a giant corporation, a conglomerate of interlocking industrial, developmental, and entertainment units as well as a primary institution of economic and public policy.

The problem is, where in this conglomerate are we to locate the teachers and the students? Today, as always, teachers teach and students learn. But the centrality of teaching and learning in the university is no longer obvious. College presidents now announce their "mission" not only in terms of the legacy of learning or preparation for democracy but in terms of their "contributions to the economic development of the region" and a new "competitive partnership with industry." The idea of the university as a corporation and its administration as management now passes almost without comment, leaving dangerously unanswered the question of what role, if any, students, professors, and democracy might play in this new corporate metaphor.

Teaching is not, perhaps, the world's oldest profession, but it shares with the world's oldest profession the satisfaction of a profound and ageless need that preceded any institution and continues to flourish no matter what institutional constraints are raised against it. There were teachers and students long before there were universities. But as long as teaching has been institutionalized and confined to "centers of learning"—now rather "centers of research"—it has been jeopardized by the very institutions that keep it alive. Never before have so many people wanted and gotten the chance to receive a "higher" education. But never before has the place of education been so uncertain in the university, and rarely have universities been viewed with such suspicion. Their incredible success notwithstanding, we read again and again, virtually every day, that our universities have failed us, undermined democracy, and violated the public trust.

We see no evidence for this astoundingly ignorant proposition. To be sure, there are scandals and fools, and a college education costs much more than it ought to. But as far as we can see, teaching in the university has rarely been better, and it has almost always been much worse. Professors are brighter, better trained, and work harder than ever before. The student body as well as the faculty is much more diverse in race, gender, national origin, culture, and socioeconomic class than could have been imagined just forty years ago. The complexion of the university is still, perhaps, overly pale, but millions are getting a decent education instead of the previous few fortunate thousands. Affirmative action, equal opportunity, and minority recruiting are becoming top priority in most schools.

It is true that more students are ill prepared for college than ever before—ignorant and even illiterate—but then many more students are going to college who are not from "prep schools" or even decent public schools, who have not grown up with books and intelligent conversation. It is only a remarkably shortsighted view of history that forgets that well into this century, the university was little more than a playground for the children of the rich, in which social and family connections counted for everything, and merit, hard work, and intellect counted for nothing. (Harvard started giving grades on the basis of schoolwork instead of social connections only in the 1930s.) "Having an education" once simply meant having gone to college. Now we actually expect students to learn something.

The single most important fact about university life—the one that we prize the most, the one that keeps us teaching in public schools such as Arizona and Texas instead of the more precious and prestigious private institutions in which we were originally trained—is the oft-mentioned but rarely honored principle of democracy.[4] Education should be available to everyone. We do not teach only the elite, the already well educated from the best private schools in the country. We educate kids from mediocre (and worse) public schools who grew up in homes without books, some of whom have never read a book for pleasure or out of mere curiosity, who cannot write a proper sentence, much less a coherent paragraph or a critical essay. We educate kids fresh off the farm and just out of the inner city. We educate kids who are the first in their families to even dream of college and second-generation immigrants forging for themselves an at least partially American identity.

It is no surprise, therefore, that many of them are "underprepared" for college, cannot write well, and do not know how to read (and have never heard of) Plato's dialogues. They are indeed "illiterate" in the Trivial Pursuit sense, popularized recently by E. D. Hirsch.[5] They cannot recognize names and terms already long familiar to those who have Ph.D.'s, who regale one another with stories about their students' appalling ignorance. But these same students are going to the university, and for the very best of reasons: They are curious, they are interested, and they want to find something in life that is more than just scraping along and "getting by."

It is our job to see that those ambitions are richly rewarded. If we are attempting to educate students from every walk of life and every type of milieu who have not had the advantage of an intellectual or encouraging background, we are bound to find a disturbing amount of ignorance and illiteracy. This is not a "problem" we face in higher education; it is our job. It is what we do.

Our universities are not mere shadows or better and worse imitations of Harvard.[6] Indeed, Harvard is something of a dinosaur in the American educational system today, no matter how loud its roar continues to be, no matter how famous its professors or smart and successful its students. Harvard may be "the place to be," but it is not necessarily the best place to teach and to get an education, and in any case, it is not the paradigm or the prototype of the schools attended by the vast majority of Americans.

Our state universities and community colleges represent a bold experiment concerning human nature and society. To participate in this experiment, it is not enough to be an accomplished scholar and an expert in an "area." One must, first of all, like and believe in "ordinary" people, trust their ability to be "turned on" and motivated, to learn and to transform themselves. It is not enough to seek out the especially talented, the already privileged, the future disciples who may (if they continue to pass the test) follow in your footsteps. The real challenge, sometimes slow and frustrating to be sure, is opening the eyes of students who have never been excited by an idea before, filling heads that are starved (not "empty," as one of our more elitist magazines recently put it). That is the challenge we put to ourselves in this book.

There have been many books published in the past few years aimed at the general public and the powers that be, warning of the fraud and subversion on the university campus. It is obvious that the authors just have not been there. Only a few of them are actually teachers, and most of them would not be caught dead on a merely average university campus. They report from Columbia, Harvard, Yale, Duke, and Berkeley. They shock the public with a dozen predictably outrageous comments and titles from a few wacky or misquoted English professors.[7] They note the tedious frequency of various cognates of the word *phallo-* (penis) in supposedly literate gatherings, they garner a few tired slogans from the dwindling Loony Left, and with a gratuitous diatribe against sex and rock 'n' roll, conclude that we are all in "deep doo-doo," as one of our best-educated leaders would have it. Perhaps such books sell because of the deep disdain for elitism in America, but the obvious fact is that, even in the Ivy League, higher education is no longer elitist. And as for widespread "subversion," one could shoot a machine gun down the halls of academe and never hit a true subversive.[8]

We will make no effort to counter cheap shots and such nonsense here. What we have in mind is a "report from the front," a series of suggestions and reflections on the actual state of teaching and learning in the university, a re-creation of the original purpose to which we have dedicated ourselves. "Re-creating" the university does not mean tearing the university up by its roots and starting from scratch, much less eliminating the thousands of institutions now making higher education available to more people than ever before. It does not mean returning to the old elitism. It does not mean bringing in the shock troops of public authority, reprimanding the legislature, demanding that the government take action, or looking for a university president who will be "tough."[9]

What it does mean is going back to "the idea of the university," revising our thinking about what it means to be a university, what a university should be, and what it should do.[10] That the university should be "re-created" also suggests that the university should be *fun*—a distinctively American concept, "recreational" in the best sense of that word. What we suggest in the following pages is nothing less than the opening up of the university, tearing down the walls and the ivory tower, flattening the bureaucracy, eliminating the red tape, putting an end to money grubbing, and creating a real relationship between the university and the community. Most of all, we want the university once again to put a real emphasis on education. This is not another bitter diatribe against what is happening in the universities. It is an enthusiastic program for re-creating the university so that it serves us all well, and at a price we can afford.

Acknowledgments

No book on sex, religion, or politics could be guaranteed to offend more of our friends than this rather straightforward prescription for the university. Such are the tensions of university life today. But to prevent at least some unnecessary hurt feelings and misunderstandings from people who have helped us the most, we should say that what follows is not drawn from or aimed at our two universities in particular. Indeed, many of our positive suggestions have been prompted or confirmed by current programs and policies at both Texas and Arizona, and we have tried to mention the actual successes of a variety of colleges and universities rather than simply criticizing deficiencies. If some of our criticism smarts as well, let's just say that such is our conception of good citizenship.

We owe a great many debts of gratitude, and special thanks, to Kathleen Higgins, Larry Carver, Paul Woodruff, Janet Sepasi, Roger Gathman, Ed Sharpe, Jim Vick, Bill Cunningham, J. Douglas Canfield, Ron Brown, Tom Miller, Patricia Gehle, the students in Humanities 350 and Classics 126 and the hundreds and thousands of outstanding colleagues and students we have enjoyed and with whom we have argued these issues over the years. And general thanks to *The Chronicle of Higher Education, Academe, Newsweek, The Daily Texan, The Arizona Wildcat,* various official budget and minority recruitment reports from the University of Texas and to Tom Philpot and Scott Henson, editors of *The Polemicist.* The book was inspired and given sustenance by Jane Isay and nurtured and greatly improved by Amy Gash. Our very special thanks to both of them.

Introduction

> We ought to view with suspicion the recent American addiction
> to easy and instant moral indignation. It exhibits the kind of
> need to find a whipping boy which is characteristically a symp-
> tom of a deep, but unacknowledged unease about oneself.
>
> —Alasdair MacIntyre[1]

We are university teachers. We love what we do. We would
do it if we didn't get paid for it (but don't tell our deans that). We would
continue to do it if we won the state lottery. We would keep doing it if we
had just a year to live. We do it despite the vitriolic nonsense about professors that emerges from the mouths of politicians, administrators, the
popular press, and embittered pundits within and in exile from the academy. We do it despite the accusations of eccentricity, the suspicions of our
motives or our politics, and the charge that we don't really "work" for a
living, where *work*, presumably, is defined as doing something that you
don't like to do in forty-hour time clock slots. We do it despite the notoriously verbose and pointless meetings that are the bane of the profession,
and we do it despite the college and departmental politics that make even
corporate conniving and third world intrigues scrupulous by comparison.
We do it despite the fact that the university clearly cares much more about
what is misleadingly called "research," and despite the pressure to publish
that has distorted the teaching profession and destroyed some of our best
colleagues and greatly distorted the self-conception of the university. We
do it despite the fact that the university clearly cares more about money
than it does about teaching and students. We do it because we love it, and
what we do, we have to keep reminding ourselves, is—we teach.

We teach classics and philosophy to undergraduates who have only
recently learned what these words mean, but also to aspiring graduate
students eager to learn the "tricks of the trade." We also lecture and listen
to our colleagues, write papers for conferences and professional journals,

and not the least of our accomplishments but by no means the most important, we write books, some of them laudably arcane and incomprehensible. We also attend meetings, head committees, interview job applicants, review applications, argue with our colleagues, and prepare graduate students for similarly rewarding professional careers. But what we do that really counts, the meaning of our professional lives, is to teach undergraduates, new adults with still-childish energy, enthusiasm, and a receptivity to new ideas and new possibilities that is (in most of them) only slightly dulled by experience, careerism, cynicism, and ideology.

We have been doing this for over forty years, and between us we figure that we have had thirty thousand students or more, some of them for three or four classes, many of them only once. Some students have become lifelong friends, while many never became anything more than a few features dimly viewed in a sea of faces, looks, and occasional gestures. We have taught tiny classes in elite Ivy League and eastern liberal arts schools as well as enormous classes at humongous state universities in Arizona, California, Colorado, Michigan, Minnesota, and Texas. We have taught students who are now making their way to the top of the field, and we have taught students who only began to get the point as the course was drawing to a close. But we cherish the latter as much as the former, perhaps even more, because with them we know that we have had a profound effect, whereas those bright preprofessional students probably would have excelled regardless of whether they ever fell into our web.

It is because we love teaching that we love university life. The long vacations and flexible hours are more than nice, but outsiders would be surprised how much of that so-called vacation time is filled with preparation and research, not to mention the inherent dangers of a job where one's desk and office are, so to speak, in one's head. There is no "leaving your work at the office"—or even in your briefcase—because the thoughts and the doubts and the ideas keep coming, even on the beach, in bed, in the middle of dinner, in the midst of an international crisis. We find ourselves awake at three in the morning, restructuring the class that will begin at ten that morning, or adding an introductory comment linking some current event with an insight about the Peloponnesian War. And of course, this inner life is matched and stimulated by an outer life that, at its best, is even better. The flurry of activity and ongoing events, the presence of so many interesting (as well as eccentric) people makes life rich and as varied as one wants it to be, and the very nature of the university is such that it celebrates the individual and the very special relationship between people and ideas that education alone provides.

The problem we address here is not that the university has failed but that in its spectacular success, it has lost sight of its mission. Its mission is to educate the "undergraduates,"[2] enrich their lives, prepare them for life in a democracy and a world in which good jobs are still available for the creative and the knowledgeable. University students are young and impressionable, but they are also strong willed, alert, and hungry. If they do not find their years in the university one of the most exhilarating times of their lives, it is at least in part *our* failure, despite the obvious confusions of the age, despite the shadow of responsibilities and hardships to come. University life is freedom for students to read, to argue, to explore, to get to know themselves, and if they do not, it is very likely our fault and the fault of the university. And the recipe for this freedom is a simple one: openness and opportunity. But too many of the responses to the current economic and social troubles in the university are proceeding in exactly the wrong direction: More control. More structure. More rules. More required courses. More tests. More coercion. It never seems to occur to those who want to run the university that these institutional demands are not the solution but a substantial part of the problem.

Our argument here is that we should "open up the university." The "ivory tower" is dead. What is taking its place is a community without walls in which teaching and learning are made available to everyone who is willing and wants them, whatever their age, their institutional status, their situation. Less than a quarter of the "undergraduates" in the United States are now in the traditional age range of 18–22, and less than half of those who attend college will receive a degree for their efforts. Older students are coming to school because they want to learn and explore. We think that this is a wonderful thing. Others at the university are beginning to realize, if often belatedly, that they are too young and not ready for college. The university is not an extension of high school, and it is not just a day-care center for late adolescents. It is a community of responsible adults who know why they are there and take advantage of all that the university has to offer.

What gets left out of all the discussion of rules and policies—except as a rhetorical aside—is the whole question of student *responsibility*. The more students are treated like children, the more they will act like children, as the "panty raids" of the "good old days" showed quite clearly. The "current batch of students," it seems, has forever been more rowdy, more "spoiled," and less responsible than the last generation. And though the "good old boys" might be nostalgic for those imaginary days of comparative innocence, the truth is that the only way to teach responsibility is to give responsibility. Rules and policies have their place, but the university ought to be the place where students build character and learn that sense of prudence, respect, and responsibility which makes rules and policies no longer necessary. It is not, as Hollywood depicts it, an *Animal House.*

The public portrait of the faculty is not much better. From movies like *The Nutty Professor* to the latest novel by David Lodge, the professor is portrayed as an ethereal fool, pampered by a security taken for granted, bitter about wealth and rewards withheld. To be sure, there are problems with faculty morale and attitudes, and we will address them here, but the usual attempt to "reform" the faculty has involved ignoring what we hesitantly call "the silent majority" and treating the faculty, too, as irresponsible children who have to be "kept in line." Every few years, the state representatives of one or another of our enlightened legislatures suggest a time clock for faculty, thus demonstrating more profoundly than one could imagine the appalling ignorance that would control the university. Such "discipline" not only stokes the natural resentment of someone who works a fifteen-hour day, much of it out of the office, but it shows nearly complete misunderstanding of the motives and rewards of a "job" that consists of doing what one loves, largely at one's own pace, in one's own way. To command and require is to undermine this self-stimulating motivation, for professors as for students and everyone else. Of course, there are professors and students who abuse their incredible freedom, and we want to remind them that the open door of the university also serves as an exit. We encourage them to use it.

We find it offensive and perplexing that a few of our colleagues should be so bitter and bored, driven by their own sense of failure and disillusionment to harass the students, attack their fellow professors, ridicule those who are foolish enough to be enthusiastic about what they are doing, and turn the university into a war zone. But their numbers are minuscule compared to "the silent majority" of faculty and students, and while several of the bitterest write the books and articles in the higher education gossip sheets on "what is wrong with the university," the fact of the matter is that they themselves are a symptom of what is wrong with the university. They have been closed in too long, trapped by tenure and embittered by their responsibilities or alienated from their colleagues. It is they who commonly call for the force of the law or public opinion to come down hard on the university, but the university is a community of self-sustained inspiration, mutual motivation, and respect or it is nothing. The idea that the university is and ought to be first of all an institution, structured by rules and requirements and managed by administrators and government, has made college life hell for many students and professors when it ought to be, and still often is, an earthly form of heaven.

The university is still a closed, hierarchical institution. The rhetoric may be "free market," but in practice the university is still a restrictive feudal guild. Admissions are still too restrictive and discouraging to older students in the community, for example, who are truly interested in an education, not particularly concerned with degrees, and often intimidated by the "objective" tests that sixteen-year-olds are trained to master. The professoriat is still too much like an exclusive club, despite the recent influx of many women and minorities, where a Ph.D. is required as a minimal credential and little recognition is given to nonacademic intelligence. Brilliant teachers who are not properly credentialed might be invited on occasion to give a guest lecture on campus, but they are rarely allowed to teach.

On the other hand, professors typically make too little effort, indeed resist the effort, to make what they do accessible or interesting to those outside the university—often including their own students. They are too specialized, not because some gemlike flame of an idea burns brightly in their bonnet but because they have been taught that the art of academic survival is to take total control of some tiny piece of territory. Ironically, some of the professors who are most vocal about the importance and the interests of the common people occupy the most exclusive, impenetrable corners of the university.

We need to open up the university, share our resources and our talents. And if this threatens the entrenched and protected professoriat or creates a challenge to "the integrity of the institution" and the "standards of the discipline," that is all well and good, and a long time coming.

What suffers most in the highly professional, exclusive university, oddly enough, is teaching. What has evolved from the commotion over requirements and the curriculum is now a senseless congeries of required courses that turn education into an obstacle course and keep many students from graduating in the expected four years. We may think that too much emphasis is put on degrees and credentials, but this "five-year fraud" shows all too clearly how not only the focus but the integrity of the university has blurred. The curriculum is filled with junk requirements taught by pedagogically incompetent technocrats and student assistants, and the pressure is on to add more junk to the pile.

There aren't enough good classes and there isn't enough support for good undergraduate teaching, and the reason for this is that the university has redirected its attention and resources elsewhere. The university has trained and hired too many so-called teachers who have little interest in, and perhaps even contempt for, teaching. They are taught to dislike, disdain, or at least be annoyed by students, and they confront no institutional incentives to feel otherwise. They live their own lives in pursuit of research, or in pursuit of the pursuit of research, applying for grants, adding little or nothing to either the world's fund of knowledge or their own skills. Meanwhile, more and more administrators are needed to supervise that research and administer those grants, to find more money, which they are always claiming not to have enough of, thereby adding more levels of administration to correct this situation. The university suffers from a structural deformity that threatens and undermines intellectual life and good teaching.

We have no utopian university in mind. "Re-creating the university" means working with what we've got, not imagining politically impossible arrangements, kvetching, and daydreaming. Some of our seemingly more radical suggestions—for example, the elimination of tenure—will in fact turn out to be in substance rather tame, whereas some of our more "obvious" and agreeable theses—for example, that teaching comes first— will (if actually implemented) cause a major disruption in university structure and politics.

Our main theme, which will outrage many educators, is that the primary business of the university is education. Our main targets, accordingly, are those aspects of the university that distract or detract from the importance of teaching, including the holy institution of tenure, the absurd overemphasis on what is uncritically designated as "research," and the feudal organizations that have emerged to service this absurd overemphasis, as well as the bloated and alienating power that constitutes "administration" in most colleges and universities today. Closer to the heart, some of our criticism is aimed at our fellow professors, even some of our best friends—as well as ourselves—who display attitudes of superiority or bitterness and participate in the polarizing politics that turns the campus into a battlefield and students into pawns (when, that is, students enter into consideration at all).

This is an insiders' account. It is not and does not pretend to be "objective." We are not looking down at the university from a privately endowed "think tank," nor are we raking muck as investigative reporters financed by any political group or ideology. We are not filing reports in the plush offices of some federal office building, nor are we sowing sour grapes in exile, trying to blow up a club that will not or will no longer have us as members. We are interested in improving our own lives and the lives of our students, supporters, colleagues, and community. By "opening up" the university, we are not inviting an invasion of the barbarians, as many of our colleagues fear. We are not suggesting giving any more power to the already overpowering forces of the administration and the state legislature. We want to defend the university as a community within a community, a marketplace of ideas that is nevertheless oblivious to the "market" that is distracting the university from its mission.

PART I

The Mission of the University

1 ▾ *The "Multiversity"*

What is a university? It is an educational community, a place for teaching and learning. Everything else is secondary, irrelevant, or out of place. Of course, an education includes learning about life, and life is not learned in a vacuum. And so it is essential that the life of the university be as rich and varied as possible. The university should provide a rich social life, filled with friendship, romance, and diversity. A university education should assist students in the pursuit of a career or profession. The university should be an intrinsic part of the surrounding community. And because students learn best in an enlightened learning environment, faculty research, whatever other aims it may serve, is essential to the university as well. It provides the atmosphere in which learning is inspired by example and not imposed by authority.

The problem is that these essential but still secondary features of the university have become ends in themselves. For most American high school students, acceptance into one or another university is the definitive event of their adult social lives and careers, a place to establish

lifelong friendships, enter society, find business associates, and form political alliances.[1] Not surprisingly, many students (with the blessing of
their parents) choose a university primarily on the basis of the "contacts"
it will provide or view the university primarily as a dating service. The
university has become, in the minds of many, a training center, whose
primary if not sole aim is to prepare students for a career. Doctors, lawyers, engineers, nurses, and architects are tested, trained, and accredited
or eliminated from the career path they seek to follow. It is no longer a
well-kept secret that the purpose of our best MBA programs is to act as
super–employment agencies for corporations rather than to "teach business skills" as such, which are, for the most part, learned better on the
job, in the particular context, and according to the particular demands
and expectations of a particular industry or company. The university sets
the standards, carries on the traditions, defines the quality, and excludes
the quacks, but in the pursuit of professional credentials, the idea of
education is often laid by the wayside.

So, too, the university is a training and testing ground for America's
multibillion-dollar obsession with sports. Of course, sports bring a
beneficial unity to campus life and provide an outlet for youthful enthusiasm as well as "school spirit" and a golden opportunity for a few talented young athletes. But as sports have become the most visible attribute
of a school, preprofessional sports eclipse intramural and honestly amateur sports in importance, and athletes who have utterly inadequate
training for academics are recruited with a vigor unknown to even the
country's top Merit Scholars. They are not "students" but candidates for
the pros, and many of them fail to make the grade both academically
and athletically. Enormous amounts of money are involved, and aside
from frequent charges of hypocrisy and criminality, it is obvious that, for
many athletes, the purpose of the university has nothing to do with
education.

A university cannot be a "great" university without a dynamic research
program and an industrious, productive professoriat. But much of the
research on campus today is only secondarily the pursuit of knowledge.
It is the search for status, for notoriety. Much of it is sheer junk, although
we know that everyone thinks of their own interests as utterly important
and essential to the future of the world. Or research is primarily a business, often hidden off campus and irrelevant to the education that has
already been paid for by the taxpayers and the students' tuition. Much
of the budget and resources as well as the energy of university administrators and many professors is increasingly structured around research
and devoted to the pursuit of prestigious research grants, which are said

to help finance the operation and growth of the university. The university has become a major corporation, its eye on the bottom line, its ambition to grow and grow and grow.

The American university is also an important instrument of foreign policy and international relations. In any international crisis, the television networks and cable channels are filled with faces of university professors offering explanations, suggestions, and solutions. And the campuses are filled with foreign faces and accents, the sons and daughters of refugee families from Cambodia, Vietnam, and Latin America, students from China, Iran, and India who have every intention of returning home at the end of their studies. The university is no longer a domestic or local concern. The university is, by its very nature, "politicized." Not only are courses and whole programs concerned with geopolitics, but at any given time the future leaders of more than half the nations of the world are being educated in American universities.[2] The state of the world twenty years from now is already being settled, as Churchill said of the "public" schools of England, on the playing fields and in the coffee lounges of our universities and colleges. The university, already a political entity, is then abused by professors who turn their classes into a political soapbox and the campus into a political battleground. Education gets sacrificed to ideology, and the students become pawns in the process.

"What is the task of all higher education?" To turn men into machines. "What are the means?" Man must learn to be bored.
—Friedrich Nietzsche, *Twilight of the Idols*

In the tumultuous sixties, the then vice-chancellor of the University of California at Berkeley Clark Kerr introduced the word *multiversity* to capture this complexity and confusion. Kerr used the word to refer to the gigantic conglomerates that were rapidly developing from his California universities. Buffeted by competing political and economic interests, universities were filled with tens of thousands of undergraduates who were falling into the cracks because they were no longer considered an essential substance. Universities had become giant corporations and served global corporate and political interests. Enormous amounts of money from federal grants and high-powered research dwarfed and eclipsed the more spiritual life of the university. Sports were no longer physical exercise and local entertainment but big business, and many universities were no longer mere citizens of communities but the economic backbone of them. "Multiversity" was an administrative shrug of the shoulders, an admission of defeat, an excuse for neglecting undergraduate education and reducing it to cost-benefit analysis.

It was about that time, in the midst of an unpopular and unsuccessful war, that the university came to think of itself as primarily a research institution. And it was about that time, when the students were not only more numerous but better and smarter than they had ever been, that the very role of students within the university came into question. They began to be treated as irritations and mere obstacles to the real business of the university, and consequently, they quickly learned to act like irritations and obstacles, too. Thirty years later, the problem of the university is still that education has been pushed to the back shelf. In the face of numerous competing interests, the students are neglected and even ignored by the university.[3]

> By the late nineteenth century, the advancement of knowledge through *research* had taken firm root in American higher education, and colonial college values, which emphasized teaching undergraduates, began to lose ground. . . . Indeed, the founders of Johns Hopkins University considered restricting study on that campus to the graduate level only. In the end, undergraduate education proved to be necessary, but the compromise was reluctantly made, and for many professors, class and lecture work became almost incidental.
> ——Ernest L. Boyer, *The Carnegie Report: Scholarship Reconsidered*

2 ▾ *The Role of Research*

The most obvious source of neglect of the undergraduates, and the loudly touted change in the university, is the conversion of the university into a research institution—the "research university." It is research, not education as such, that is said to have become the mission of the university. It is, our colleagues say, what they are paid for. It is, in fact, the basis of promotion and tenure. But although research may be essential to the life of the university, the nature of research is often misstated and misunderstood, and its role in the university is often oversimplified.

Spokespersons for the research university insist without hesitation that research is essential both to its educational functions and to the financing of the university. Neither of these claims is obvious. Students, on the other hand, complain that the university emphasizes research at the expense of teaching. This is a misunderstanding. Research and teaching are not incompatible and to a large extent reinforce each other. Graduate students and some advanced majors directly benefit from the fact that their teachers and supervisors are involved in the latest issues and techniques and therefore have access to the most up-to-date equipment and leading figures in the field. What is problematic is the relationship between research and most undergraduate teaching. Does a professor's research help his or her teaching, or is it a disruption or a distraction? Does the money coming into a university for research in fact support undergraduate education, or is it a drain on school finances that actually undermines education? Indeed, why should so much research go on in the university at all, when so much of it could be (and in the past has been) sponsored and carried out elsewhere, in government and corporate laboratories? Indeed, what makes a piece of research worthwhile, and why should parents and citizens of the state be required to sponsor it?

Research is not a homogeneous activity. The public and the legislature, when they think about research, immediately think of inventions and technological progress and an economic boon to the community. But research in the university also includes the participant-observer project of an anthropologist studying the music and rituals of a tribe in New Guinea, and a literary critic trying to convince her colleagues of the inherent sexism of *Moby Dick*. Research also includes the multibillion-dollar "big science" enterprises of basic particle physics and the genome project, which may or may not offer the sort of commercial rewards that one might expect, say, of a new and improved technique for refining petroleum or the development of a lighter, tougher metal for airplane parts and structures. Research includes the archival scholarship of a historian or a classicist, not to mention the work of those in the fine arts or music school whose "research" is rather a painting or a new composition. Much of what is called "research" is in fact critical and speculative, not a matter of experiment or discovery but of argumentation and polemics. These are not all the same. They require different kinds of support and have very different implications for the relation between teaching and research.

Some research projects are directly relevant to the classroom. When a scholar deepens his or her knowledge of the text being taught, it is of obvious importance to the students, even if the discussion only scratches the surface. When a scholar is deeply involved in the text, this devotion and enthusiasm are apparent to the students, who will be affected and, better, infected as well. The university does and ought to support this sort of research, as part of its teaching budget. But when research is a distraction from teaching or teaching gets viewed as a disruption of research, then the question must arise: Why is this research going on in the university rather than in a self-supporting research institute (even if it is perhaps affiliated with, but not financially supported by, the university)?

In the often-polarized debates over research—is it relevant to teaching or is it not?—what frequently gets confused is the exciting idea of research as breaking through the frontiers of the discipline and the much more mundane importance of *keeping up with the field.* As so often, the argument here is of the fallacious "either/or" variety: Either one does original research or one falls years behind and is incapable of giving the students adequate information on the subject. But good teaching may require only the enthusiasm and interest to keep reading and going to conferences and looking up the latest research. It does not demand actually breaking through the boundaries and advancing that research. Indeed, some of the most spectacular teachers we have met have been strictly of the "enthusiastically keeping up" variety. Not everyone can advance the field, and not every teacher ought to be expected to.

Anyone who minimally qualifies and continues to qualify as a university teacher should have and continue to maintain the enthusiasm and the motivation to enrich his or her field and try, in his or her own modest way, to add a comment or a detail here or there. If that is what one means by research, then requiring it of all professors is fine and dandy. But don't turn this into the mission of the university, the job of the professor, the criterion for continuance, and don't try to fool the public or the legislature by promising any great financial return on their investment in research.

The university is not "paying us to do research." The university is paying us to teach, and doing research is, in part, what we must do to master our subjects and teach well. The luxury of time that it takes to do research is one of the best "perks" of the teaching profession, but it is not, as such, our job.

3 ▾ Education Is the Mission of the University

The mission of the university is education. The primary concern of the university is to serve the students.

Our insistence on this single-minded mission of the university is not a nostalgic attempt to "set back the clock" or return to the ivory tower, nor is it to deny the legitimacy or desirability of the many other functions of the university. Our aim is to provide a focus, to call for an end to the unprincipled war over funds and prestige and the near-total neglect of the undergraduates, whose value lies these days only in their future employability and their potential generosity as alumni and alumnae.

> Everything else that goes on in a university is peripheral to the core business—the students.
> —Peter T. Flawn, *A Primer for University Presidents*

There are few college presidents who do not insist—in their speeches to parents, legislators, and graduating seniors or writing in their memoirs—that the mission of the university is educating the undergraduates. But their activities in office too often show them to be thoroughly mistaken in their implementation of this education and too often dismissive or distrustful of students.[4] In response to a Carnegie report that chastised universities for neglecting undergraduate education, the only action a number of embarrassed public university presidents could take was to create new deanships of undergraduate education, appoint faculty study groups and committees on undergraduate education, increase the number of basic education courses without allocating funds to teach them, and encourage the recruitment of more minority students without any plan for making the campus more accommodating to them. The executive director of the Alliance for Undergraduate Education claimed that "these new appointments send out an important signal that undergraduate education is important."[5] Henry Koffler, then president of the University of Arizona, publicly dismissed the Carnegie report, noting that "the emphasis should not be on teaching but on learning."[6]

In the present scheme of things, the university is clearly not administered for the benefit of undergraduate education. It has become a multimillion-dollar corporation that thrives on much, much more than receiving tuition and issuing baccalaureate degrees. In addition to tuition, the university requires hundreds of millions of state tax dollars, but this still feeds only part of its voracious appetite. The university survives only by attracting more hundreds of millions of dollars from the federal government, private donors, the local pizza parlor, *Fortune* 500 companies, and anywhere else it can. It demands one fee after another from students, solicits donations from faculty, shamelessly sells its logo on T-shirts and shot glasses. It sends fund raisers overseas to court foreign capital, markets its research products, and solicits huge sums for investment purposes. No university, it seems, ever has enough buildings, and many universities now seem to be in the real estate business.

Because the university mission has become so business oriented, the university views the students as part of its business, the purpose of which is to supply the corporations as well as the state and federal governments with a commodity—trained employees. Education, accordingly, becomes training. It is the process of providing skilled, disciplined, narrowly knowledgeable technicians, managers, and professionals. The real virtues of a university education—the time to explore one's talents and possibilities, to cultivate a rich and creative mind, to learn those things that one could not learn before and may never have time to learn again—these are sacrificed, sometimes totally, in the name of career preparation and training. Insofar as "educating the undergraduates" is what the university is all about, it is only to protect its investments and thereby serve the larger economic interests of the community.

> Universities are full of knowledge; the freshmen bring a little in, the seniors take none away. . . . the knowledge accumulates.
> ——Mark Twain

4 ▾ The University as an Investment

The argument that the university is an "investment" in the future and should make a contribution to the surrounding community sounds great to legislators and local taxpayers. But the notion of investment slips from the legitimate concern for the future of the community to the narrow, destructive emphasis on short-term returns. The real interests of the students and the community get sacrificed to an overly restricted commodity and production model. It does not allow for perhaps the single most important fact about an education, and that is how much searching and reflection, how many false starts and wrong roads, how much "waste" an education often requires. A decent education includes any number of "useless," "impractical" subjects as well as skills with some—we hope—immediate application, and that means that the very idea of the university as an investment institution is in error.

The taxpayers have a right to expect and demand that they are "getting their money's worth," but this is not to say that the university should literally "repay" their investment in the short run or, worse, have to "pay as it goes." Such thinking reduces the university to purely economic interests in which the concerns of education give way to a cost-benefit analysis of programs and policies. The result is a backward set of priorities in which those activities that have the least to do with education and undergraduates get the most attention, and those that are most central to education—ordinary writing and reading courses, languages, and literature—get the shortest schrift.

When the university turns out to be an expense instead of a profitable investment, the corporations and communities that find themselves facing shortfalls try to soak the university and its students for immediate gains, through increased student taxation and tuition, reduced academic services (e.g., fewer tutorials, remedial classes, and other aids for weak or disadvantaged students), and by way of renewed corporate favors and financial deals. By so doing, the university sacrifices its most important contribution to the future of the community, and the mission of the university is aborted.

Some would say, of course, that the idea of a "mission" for the university is simply a mistake, a matter of being one-dimensionally idealistic or, worse, simpleminded. The university serves many functions in society, as we have already pointed out, from providing the community with

> Sometimes I wish I were running a small liberal arts college, so that I could say, simply, "this is our mission." But this is the University, and we have to balance several different missions.
>
> —Ed Sharpe, president, University of Texas of the Permian Basin

thousands of jobs and high-profile sports and entertainment to doing research for future technology and preparing tomorrow's technicians, technocrats, and professors. But the matter of "mission" is something quite different. The very word *mission* implies one's primary reason for being. It is very self-conscious. It is the one activity in which failure is not just regrettable but fatal. "Investment" fails to capture that one essential activity.

Several universities in recent tight times have severely cut the number of staff and custodial workers; that is a tragedy for many of those people and an inconvenience to the remaining members of the university community, but it does not indicate the failure of the university. Universities often have losing football teams (even Texas and Arizona), but though there may be grumbling among the alumni and sarcasm among the students, no one would declare the university a failure for that reason. There are many colleges and universities that help their local communities prosper, if only by way of the thousands of students renting apartments and buying books, gas, and hamburgers, but it does not mean the university is a failure if it turns out to be something of a financial drain on a community. A large research university attracts industry and business, but the university is not a failure if it does not "pay off" or fulfill its promise to be the source of new technology or new business.

The university is a failure only if its students graduate without the competence to hold a job in their chosen area of interest, if they no longer have any desire to read a book or keep up with the news, if they have not developed the basic ability to think for themselves, to articulate and argue for what they believe in, if they cannot write a simple letter of inquiry or a letter of protest to a member of Congress or a love letter. The university is a failure if its graduates are not familiar with the names of the most influential figures in history, if they cannot date the American Civil War or find England or Indonesia on a map, if they do not know what "the red badge of courage" refers to or that Cyrano suffered the fate of his proboscis several centuries before Steve Martin coped with a similar problem in a Hollywood movie. The university is a failure if a graduate cannot converse in any language other than English, if he or she has never heard of Borges or Thucydides or Márquez or Joyce or Mishima or Mao or Mecca or Angkor Wat.

It may be a bit perverse to measure the university's mission by its conditions for failure, as it is to measure an investment solely by the potential loss. But what becomes obvious in this now-standard litany is that a distinctive mission for the university is presupposed even by those who most vehemently attack the university today. Critics may complain about ethnocentrism and male chauvinism and cultural imperialism, but you can bet that they would rather die than be found to be *ignorant* of one of the figures they are demeaning. One can legitimately attack Shakespeare in today's university community, even dismiss or ridicule him—but it is expected that in any case one will have read him.

The university is an investment in a culture, in continuity and intelligence. It is not primarily a financial investment, and the rewards are not necessarily financial either. There is more than one way for a community to become "rich."

5 ▾ *What Is an Education?*

The Japanese word for *teacher* means roughly "he who pours," but if that sounds offensive to students, we should think of some of our own metaphors of passivity, of students as empty vessels, sponges, and raw materials. But the real problem here is not only the reduction of the active, grasping mind and restless personality of the student to a static, passive receptacle. It is also the misunderstanding about what it is that gets learned.

For a few thousand years, philosophers and sages have distinguished between information, knowledge, and wisdom. Information has simply to do with input and output, with memory and recognition. One does not get an education by memorizing the Denver telephone directory, even if it is filled with useful information. It would not be much different if the book were Gray's *Anatomy* or the chronology of English kings. Nor would information become an education if one were to memorize the definitions and details of E. D. Hirsch's now-infamous list of "things that a literate person should know." Education is not just information, nor is it the processing of information, as popular as that phrase has become since the computer revolution. If it were, we would not need teachers or, for that matter, students. A good computer can hold more information—

and retrieve it more quickly—than even the most brilliant student or teacher.

Of course, a considerable amount of information is necessary just to provide the skeletal framework within which further research and understanding can take place. But information alone does not provide understanding nor carry with it instructions for its use or about its significance. It is knowing how to handle information and what to do with it to understand the world and oneself that counts as an education. "Just the facts" may have been good enough for Sergeant Joe Friday, but it is not good enough for us. We do not want students to learn just facts; we want them to acquire knowledge as well.

Students are not information processors, although information and its digestion are, of course, part of the educational process. They are, first of all, seekers after meaning. They want to be excited by ideas. They want something that they can use, or something that intrigues them, something that answers questions, including the questions that a talented teacher has only recently planted in their minds. Students, unlike computers, require motivation. Knowledge, ultimately, is that motivation. Knowledge is not a discipline but a passion. In order to succeed, knowledge acquires what discipline it requires. Allan Bloom was right, although most of his critics simply ignored this part of his message, when he compared education to an act of love (*eros*). He was returning to what was the very best in the ancient Platonic model of education—the education and inspiration of souls and not merely the transmission of information.[7]

But education is not primarily concerned with knowledge either. Here we have to disagree with John Searle, who identifies the university as a "knowledge institution."[8] To be sure, it is that, but it is something more besides. Knowledge is still too impersonal, too specialized, just as the idea of the professor as an "expert" is too narrow to explain his or her importance to the education of a student. Education is also an enriching, a deepening of the personality, a stimulated curiosity, and a certain love, even reverence, for learning. What the university does in its dealings with particularly impressionable and vulnerable eighteen-year-olds and older students is to open up their minds. That is not, as the current insult has it, to let their brains fall out. It is rather to give them the freedom and the knowledge to gain wisdom. That presupposes a great deal of information and curiosity, and it requires a great deal of knowledge and its accompanying skills. But we all know how information can eclipse common sense and how knowledge can lead to great pretense and foolishness. Wisdom, on the other hand, is the passion for living well.

> Without virtue, without the education of the heart, expertise and ambition easily become demonic. How can society survive if education does not attend to those qualities it requires for its perpetuation?
>
> ——James T. Lancy, president, Emory University, "The education of the heart"

Wisdom is, in modern terms, having one's priorities straight. Young professionals fresh out of college work seventy-hour weeks in order to afford a Porsche, forgetting about the virtually costless pleasures of a good book or a deep conversation. With a little wisdom, the smart ones will see their way through it, and the point of an education is to show them the way. A wise friend once said that the most important decision a person ever makes in this society is how *little* money one needs to live on. The wisdom behind that homey bit of advice was, of course, that money is a mere means, and if you do not understand what it is you really want, the means may readily eclipse the end. It has also been said that "You can never get enough of what you didn't really want in the first place," and this seems to be all too true of a great many people in our society. Wisdom is knowing what one wants, what is important, what is really worth working and living for, and why. Wisdom means understanding oneself and other people, having a deep appreciation of emotions and the calamities that can befall a human being. One cannot be both insensitive and wise.

One of the most important sources of wisdom can be found in the professor who actually exemplifies wisdom as well as teaches it. Very few people actually "have" wisdom; even Socrates insisted he was just in love with and in search of it. But in the love of teaching and learning, in that rare satisfaction with life, the professor has always been a potentially inspiring figure for those who seek something more than the fads and fallacies of our consumer society.

As for the students, growing up, acquiring wisdom, and "finding oneself," as the expression goes, are essential to university life even if they seem like a continuation of adolescence and irresponsibility. (For some graduate students and professors, the continuation of irresponsibility seems to be a lifelong project.) But the idea of growing up, corralled into its proper university context, is an important supplement to the usual too-restricted emphasis on the passing down of information and the acquisition of knowledge. Great literature, for example, is not just a source of knowledge, much less a source of information, and philosophy is not just protolegal training in argumentative techniques. The classics are not just a vocabulary lesson in preparation for the more arcane jargon of medicine and the law. These subjects and the rest of the world "humanities" are profound mirrors of the soul, the source of the most basic understanding of ourselves. They may provide only minimal information and little by way of knowledge as such. But they are the source of wisdom, which for every student, no matter what his or her career or professional objectives, is the ultimate goal of a university education.

For the students, then, the most important prerequisite for higher education is positive motivation, the right kind of attitude. This is much more important than the usual "requirements" for college entry—professional ambitions, higher-than-average SAT scores, and an impressive grade point average. The ideal student is one who really wants to learn, who has a thirst for knowledge and a desire for wisdom, no matter what his or her IQ, test-taking ability, or accomplishments in high school. What good is a 1300 SAT if a student is bored and only wants to sit in the frat house and drink beer? Admissions officers take note, but there is no way to quantify or test such attitudes with computer-graded examinations.

And as for the faculty, teaching should be challenging and inspiring, even (dare we say it again?)—*fun*. For what we teach is not "the facts," nor do we just impart knowledge or display our own wisdom. What we do is inspire wisdom in our students to learn and keep on learning.

6 ▾ *Democracy: The Great Experiment*

What makes university teaching today so challenging and exciting is that we as a nation are attempting a noble experiment of enormous importance, the "higher" education of almost half the population. European aristocrats scoff at the attempt; most countries of the world could not even begin to afford it and, in any case, would not tolerate the threat to their various hierarchical, feudal, and religious traditions. Few societies have ever made the effort to spread the skills and wisdom of its cultures to as many people and as large a proportion of the population as we have.

> Let us begin with a simple proposition: what democracy requires is public debate, not information. Of course it needs information too, but the kind of information it needs can be generated only by vigorous popular debate. We do not know what we need to ask until we ask the right questions.
> —Christopher Lasch, "The lost art of argument"

Of course, the experiment has its flaws, and it sometimes seems as if we have bitten off more than we can chew. It would be much easier to reduce our system of higher education to a few elite schools funded by the wealthy for their own children and filled with faculty who would pamper the students with wisdom from Plato and puff up their already elevated sense of their own superiority and privilege.

But this is not the American way, and we no longer tolerate such unabashed elitism in the name of higher education. The alternative is not, as we so often hear, the "leveling" (or "dumbing down") system of egalitarian mediocrity (mediocracy) in which the best minds are wasted and all resources go toward improving ever so slightly the most hopeless students among us.[9] Nor is our democracy primarily a matter of rigorous competition within which even the poorest students can eventually "prove" themselves. The university is not a race or a competitive sporting event but an opportunity. It offers a luxury once reserved for the idle rich to anyone who is ready to take advantage of it.

What is so beautiful about our system of higher education—as opposed, for instance, to the still-closed systems of Japan and Europe—is that there are so many institutions and so many levels of learning. Virtually everyone who wishes to be a student can find his or her place and intellectual identity. Most students do not aspire or cannot afford to be at Harvard or Haverford or Mount Holyoke, but that does not mean that their education is any less important to them or to us.

In some parts of the country, a student can attend an excellent state university for a thousand dollars tuition a year. In a good honors program or with a sufficient amount of initiative, he or she can get an education as superb as that available anywhere, including the "best" schools in the country. Our problem is that we fail to distinguish two distinct meanings of *elite*. Originally, the word referred to the "aristocracy"—"rule by the best." But this was turned into a cruel, self-serving tautology—namely, the best are those who rule. *Elitism* thus came to refer to privilege rather than excellence. Traditionally, American universities were instruments of privilege. Today the watchword is excellence, and this is the very opposite of inherited or unearned privilege.

It is no longer true that one has to have a privileged institution to have excellence in education. Some of the best-educated students we have ever met have come from financially strapped, so-called third-rate colleges with a couple of dedicated teachers. And need we say that some of the worst-educated students we have ever suffered have come from the "best" schools, where they never talked to a teacher and did not take even the most minimal advantage of the opportunities available to them. Elitism means encouraging the best, not extending privileges to those who do not deserve them.

Democracy in education cannot and should not be taken for granted. It has not always been a part of American life, and it is continually threatened by public policies, by parents, and by elite institutions and professors who insist on retaining the fantasy that there is something natural if not God-given about the right to educational privilege rather than the right to an education. The origins of the democratic university are very recent, dating to the institution of land-grant colleges at the end of the last century, the "liberation" of women, and the GI Bill that followed World War II. (The purpose of the GI Bill, however, was not to spread knowledge and learning but to keep returning soldiers out of the already-tight job market. There are many voices today that still suggest that the main importance of the university is to keep kids off the streets.)

In central Texas, recent poll: 94% believe it is important for their young people to go to college. 71% thought a college education helpful in leading an enriched and happier life. 64% thought that a college education would make a person a better citizen.
——Harte-Hanks Communications

Whatever our elite Founding Fathers may have thought about the importance of a good education for "the pursuit of happiness," they made few allowances for general education, much less for "higher education." The great universities they supported—Harvard and the University of Virginia, for example—were hardly "equal opportunity" educators. Harvard has become a "meritocracy" in which students are graded on the basis of their efforts only in the lifetime of some professors still teaching there, an embarrassing bit of history. Twenty years from now, it will be equally embarrassing to see how many potentially great universities sold their souls (for a remarkably small price) to local developers, aspiring politicians, and fast-buck industries.

The health of the economy is important, but the health of the economy in a democracy does not depend on the training of a robotlike army of industrial ignoramuses. The health of the economy depends on the health of democracy, and it is the mission of the university to teach the meaning of democracy—that is, critical thinking and a sense of political responsibility combined with a healthy skepticism. There is no better "career preparation" than learning to participate in this democratic marketplace of ideas.

PART II

"The Marketplace of Ideas"

7 ▾ *Money and Metaphors*

> Our concepts structure what we perceive, how we get around the world, and how we relate to other people.
>
> —George Lakoff and Mark Johnson, *Metaphors We Live By*

The concepts through which the university is defined and the metaphors through which it is perceived inevitably reflect the larger culture within which it is situated. The "ivory tower" metaphor was appropriate for the medieval university, with its religious virtues of devotion, fidelity, and pure-mindedness. During the Renaissance, as a secularized society became entranced with the classics, the universities became more like museums, with scholars collecting and preserving old pagan manuscripts, studying them, and sometimes translating them into the contemporary idiom. In the nineteenth century, as Europe asserted its superiority, the university became one of the instruments of that superiority, celebrating and exaggerating the virtues of "European" civilization. As the world's wealthiest civilizations converged in the international marketplace, so too, there came to be a much-celebrated "marketplace of ideas," a place where ideas, as well as money and goods, could be negotiated, examined, and exchanged. Today in America we live in a capital-intensive, consumer-driven, "postindustrial" corporate society. Thus it should not be surprising to find that our giant universities pride themselves on being well-managed, multimillion-dollar corporations.

Behind the rhetoric of free enterprise and the marketplace, the university is an inherently conservative institution that retains its medieval roots. The university is still a feudal institution. Feudalism has its virtues as well as its obvious vices, however. As an isolated, closed, inegalitarian system, entrenched in tradition and inherited privileges, we reject it. But the fact that the feudal university is self-consciously old-fashioned and in that sense not so much conservative as self-contained, aloof from the financial pressures of the marketplace, has always seemed to us to be something of a virtue. It tends to free the university from the political fashions of the day, however much these might be discussed in classes and in the halls.

The contemporary self-image of the university, however, is anything but feudal. It is rip-roaringly twentieth century. The old "ivory tower" imagery has been relegated to the museum of outmoded metaphors, and the language of economics has come tumbling in—and with it previously unimaginable money from corporations, business, and government. "Free enterprise" has become the metaphor of choice, although it was not at all apparent what was freedom for whom or to do what. Indeed, the "enterprise" in question appeared to exclude rather than include what would seem to be the central freedom—the freedom to teach and to think without concern for practical and material consequences. The "marketplace of ideas" became a market for competing corporations, national defense contractors, entrepreneurial professors, and profit-seeking presidents to turn the already rich university into a money-making machine.

Free enterprise signaled a new competitive spirit, and professors started selling their services to the highest bidder. There had always been an outside market for a few ambitious or brilliant professors, but this was rarely discussed in polite academic company. Most academics trained and stayed in their professional guilds and depended on the small network of like-minded senior professors to find them a job. Equal employment opportunity laws may have put an end to that practice, or rather, they may have driven it underground, but academic life has in any case turned from the guild to the market mentality in only two decades. Professors are now for sale.

In the new "marketplace of ideas," economics determines whether or not an idea or a hypothesis will be investigated. Economics determines how much an idea is worth and whether or not a program will be continued. Consequently, economics controls the flow and realization of ideas as well as the language, the self-image, and the administration of the university. Entrepreneurship becomes the new professional virtue, and the best departments and programs are those that "pay for themselves." "Hustling" is an academic virtue and not, as it was only a decade or so ago, a matter of "selling out."

The dean's favorites are those who bring in grants from outside sources and start "programs" financed by foundations or philanthropists. Presidents lust after new multimillion-dollar buildings, vice-presidents get promoted on the basis of a six- or seven-figure gift or two. Administrators, professors, and staff—and consequently the students—spend much of their time chasing money. As Gordon Gekko proclaimed in *Wall Street,* "Greed is good." In the university as well as on Wall Street, money talks, but it does not teach, and it shows increasingly little patience for the inefficiency and intangibilities of education.

8 ▾ *Education and Free Enterprise*

The idea of the "marketplace of ideas," an intellectual bazaar where competing ideas, theories, and interpretations confront one another and get worked out is an inspiring, invigorating notion, and we want to accept it as the central metaphor of our approach in this book. But the marketplace of ideas like many other markets has been too restricted, too hostile to new entrants, and too easily manipulated for purposes that have nothing to do with ideas. The market metaphor has been used to defend the corporate image of the university, and it has been used to justify all sorts of behaviors that undermine the mission of the university. The truth is that people and projects as well as ideas compete for the highest bidder. The market is, above all, competitive, and it is not always the university, much less the students or the public or for that matter the best idea, that wins. The concept of the "marketplace of ideas" is an inspiring metaphor, but it is much abused.

The students do not seem to have much of a place in this marketplace of ideas. They are the vessels in which these ideas are stored and transported. Or it is sometimes said that the university is a factory, in which students are the raw material, educated graduates and research are the products, and efficiency in production the test of success or failure. Or the university is a service corporation, selling instruction, certification, and credentials to consumers (the students and their parents), with customer satisfaction and the smoothness of the path to a degree being the measures of success or failure. Or the university is a training institute for the employees of our corporations or, perhaps, an employment center, a way station on the road to high salaries.

According to any of these conceptions, the students are subject to the law of supply and demand, but it is not clear that their demands, much less their needs, are in turn taken into account. After all, there is no profit in satisfying the students. It is quantity that counts—whether it be the size of the endowment, the number and size of government grants coming in, the amount of tuition collected, the number of Merit Scholars or average SAT scores, the number of degrees granted, or the "quality" of education, measured by such tangibles as the ratio of students to teachers.[1]

As for the professors, the market mentality is advantageous only for a very few. It rewards fame rather than accomplishment, and it tends to distort "the market" by overemphasizing the importance of a few top professors and neglecting those who do most of the work. It engenders envy and resentment. When a new "hot shot" enters the department at a salary ten thousand dollars higher than colleagues who have a few years' seniority, the results can be poisonous. Professors who were otherwise perfectly happy and devoted to their institutions are forced out on the market to prove their "worth," realizing their only chance to get a raise is to receive an offer from another institution. Their only aim, of course, is to get their home institution to "appreciate them." But to do so, they commit a kind of fraud, distract themselves from their work, throw the faculty and administration of some other institution into the six-month paperwork frenzy that accompanies all tenure hiring. Thus the marketplace disrupts university life, not to mention family life, and encourages envy, fraud, and waste.

Even worse, the disparity between those departments and colleges for which the market is strictly limited—most of the humanities, for example—and those that must compete for faculty in the larger domain of business and industry can be enormous. There is no reason why an assistant professor of accounting or surgery or torts should make two or three times more than an assistant professor of German. There is no reason why a full professor should make three or four times as much as a secretary who has served the department for years. There is absolutely no excuse for all those administrators who make six-figure salaries, let alone football coaches who, even after being fired as coach, get paid over a hundred thousand taxpayer dollars a year just to live out their contracts.

Of course, all these injustices are glibly defended by appeal to "the market." But arguments about "the market" are as fraudulent in academia as they are in many areas of the corporate world. Chairpersons of *Fortune* 500 companies are not paid several million dollars because no one equally competent would do the job for less. The chairpersons of the top companies in Tokyo do it for about 70 percent less.

There is no good reason why university administrators are paid so much while irreplaceable staff are paid so little. University life is a life of love. If we were to equalize salaries and end the petty competition, then perhaps more professors would just pay attention to what they are supposed to be doing, and administrators would stop thinking of themselves as corporate leaders. To the argument that no one qualified would be a college president or dean or senior professor for less money and perks, we simply respond, "Why don't we try it and see?"

> **The crucial point is that many human needs cannot get themselves expressed adequately as market demands. When [former University of California chancellor Clark] Kerr speaks repeatedly of the multiversity's responsiveness to national *needs*, he is describing nothing more than its tendency to adjust itself to effective *demand* in the form of government grants, scholarship programs, corporate and alumni underwriting, and so forth.**
>
> **—Robert Paul Wolff, *The Ideal of the University***

The heart of the entrepreneurial university is research. Research not only promises to pay for itself and pay for much else besides; it also promises enormous dividends in the future and opens up lucrative opportunities with the business world, not to mention the military. The research that is most likely to be funded is commercially aimed, technological research, not the search-in-the-dark research of the basic sciences. But even the most "targeted research" requires more fundamental exploration in the basic sciences and exploration that is motivated by "inspiration," "curiosity," and "the search for knowledge" rather than the entrepreneurial market motive. It may pay off, but it very well may not, and so the entrepreneurial model makes administrators very uncomfortable with basic research, and they have to justify it in the stretched-thin hopes that, "in the long term," it will show practical application. But what happens to the integrity of the university when lying and false promises become the preconditions of research and its increasingly fragile support?

If we really want to talk about education and free enterprise, the first thing to be said is that the vitality of democratic capitalism requires something more than entrepreneurship and efficiency in the university. It requires an educated work force that can react to a fast-changing environment and is ready and willing to articulate its opinions. It requires managers who know how to work with people as well as solve routine problems. It requires executives who can see beyond the quarterly reports and the demands of the current stockholders. A free market requires free and educated people.

9 ▾ The University Is Not a Corporation

The basic unit of economic competition today is the corporation, the megaorganization that requires professional management and a keen eye for finances and the bottom line. But the university is not a corporation.

Not only is the university not driven by the "bottom line" (most good corporations are not either), but the corporate mentality infects the university administration in more insidious ways. Instead of viewing themselves as fellow academics in for a life of learning, administrators who are hired for four-year terms come under intense scrutiny within a few months after entering office. The temptation to *do something,* to introduce new programs and policies or attract new donors, is overwhelming. All too often a new administrator will suggest some half-baked radical change in university structure or the undergraduate curriculum before he or she is even familiar with the new environment and then leave for the next assignment just when the established order is thoroughly disrupted, the faculty polarized while the new suggestions are still in limbo. Whatever else it may be, the university is an established community with deep roots, a long history, a long-term outlook, and a resistance to short-term solutions. Insofar as the modern corporation violates these prudential concerns, it is no model for the university.

The best corporations, of course, are those that are focused on and devoted to the long term. But there are other reasons to resist the corporate metaphor. The corporate metaphor shifts all of the attention and much too much of the resources of the university "upstairs," to the administration, now self-conceived as "management." We have all seen the extravagant abuses in corporate life as CEOs receive multimillion-dollar salaries and bonuses while their companies are failing and they are closing plants and laying off workers. Following that same gruesome practice, the highest-paid university administrators now make salaries unimaginable to most of the faculty, with perks (including a free half-million-dollar house) that increase it several times more while laying off instructors and staff who are directly responsible for undergraduate education.

Administrators come to think of themselves as the university, just as corporate management has come to think of itself as the corporation. Consequently, the faculty are reduced to hired staff, a status that rightly offends their sense of themselves as dedicated teachers, scholars, and scientists. Students are reduced to—what? Raw materials or ignorant consumers, and all too often they become merely an excuse for the legislature to keep the "company" going.

> **God bless the corporation and bugger the individual.**
> ——John le Carré, *Russia House*

Moreover, in the shadow of the corporate metaphor, the university is now making some of the same terrible mistakes that corporations have been making, and possibly at greater cost to itself: an overconcern with finances as opposed to substance and real productivity. An indifference to or disdain for employees that results in massive insecurity and resentment, "poor faculty morale." Costly acquisitions and unfriendly mergers in the name of the "bigger is better" philosophy. Many universities, like some of our largest and once most successful corporations, have overextended themselves, gone into debt unnecessarily, and gotten into ventures they never should have undertaken. It was all the rage a few years ago, for example, for universities to go into the real estate development game, and many of them got stuck when the crash came in the late eighties. Ambitious research projects and the buildings that house them have become white elephants—expensive to feed and without any redeeming pachydermatous charm.

Universities, like some corporations, have spun off their most profitable divisions, putting them into the hands of those who are quite indifferent to or unsympathetic with the aims of education, and too often, universities, like newly merged corporations, have insisted on keeping the unhappy halves of a hostile merger together, with all the consequences of a bad marriage. Professional schools now sit side by side and fight for funds with liberal arts colleges; religious institutions hungering to be big-time universities now find themselves replaying the fight over the separation of church and state within their walls, and on a smaller scale, English departments across the nation are turned into war zones as more and more disparate assignments are forced into a supposedly single but unstable amalgam.

It is no secret that corporate America is going through a traumatic restructuring these days. By their own admission, most corporations are top-heavy, overmanaged, cumbersome, and uncreative. So why are our universities, which not long ago provided the most obvious and the best alternative to corporate life, now so enamored of their already archaic structure?

10 ▾ The Virtues of the University: Waste and Anarchy

In theory, the corporation manifests the virtue of efficiency. In fact, most corporations represent an enormous amount of waste, duplicated functions, excessive executive salaries, poor and complicated communications, and much too much paperwork. But what the corporate world cannot possibly understand, much less "manage," about the university is what in the workaday world would be considered leisure time and just plain waste. Students "waste" their time reading books and talking and variously wallowing in their postadolescent travails. Teachers "waste" their time giving individual attention to students when they could just as easily hold a lecture for thousands in the university entertainment center. The faculty has as its profession a life of "wasted" time reading and poking around, waiting for ideas to come to them. Researchers "waste" an enormous amount of time pursuing the wrong hypothesis and looking down the wrong path for answers.

If one wants efficiency and time clock accountability, one could not find a more formidable time manager's nightmare than the university. But to eliminate such "waste" would be to eliminate scholarship and serious study, intellectual perspective, criticism and controversy, the best teaching, and almost all promising research. Indeed, when the best management theorists talk about innovation in the corporation, their primary message is "Cultivate chaos."[2] The university should not be more like the corporation, and at least in its R&D department, the corporation would do well to be more like the university.

So, too, the single most important political feature of the university is its anarchy. A university of any size may need the careful organization that goes into the curriculum and scheduling. But the process of teaching and learning presupposes sufficient dedication from the outset that external controls are not needed and only get in the way. Just as the ever-watching eyes of top management often make it difficult for corporate employees to be creative or innovative, even when that is what they are told to do, the scrutiny of the university administration and the tenure system make it extremely difficult for college professors to be creative or for that matter even to do what they are supposed to do.

> Universities are partly to blame for claiming to do what they cannot do. Whether they can be defended in any way in a manner which will satisfy our sophists and calculators, without making such false claims, is another matter.
> —Michael Oakeshott

Just as the stockholders, who may know little about the company, sometimes make it difficult to do what is best for the employees and the community, the taxpayers, legislators, grant-giving institutions, and corporate sponsors of the university, in their concern for the well-being of the institution, may well make it difficult for the best administrators, faculty, and students to do what is best for the university. In the name of efficiency and accountability, it is all too tempting to enforce guidelines and cost-accounting measures, to insist that faculty punch time clocks on campus, and that students be forced to take what is good for them. But what makes the university work is its freedom, the open-ended possibilities for discussion and exploration. The American corporation is far too hierarchical and authoritarian, a no longer healthy residue of the military mode of organization that fell quite naturally in place after the two world wars. The best management gurus are predicting and promoting an end to that authoritarianism, so it is ironic that it is becoming so fashionable in some of the best universities.

11 ▾ *Management Mania*

> Management is the organ, the life-giving, acting, dynamic organ
> of the institution it manages. . . . Without management there
> would be only a mob rather than an institution.
>
> —Peter Drucker, *Management*

One of the prominent themes of the much-touted "managerial revolution," announced by management guru Peter Drucker two decades ago, was the idea that management was a heroic profession, the *sine qua non* of success for any organization, whether enormous or minuscule, private or public, a corporation, a hospital, or the university. In the minds of the administration and the legislators who supported them, the answer to the problems of the university was at hand. What the university needed was management. Administrators would be managers.

A corollary of the management revolution was the idea that *a good manager can manage anything.* It is not surprising, then, that many university administrators are no longer professors or ex-deans but former city managers, state bureaucrats, up-and-coming politicians, and semi-retired or would-be corporate executives. And it is not surprising that, as conscientious managers, their focus and interests are on the budget, cost containment, new sources of revenue, the bottom line, and minimizing expensive and distracting campus debates and disturbances. Education as such does not fit easily into their program, and many of them even admit it is none of their business. A manager's job is to manage, and the substance of what is managed is of no special importance.

Consequently, education has to find its own way through the interstices of the bureaucracy and the trickle-down resources of the research budget. Indeed, this is how many faculty and the best students have come to see themselves, as subversives who teach and learn interesting material *in spite of* the university structure. Teachers are paid for being warm bodies in the classroom, pouring as much information as possible into the students, and preparing them for jobs. Giving good lectures or running exciting discussion sections is, in effect, something they do as an extra, above and beyond the call of duty. Actually learning and getting excited about the material, instead of simply memorizing it for the exam, is viewed by most students as something of an extravagance, not part of but in spite of what is expected of them. Meanwhile, the managers manage the institution, some of them all but indifferent to whether it is a university or a hospital or a sewage treatment facility (which similarly takes crude matter and turns it into usable commodities).

To point this out with some slight sarcasm is not to deny that every institution including the university needs competent management and that at least some of that management is concerned with high finance. But the question is whether these managers should be allowed to be indifferent to the mission of the university, aloof from and superior to the students and faculty.

The best university administrators make it a central point of their job to meet regularly with faculty and students, and though one might wonder whether they should expect to or do get candid reports, the gesture is of much more than symbolic importance. On the other hand, there are too many administrators who make it a point *not* to meet with faculty or students. They are understandably wary of being asked for favors or being bombarded with complaints, but the result is only predictable ignorance of and even hostility toward the interests of students and faculty. The feelings become mutual, of course, and so the worst suspicions are confirmed, and accordingly, the distance is increased.

One need be no radical to complain that the university has been corrupted by big money. Too much money, like too much power, eventually breeds corruption, but first it breeds management. When the mission of the university shifts from education to financial management, however, the result is apparent in the headlines. Stanford University confesses to massive fraud in its use of research funds, and prominent university scientists prostitute themselves to work on the "Strategic Defense Initiative," the biggest, most fraudulent research boondoggle in history, whose scientific foundation is a presidential fantasy based on *Star Wars*. They know that the project is impossible, but where else can they get so much money for their work? And besides, "If I don't take it, someone else will."[3]

According to the management mentality, it is consensus, not debate, that indicates a healthy corporate atmosphere. But the university is all about controversy, not closure, and the stifling of debate in favor of efficiency is almost always a mistake. Of course, this makes it extremely difficult to get anything done in the university, but this is probably just as well. Single-minded programs to reform the curriculum or improve the faculty rarely do either and typically damage both. But managers insist on managing, even if they thereby destroy the very institution they have been hired to help.

12 ▾ *Evaluation Frenzy*

Administrators like to have a bottom line, a way of keeping score. The size of the budget, the size of the endowment ("Ours is bigger than yours"), the amount of alumni contributions and research income are often tantalizing measures of competition and quality. But universities also boast about their number of Merit Scholars, their students' average SAT scores, their teacher/student ratios, and their number of Nobel Prize winners. (Only the Nobel really seems to count. Pulitzer and more regional and area-specific book prizes are of merely local significance.)

Every year there is a new ranking, by a congeries of college presidents or one or another popular news magazine, of the best universities, the best graduate schools, the best undergraduate programs, not to mention the weekly rankings of the best football and basketball teams. But the quantification of the university, or what we call evaluation frenzy, has reached pathological proportions. These measurements are no longer mere signs or symptoms of health or trouble in the university but have become themselves the criteria for success and failure and the main determinant of educational policy.

If you give economists a question about the well-being of a people, they will predictably give you an answer in terms of financial prosperity. Push the point and they will admit that economists cannot really measure "well-being," so you will have to settle for the finances, which are easy to measure and compare in dollar amounts. So, too, ask administrators about the freshman class and you will hear about college entrance exam scores, percentiles of graduating classes, and the statistical breakdown indicating increasing cultural diversity. This is understandable, perhaps, but it hardly answers the question. What one wants to know is what these students want out of college and out of life, how they see themselves, who they are as individuals, and whether they are ready for the university.

So, too, assistant professors joke routinely about "another line on the résumé," knowing full well that this is not a joke but indeed another weight on the measurement scale. Associate deans count citations as evidence of "influence" without bothering to read or evaluate the books or articles cited, and professors accordingly amass publications without concern for their ultimate merit, contribution, or readability. It is quantity that counts. Nothing else can be objectively measured.

Institutions need feedback, and there is good reason to compare universities, if only so that prospective students can make an informed choice among the many alternatives and so that universities can improve themselves. But when the measurements become ends in themselves, education is bound to suffer. The recent national mania for testing will redirect teaching to focus on passing the tests. But whether tests accurately measure accomplishment in a course is a dubious proposition at best, and whether general "aptitude" tests actually measure anything like potential for getting a good education is more dubious still. Moreover, there is a self-fulfilling aspect to this process—namely, that as more and more of college life is dominated by tests, success in college life will indeed be tested and predicted by tests. If the SAT is in fact an accurate measure of success in college, then we ought to condemn the state of college education rather than applaud the tests.

No statistical evaluation procedure can adequately evaluate the quality of undergraduate education at the university. The number of Nobel Prize winners has notoriously little to do with the quality of undergraduate education, as the riots in Berkeley made so clear thirty years ago. The teacher/student ratio says little about the dedication of the instructor, not to mention just how the courses are taught and what is taught in them. The test-taking ability of an undergraduate body has little to do with their attitude toward education, except where low test scores prematurely discourage some students. And those financial comparisons—the size of the endowment, alumni contributions, and the number of research grants—have nothing to do with undergraduate teaching either. The proper measurement of the quality of education is a happy, productive life full of learning and the love of learning, the enjoyment of books, and a joy in ideas and lively conversations. Who really cares about how one university "stacks up" against the others or how a student might do on some arbitrary test or two?

Testing tyrants have come to run the university, ultimately (with legislative backing) garnering more power than the president. One of our best freshman honors students, who made the mistake of running afoul of the state-legislated testing mafia, was thrown out of school for failing to take a test—a test whose stated purpose was to diagnose learning problems before the student entered college. The president of the university was powerless to intervene. But it is an apt illustration of what Hoffman has called "the tyranny of testing," which governs and subverts not only the classroom but the university as well.[4] Some of the fanciest offices at the University of Texas belong to the testers. One wonders how well that money could have been spent training teachers instead.

Since university administrators cannot give concrete figures on how their institution is doing, and if prospective students cannot be fairly preselected for their abilities and attitudes, undergraduate students should be admitted to the university on a trial basis. Let them prove themselves. Why should they have to do so beforehand? And if the university is really concerned with education rather than running a horse race, let's stop the barrage of testing and grading as well. Indeed, it is also time to re-examine the most sanctified measure of a university education—the credential or "degree."

A bachelor's degree today means little more than a high school diploma did thirty years ago, and Ph.D.'s are routinely handed out like military ribbons in a bully campaign. Why should the whole apparatus of the educational community be organized toward the attainment of what is ultimately a meaningless piece of parchment? Frank Baum had it right in *The Wizard of Oz* when he provided the straw man with a diploma instead of a brain. Successful students in almost every walk of life are "dropouts" from college, often a year or even a course short of graduation. The best students in the university today are often older students who are there only because they want to learn. A degree might be something to show the grandchildren, but is it ever really much more than that?

The idea of the university as a "degree mill"—another economic metaphor—has outlived its day. The idea that the student has "successfully completed" his or her education is antithetical to the very idea of an education. Education is a process, not a product. It can be measured, if at all, only in its continued employment and enjoyment throughout one's life.

13 ▾ The University as a Social Welfare System

We will always face the unflattering image of students (and often the professors, too) as welfare recipients, living well on the public dole while giving nothing in return. The focus is still on money, but instead of thinking of the university as a money-making proposition, it is now thought of as a drain on finances. Of course, other more money-making aspects of the university are still trotted out in defense of the institution, but the educational component, or at least undergraduate liberal arts education, is admitted to be a financial washout. According to the standard calculation, students pay less than a third of the cost of their education, and no obvious job possibilities are in sight! How else to view them, then, than as welfare recipients, mere parasites. And they even dress the part in their designer-torn jeans, sweatshirts (some with obscene slogans), costly recreational shoes, and multipierced ears.

Universities are by law "nonprofit" institutions, supported by tuition, grants, donations, and tax dollars. Their contribution to the nation and its economy is indirect, although it is nevertheless presumed to be substantial.[5] "Why should my tax dollars support some Marxist?" is but one of any number of taxpayer complaints, unusual only in its specificity. "Why should my tax dollars support kids who drink beer all the time?" is something of a generic objection and a favorite Hollywood movie theme.

Once one sees the possibility of a return on investment—for example, the training of much-needed engineers or the creation of a young entrepreneur who will enter into the business community and enrich us all—such objections are mollified. But this does little good for the liberal arts, for which the question "Of what use are you?" has always been an embarrassment. Insofar as the university has as its defense some woolly and economically inert ambition as "the creation of a well-rounded individual," it does not seem all that different from a welfare service. Taxpayers give to the needy and the unneedy alike, some of whom are "cheats" and abuse the privilege, not to mention those who could well afford to pay for the services themselves.

Any justification of the existence of the university at the expense of the taxpayers must establish that the university contributes to the larger

> This is the first time, outside the Chinese revolution, that it has been seriously questioned whether it is better to be educated or uneducated.
> ——John Passmore

well-being of the community. This contribution should not be expected to take the form of immediate returns. The university's contribution to the community is too readily invisible to short-term perception (except for training professionals and providing televised sporting events). In the longer vision, however, the university becomes the essential institution of democracy and the key to a good life and financial and cultural wisdom. But to gain a proper appreciation of this, we have to jettison the economic social frame within which the corporate and marketplace metaphors are subsumed in favor of another in which cost efficiency, finance, and investment are peripheral. Business metaphors have their costs, not the least of which is the economist's blind eye to virtually all human interests and activities that are not part of the financial economy.

PART III

The University as a Community

14 ▾ *The University Is, First of All, a Community*

The idea of the university as a community accounts for not only the variety and richness of campus life, with all of its seemingly distracting nonacademic activities, but also why it is that "commuter schools" and "get a degree at home" programs often seem so impoverished. Without an academic community, books and classes alone do not provide the enveloping context for intellectual life. Shared enthusiasm is the glue that holds the university together. The supposedly "ideal" student who does nothing but attend class and study is getting a second-rate education, and the faculty member who does nothing but teach class and put in the obligatory office time provides a second-rate role model. A university education also includes those on-campus lectures, films and concerts, events and festivals, long meals filled with conversation, a beer and an argument in the late afternoon, an earth-shattering discussion on a walk or on the bus. Who knows how many great ideas have been invented or at least communicated on the most pedestrian modes of transportation on or near the university?

The architecture of the university is particularly important. With the exception of one or two "cathedrals of learning," the university is not a tower but a well-protected, green, and comfortable quadrangle, students sitting on benches and on the grass, faculty standing around chatting, a bookstore, a luncheonette and a couple of pubs just across the way. Even in the busiest city, the core of the campus is an enclave, an intellectual haven within which the conversation of humanity continues. On-campus housing for students is essential, and though there may be arguments both aesthetic and sociological against the monstrous high-rises that blemish a great many campuses these days, the alternative—students scattered around the city and an empty campus at night—is intolerable.[1]

A community is not a nine-to-five proposition but an all-day, all-night conversation. Although donors and administrators may prefer to think of the continuous construction on campus as "improvement" and "progress," the fact of the matter is that most of it is disruptive. What most campuses lack is not "space" but what in a few quaint cities is still called "the commons," the place where people get together, the place where community finds a home, the place Martin Luther King, Jr., dreamed of—an "educational park" open to all.

Small liberal arts colleges have never lost the idea that they are communities of scholars and students. What is necessary is to extend this conception to the university, even those gargantuan state universities of forty, fifty, sixty thousand students. Too many of the students who attend the university have no idea that they should have access to and share interests with their professors, and too many professors see themselves as isolated and threatened rather than nurtured by the university, lone voices in the wilderness of their own specialty rather than members of an academic community. Too many administrators, whatever their rhetoric, remain aloof from the enthusiasm of intellectual life and think as well as live as corporate managers. Unfortunately, the one force strong enough to guarantee unity and a sense of community in the faculty seems to be not their shared intellectual enterprise but their shared contempt for the administration and the institution.[2]

What the university needs is not more structure or authority but an expanded sense of community and more communities within the university. The old "college" system still has much to recommend it, but where the formation of such independent communities is impossible, there are any number of gregarious programs that can reproduce some of the same results: groups of students and faculty who remain together through various courses, activities, and informal affairs from the first year until graduation; more yearlong courses supplemented by not only discussion sections and laboratories but pizza pig-outs and picnics; the replacement of "majors" as an administrative category defined in terms of so many courses by "associations" of students who share an interest in the same subject, meeting regularly, supported by the faculty, forming bonds that are only in part structured by a shared regimen of courses.

Despite the current attack on fraternities and sororities, those organizations should be multiplied and expanded together with community cooperatives and more special "honors" programs. Students should be encouraged to work more with other students. Voluntary study groups (not high school "study hall") can be loosely sponsored and organized as part of each class. Students can organize their own tutorial and advising system, with faculty and administrative advice and support.

So, too, we urge more faculty seminars and cross-disciplinary groups in which professors and students can get to appreciate and really talk with one another. As it is, most faculty meet one another only in onerous administrative committee meetings and quite naturally learn to despise one another. Indeed, that handful of faculty who enjoy such meetings (however much they may dutifully complain about them) and enjoy the appearance of power too readily supplant all less political groups whose sense of community is not shared power but genuine mutual curiosity. We have never met a faculty member who did not complain that the cheap currency of campus politics too readily drives all other conversation out of circulation.

15 ▾ *Leaders, Not Administrators*

The university community is not a captive crowd. Students are there because they have chosen to be, presumably because they want to learn. Faculty are there because they want to teach and study. And this university community is dynamic. It creates and cultivates itself, molds its members and its own traditions, selecting them on the basis of their interest and enthusiasm. The university community is not the product of authority or mandated requirements but the confluence of those shared interests and enthusiasms.

In the university community, organization and authority may be necessary, but only insofar as they minimize friction and conflict. Politics may be inevitable, but it is tolerable only when it supports rather than fragments the sense of community. Competition is natural, but when it becomes destructive rather than inspirational, it, too, is out of place. However fractious it may be, it is mutual respect that holds the university together. Peer pressure is the most powerful force among the faculty as well as among the students, and group solidarity should depend not on the threat of outside interference but on the shared goals that got everyone together in the first place.

This is why the university, unlike most other institutions, does not have to be "managed." It does not need administrators. Indeed, almost everything that counts as management is destructive of the university community. In order to inspire good teaching, for example, the administration gives teaching awards to a few illustrious faculty. No matter how well deserving the recipients might be, the result is widespread envy. In order to assure uniform compliance with teaching responsibilities, the legislature mandates minimum, quantifiable teaching loads. The result is general resentment, all sorts of departmental schemes to get around the rules and use them to reward and punish colleagues, and endless faculty and student meetings to debate the proper quantification of that which is intrinsically unquantifiable. Management in education is interference, not organization.

On the other hand, there is an extremely important place for leadership in the university, so long as we do not confuse leadership with power. The leadership of the university, whether or not it calls itself the "administration," shapes a collective personality and a shared mission or *telos,* a high purpose. The leadership sets the values, the perspective, and exemplary ways of doing things. One leads by example, not by mandate or according to a "plan." A university president who loves great books creates a climate conducive to readers. A president who loves wisdom will create a community (hardly an "institution") of "higher" learning. A president who luxuriates in power will create an organization of petty power mongers, and a president who insists that money is the root of all education will create an institution of money grubbers. We do not need the extra bureaucrats and hidden power mongers. Let's have a few inspirational leaders instead.

Here is a homely analogy: An amateur softball team is held together by its shared enthusiasm and enjoyment of the game, its interest in winning or at least playing well, and the bonding that results from working together to coordinate a number of uneven talents and prepare for the many eventualities of the game. The team may well be able to use a good coach, but does it really need a manager? Not until it accrues so many incidental concerns—uniforms, scheduling, transportation arrangements—that it is no longer sensible for the team members to take up their time with them. Will it then require someone with authority? No, only someone with certain specified and clearly secondary responsibilities. The game and its players are primary. The organization and operations are secondary. If they lose sight of that, they give up the game.

On the other hand, what will make the team "click" is one or two excellent players—players who will not lord their excellence over their teammates (much less boss them around). They will inspire others through their own performance and knowledge of the game.

There has been much agonizing over the loss of "authority" in the university (for example, by Robert Nisbett, in *The Academic Dogma*), and one of the leading complaints about the infamous sixties was the "undermining of administrative authority." But this panic about authority is misdirected. The university should not be a hierarchical institution that depends primarily on authority and in which obedience is accordingly the highest good. Indeed, one could argue, as do we, that something akin to disobedience is one of the surest signs of health in the university, and a good education not only encourages but requires precisely that sort of back talk and going off in one's own direction that is every manager's nightmare. Thinking for oneself and critical thinking are an essential part of the mission of the university, and although such acts of intellectual rebellion can be taught, they cannot be "managed." And if, despite the lip service given to these goals, some professors and administrators remain adamant about the need to maintain their authority and "respect," that is a clear indication that the university has failed, not to control the students but to provide the leadership that makes the mission of the university unmistakable. If people share an interest and a purpose and join together in a mutual pursuit, that interest, purpose, and pursuit provide all the "authority" that is required to run the university.

But what about standards? What about quality? Who will maintain the integrity of the institution? How can we assure that the university will not become a playground for like-minded idiots? To return to our little analogy, the players on a softball team will quite naturally admire the skills of the best batter and best pitcher and give them those positions and that authority they require to exercise those skills for the good of the team. The nature of the game provides its own impetus to excellence. In a university people who gather together to learn will similarly seek out and admire the skills of those who know most and can teach the best. Those people, without any authority, will occupy those positions that allow them to exercise, share, and augment that knowledge and teach as effectively as they can.

The idea that one needs authority to teach implies either that one is not a good teacher or that the community of the university is lacking. Or too many students who do not belong there, too many required classes breeding too much resentment, too many teachers who aspire to authority rather than teaching. So, too, the idea that only one's immediate peers are in a position to judge competence and expertise is nonsense. If a professor can't explain and make ideas exciting to others not in the field, including students, then that is *prima facie* evidence that he or she is not competent. In a community moved by the desire to learn, quality will emerge of its own accord.

16 ▾ *Academic Ethics*

> I strongly sympathize with any businessman who thinks it something of an impertinence for a professor to lecture to businessmen on business ethics; if such a businessman were to ask "Why should I not give lectures to professors on academic ethics?" the only appropriate reply would be "Why not indeed?"
>
> —Alasdair MacIntyre[3]

As a community with a mission, the university is an ethical institution. By this we do not mean merely that it teaches ethics, although that is surely part of the mission, nor do we mean that the university obeys the laws and customs of the larger community of which it is a part. That goes without saying. As an institution, the university is exemplary, defining the ideals to which the society as a whole aspires. Accordingly, its failings are not merely mistakes or letdowns, like a missed deadline or a poor second quarter. They are ethical violations, the failure of a whole society. A poorly educated student is not just a disappointed consumer but a national tragedy. The professor who is paid to teach but thinks wholly in terms of publication and personal advancement is a parasite. The world-renowned university that fails to offer well-taught courses to all its undergraduates is a fraud.

Academicians are fond of studying the ethics of others. Academics have always been suspicious of big business. They have always seen lawyers as sophists. Compared to the supposedly pure life of ideas enjoyed by academics, all other professions and careers have seemed inferior and impure, even the priesthood, from which many of the original academics first emerged. But the call to commune with the eternal verities makes no mention whatever of our obligation to our students. Academic life is often thought to be most pure only when it is most irresponsible.

The "life of ideas" may be a wonderful way to summarize a shared mode of living in which money and prestige and the ordinary pleasures of life are secondary. But it doesn't take very many conversations with academics or departmental meetings to make it obvious that politics and intrigue, professional feuds and rivalries, ideological battles over minor merit raises, and wholesale warfare over hiring and promotions utterly eclipse whatever shared life of ideas may in theory tie faculty members together.

Janice Moulton and George Robinson criticize the myth of the ivory tower as a denial that ethical problems exist in academia. One can find hundreds of books (by academics) on "business ethics" and "medical ethics" and "ethics and the legal profession." But until the past year or so, one could find only a handful of titles referring to academic ethics.[4] This is a humiliating revelation. Instead of taking on the necessary self-examination ourselves, we waited for outsiders—bitter ex-academics, politicians, and journalists—to force the mirror before our faces. And they, of course, depict our flaws as fraud and our vices as subversion of the very worst kind.[5]

The popular press is filled with tales of corporate corruption and back-stabbing abuse of power.[6] Perhaps because the financial stakes are so small and the dialogue so tedious, the public has not had much interest in comparable academic scandals. But the viciousness and corruption of academic life are a match for all but the most brutal corporations. With business ethics booming, no one needs a renewed emphasis on ethics more than the university these days.

It would be a mistake to think of academic life primarily in terms of rules and procedures. It is a shared life, whose ethics is defined by its ideals. Thus there is no rule that academics should love and read books, but one has no place in the university if he or she does not. Thus there is no rule that academics should respect and care for their students, but that is certainly one of the central expectations of academic life. There may be rules against cheating, but what is wrong with cheating is not that it breaks a rule. What is wrong with cheating is that it undermines and makes a mockery of everything the university stands for.

Academic ethics quietly defines the life of the university. There are ethical questions about grades and grading and consequently about power and the very nature of personal relationships. There are inescapable questions about student-teacher relations. There are responsibilities and obligations with regard to research and scholarship and with regard to the institution itself. There are more universal concerns such as racism and prejudice and the responsibility of the university toward such social ills. There are difficult questions surrounding the justification and implementation of affirmative action, questions about job security and justice, not only for faculty but for administrators and staff as well. There are questions of rights and restraints, too often buried beneath the rhetoric of academic freedom. There are rules particular to the practice, the profession and its responsibilities, and there are ethical questions facing anyone in any profession—concerns about sexual harassment, cheating on one's finances, confidentiality, and honesty.

Our primary concern in this book is the role of the university in education and the critical role of the professor in the classroom. One of the most enviable aspects of university life is the enormous freedom to be found there, but it is a freedom that is too easily taken for granted by faculty, and it is often far too dazzling not to be abused by undergraduates fresh out of high school. Under the banner of "academic freedom" the ethical questions of responsibility get lost. Authority is allowed to overshadow fairness, and concern with status undermines respect for others. Accountability is sacrificed to a sometimes dubious freedom, and professional self-regulation is ignored in the name of autonomy. But professional self-regulation means the recognition that we have a shared mission and a primary responsibility to the students, not just to our own careers. It means a modicum of common sense, mutual respect, and decency. Academic ethics, ultimately, means living an exemplary life, dedicated to the well-being of others, comparatively free of greed and resentment, full of integrity as well as ideas.

One particular concern for academic ethics is the one that most academics do not like to talk about—money. It is not the only root of corruption in today's university, but in the past ten years or so it has become the most obsessive. Most professors are deeply concerned with their salaries. They tend to measure their success and respect by the comparative size of their paychecks, and there are shocking differences between the salaries of professors of similar rank in the same department. There are glaring differences between the salaries of older and younger professors, professors in different departments, professors and administrators, and most serious but most neglected of all, professors and the staff, who do so much of the work and are mercilessly exploited.

17 ▾ *Academic Fraud*

The university slips from mismanagement into fraud by way of misplacing its mission, celebrating fame and research instead of the love of teaching, putting money ahead of education, implementing management practices where academic life would be well enough left alone. A glaring example of mismanagement that corrupts the very idea of the university is what we call the five-year fraud, which is currently being perpetrated against students and their parents. The "normal" course of a college career is four years. Parents who have been planning and saving for ten to twenty years have depended upon this, and students looking forward to the rest of their lives have been assuming it. Today fewer than half the undergraduates in supposedly traditional programs of study graduate in four years. Many of them find, in a final "degree check" the year they are supposed to graduate, that they lack some required course or other. And then they often find that they cannot get into the overcrowded courses required of them. One of our most creative writing students found that she had to stay around a ninth semester to take another English course, and the only course she could get into was an "English for Secondary School Teachers" class that had no relevance whatever to anything but her finishing her degree.

To the faculty, the question of how long a student stays around is of little interest. Required courses rather assure the dull and incompetent that their classes will be filled and the demands on them will be minimal. To the administration, of course, the longer a student stays around, the more tuition gets collected (though, to be sure, the admissions office and the classes will always be full, so it doesn't much matter whether any given student stays or goes). But to the parents, the five-year fraud presents a genuine hardship, not to mention inevitable misunderstanding and friction with their college son or daughter. To the student, the five-year fraud means not only delay and disappointment but a kind of poisoning of his or her entire college experience. The university is not honest about what it wants or requires, and it does not seem to care about the quality of the courses it requires. "The university only cares about the numbers," complain an ever-increasing number of students— and they are right.

Within the faculty, ethical lapses are as glaring as the elegance with which they are justified. Faculty appointments are railroaded through by powerful professors with no sense of due process, confident of their own judgment. Specialists in subjects of little interest to anyone fill the department with others just like themselves, indifferent to the needs of the students and the interests of others in the university community. Alternative appointments are blocked in the name of "the integrity of the profession." Assistant professors who have done good work for half a decade are fired because they do not fit into one or another ideological camp or have the misfortune to get on the wrong side of an overly opinionated professor, all in the name of the "excellence" of the university. Supposedly democratic processes are undermined by backdoor visits to the dean's office and kangaroo courts, and even the most minimal requirements for equal employment opportunity are sabotaged by dummy interviews, prejudicial rankings, and what remains of the "old boy system." The latter is now more often defined in terms of ideological compatibility rather than mere acquaintance and can be found today not only among the "boys" but in the mirror image of feminist "networking," in which, once again, positions are sometimes secured not by merit or fair competition but by academic sisterhood and ideological correctness.

"The pure life of ideas" and "the pursuit of truth" get compromised if not splattered across the windscreen by other faster-moving motives—to get ahead, to be recognized, to make a better living, to impress one's seniors, to get money out of the dean or the NEH or the NSF. The students, in turn, learn to despise not only the hypocrisy of the high-flown rhetoric but the education, too. They develop defenses rather than curiosity, they talk back rather than argue, they flirt, they read the newspaper in class and the textbook during the exam. And yet, in this bastion of inquiry and truth, they will still argue, "Everyone does it," including their professors and the illustrious people who run the university.[7] What kind of an education by example are we giving them?

18 ▾ The University as a Feudal Institution

With the ideal of an academic community in mind, let us return to the archaic but strikingly accurate image of the university as a feudal institution. Administrators and politicians talk as if the university stands at the front ranks of corporate society, its training ground and its *avant-garde*. But the fact is that the life of the university is very resistant to change. Say what you will about free markets and corporate metaphors, life among the faculty and the students remains in many ways the same as it has been throughout the past seven or eight hundred years. That is a long time to establish a way of life that will not bend with the wind of this or that new administration or public policy. Even if the university is at the cutting edge of science and the arts and a harbinger as well as an experiment in social change, one of its primary virtues is to act as an anchor with its roots set deep in the past.

The news is full these days of the plight of the universities, their need to "do more with less," and the inevitability of radical change. In fact, the university has almost always faced cutbacks and financial exigencies, and it has always been threatened with "radical change," but the university has always survived. Despite the pleas of administrators and the tightfistedness of legislators, the university has always been a community that is all but impervious to the changing fortunes of the economy. What feudalism has going for it is its inherent stability.

What feudalism has going against it, on the other hand, is its resistance to change. Indeed, that is how the university and its more vocal members can bluster about radical change while remaining secure—even arrogant—in the knowledge that nothing essential will change. Feudalism begins with a sense of community, but what distinguishes feudalism is the insulation from external influences, its exclusionary character, and its insistence on the academic equivalent of bloodlines, one's academic lineage. Despite a decade of affirmative action, the royal bloodlines (the Ivy League, Oxford and Cambridge, Chicago and California) still define the profession and provide even the populist rebels. The fact that one has "studied with Professor So-and-so" and has the appropriate laudatory letter of recommendation is often the primary consideration for academic employment. Although contemporary university politics obviously provides much more mobility than feudal bloodlines and birthrights, one cannot underestimate the extent to which this medieval structure renders the university impervious to real change.

One does not have to look very far beneath the exploitative relationship between tenured professors, untenured professors, and their graduate student assistants to see the old apprenticeship system at work. Graduate students and untenured instructors are the serfs in his or her lordship's realm. Seniority defines the pecking order in the university. Not surprisingly, the serfs do most of the work, and the lord gets most of the credit. Bordering on the obscene, we might also suggest that the feudal ritual of the *jus primae noctis*—wherein the feudal lord has first rights to the bride—applies all too well to coauthored research and sometimes elsewhere as well.

The age of feudalism was also the age of the monastery and the intellectual oasis.[8] It is within the protection of the walls of the academy that a level of dissention, debate, and disagreement that is intolerable in the workaday world can continue to take place, and ideas and interests that seem like nonsense or "a waste of time" can be pursued.

What defined such a community was not simply shared interest. It had *standards*—standards of research, expectations of ability (notably, to read ancient languages)—and it typically saw itself not as a self-enclosed island of study but as a standard bearer of civilization, protector of the truth. There were also the guilds, in which mutual recognition and accomplishment were essential. It is this often-exclusionary insistence upon standards that still defines much of university life among the professoriat. Guilds were medieval institutions, of course, which one might think makes this metaphor particularly inappropriate for the contemporary progressive university. But we would like to suggest that one cannot possibly understand what is wrong with the university today unless one recognizes how alive and influential this guild mentality still is.

We think that the feudal nature of the university is in mortal conflict with free-market metaphors, and the security too readily assumed by critics inside the university is no longer to be taken for granted. Accordingly, we want to save the community and the marketplace of ideas but do away with both feudalism and the market-minded corporate mentality. We want to expand the university, open it up, and level the hierarchy. The university is and ought to be a democratic institution, in which professors have status over students only by virtue of their knowledge and their teaching abilities, and administrators who are not educational leaders are tolerated only because of their utility. Everything good does not have to be modern (or postmodern). Back to the monastery, we say, but a monastery that is also a market without walls.

19 ▾ *The Museum Metaphor*

The idea that the university harks backward rather than forward is most straightforwardly expressed in the traditionalist idea of the university as a *museum*, a sacred repository of the wisdom of the past, a reliquary of the best that a culture has accumulated. Malcolm Arnold's too-often-employed line, "the best that has been thought and said," is typically quoted in this context, in which professors act as guides and curators and students are supposed to be awestruck in the face of a dazzling tradition.

In confrontation with the vulgar "utilitarian" challenge—what is the *usefulness* of a university?—traditionalists can rightly reply that there is usefulness beyond vulgar pragmatics, and the maintenance of a culture, a tradition, has its rightful place in even the most "pragmatic" and business-minded society.

The idea of the university as a sacred place, without which the past and our shared identity would disappear, runs deep in the conservative arguments concerning the university. Roger Kimball, William Bennett, and Allan Bloom warn of the "demise" of Western civilization if the classics are neglected, while their critics harp on the scope and content of that "our" in "our shared identity." To be sure, both have a point. But our interest for the moment lies just in the idea of the university as a depository for the past.

If this idea were taken seriously, science and technology would be sent off campus, to be replaced only by a rather modest department of the history of science and technology. There would be no science research, no engineering, indeed, no professional schools of any kind, for it is their very nature to teach the most up-to-date material and reach out into the future. One might have a subsection or a professor in the history department concerned with the history of medicine and another with the history of law, perhaps one concerned with the history of commerce, but there would be no medicine, no law, no business. Rarely is the traditionalist argument put so baldly, of course, but it does not take much by way of conversation with many scholars and academics, particularly in the humanities, for these prejudices to emerge. Indeed, the same prejudice emerges from those who declare themselves against the tradition. They are equally dismissive or disdainful of the place of science, technology, and the professional schools in the university. The main difference between them and the traditionalists is that they want to destroy this particular museum and put another in its place.

It is possible to reject the museum metaphor and still hold on to the value of tradition and culture. Even if one of the functions of the university is to make available and teach "the classics," the university's mission is not just to maintain and defend the classics. It is to teach the students, teach them to use the classics in their own way—to think about them and to criticize them as well as appreciate them. Anything that works, anything that piques their intellectual curiosity, is legitimate. This does not mean that Shakespeare is no "better" than Bugs Bunny or could be replaced by cartoons. The classics play an essential role in teaching, not because they are the classics but because they are exemplary. They are good to teach. And their exemplary quality is not diminished when coupled with student concerns about their future in the professions or with "Star Trek" or the Three Stooges.

What is wrong with the museum metaphor? Too often the museum is assumed to represent a culture as something strictly past, an heirloom rather than (as it is said) "a living legacy." Living authors were not until very recently part of the British or German educational "core," and twentieth-century American authors (Faulkner, Hemingway) have only recently made it into the curriculum. It was only the *avant-garde* and the loose cannons who taught Pinchon, Barth, and Mailer, who bordered dangerously close to "pop."

Worst of all, the museum metaphor brutally separates research and scholarship—science and the humanities—in a way that is detrimental to them both. It reduces the role of the students to mere sops for appreciation and historical information, not much less degrading, we would think, than reducing them to raw materials or mere "numbers." The university is not a museum, a mausoleum of old artifacts whose value is insured and augmented by scholarship and "education" as nothing more than appreciation. How readily we can smell the *dust* behind Allan Bloom's polemical prose and praise of Plato and other old and noble things! The university is first of all a *living* entity, and the museum metaphor makes that fact—and the presence of so many students parading around its exhibits—extremely dubious. The university is aimed at the future as well as at the past, and at its heart are the students.

20 ▾ *In Praise of Eccentricity*

All of this emphasis on community must not undermine the fact that the university is a community of individuals—often extremely eccentric individuals. Many of the faculty on any university campus would find themselves wholly at a loss in the "normal" world of polished images and practiced politeness. Indeed, some of them have a great deal of difficulty even negotiating a shopping mall or a checkout counter. That is part of the charm of the university.

The "absentminded professor" has always been a delightful target, beginning with Aristophanes's parody of Socrates in his play *The Clouds* and continuing on through the Disney versions of "the nutty professor," who was a genius and a goofy charmer. In today's university, we hear of history professors who swing swords around in class, demonstrating a point. We have watched a physics professor lie down on a bed of nails, and one chemistry professor, after boasting in class that he could recite the complex chemical table while standing on his head, accepted the challenge and did it.[9] One of us confesses that he once showed up for class wearing two different-colored shoes. One of our colleagues continues to wear beach "floppies" to class despite the constant comments from his students. It's not that he is obstinate or adamant; he just can't imagine what else he would wear.

The glory of eccentricity, however, emerges not in such social oddities but in the intensity and focus with which academics apply themselves to their chosen corner of the world. One scholar spends twenty years rummaging through a great old poet's notebooks and letters, digesting them, organizing them, analyzing them, alternatively identifying with, falling in love with, and despising the subject. What "normal" person would engage in such an extreme act of devotion? Another spends a decade sitting in the woods, observing the mating habits of a peculiar kind of frog. What an odd and wonderful cast of mind it takes to motivate such curiosity.

In fact, one way to define the purpose of the university would be to say, it is the place where such wonderful eccentrics can devote themselves and inspire others as well. To be sure, everyone does not need to know the letters of the poet or the mating habits of the frog, but everyone is richer just by virtue of the fact that someone does. To study with people with that sense of dedication is one of the most important lessons in life, not the subject but the very idea of dedication. Indeed, the single most important division between students at the university is between those who pick up that sense of devotion and learn to apply it themselves and those who do not, whether to education, law, medicine, business, plumbing, or public policy.

The concept of eccentricity also has some unfortunate implications. Culturally and intellectually, it tends to reify the cult of genius that is endemic to the university and overemphasizes the abilities and contributions of individuals as opposed to cooperative group work, and politically, it tends to celebrate individual creativity but thereby ignores or looks down on cultures that do not share this anthropologically odd emphasis on the individual.

Within the university, it endangers the very idea of a community with shared practices and a common set of values, not much different from the individual egoism of certain sports players who wreck the team while reveling in their own performance. The lack of cooperation becomes the core of the academic "message." Especially in the liberal arts, cooperative research is discouraged. Joint papers are often discounted in a tenure or promotion decision, for example, and students studying and working together risk the very great danger of being charged with cheating if their work is in fact very similar.

Eccentricities are not always charming either. We may be amused by our colleagues who every day forget where they parked their car, but we are not charmed by those who forget to go to class or forget to prepare the lecture or lose students' exams.

> She began to realize that being clever, brilliant, even what gets called "well-educated" is not to be equated, necessarily, with being considerate, kind, tactful, even plain polite or civil.
> ——Robert Coles, *Harvard Diary*

Professors, for all their eccentricities, serve as role models for their students. This may give parents serious pause, but the influence is for the most part only temporary and a healthy antidote to the overly button-down exemplars and the heavily muscled murderers students are taught to admire in the professional world and on television. In academia, even the law professors manage to be a bit odd. But eccentricity leads to a wide variety of teaching styles and social (and antisocial) behavior, and one of our concerns in this book is to defend a university that leaves ample room for all the variations and oddities of those who teach well and distinguish them from mere irresponsibility.

21 ▾ The Social Responsibility of the University

It is sometimes suggested that the mission of the university is to solve social problems. This is confused with the reasonable position that the university, as a public institution, has profound social obligations. In a much-publicized book, President Derek Bok of Harvard complained that the university is failing in its "dual mission," to solve such social problems as poverty, low productivity, and racial tension, on the one hand, and to inculcate a sense of moral responsibility and a social conscience, on the other. Conservative critics object with some reason that the university has its own mission and has no business in the public arena, trying to solve problems that are not of its own making and concerning which it has no special expertise.[10]

Is the university essentially a self-enclosed community with its own ends and its own agenda, or is it at least part of the mission of the university to serve the extramural community? We think that both options are wrong and the choice misleading.

The university has a set of aims that are inseparable from the public interest but that nevertheless are not those public interests per se. Of course, one can and should encourage individual contributions to the local community—teaching for two years in an inner-city public school, working in a soup kitchen on Saturday afternoons, or working on a rural poverty project—but there are limits to what the university as such can do. Whole courses in some schools require students to go out and volunteer in social programs, but what one cannot expect of the university is an institutional mandate to "end racism or poverty." The university is not a school of social work much less a social worker. Its mission lies elsewhere if it is to have the desired impact on society.

Take, for example, the difficult problem of race relations. The university has no obligation to staff street-corner missions or even to research racism. But this does not mean that the university should be oblivious to this pressing, tragic, and humiliating problem. A university that simply ignored the issues of race would be failing in its educational mission. A university that condoned or encouraged racial tensions on or off campus would be violating the very idea of education in a democratic society. At the very least, the university should insist on collegial race relations on campus.

The university can by its very nature do more than "put its own house in order." The university can make a special effort to recruit underrepresented minorities and take care that they get the assistance they need to succeed in their programs. That is part of the university mission, but it is also the key to the larger problem of racism in society. It is not as if the university should set out to solve an enormous social problem, but by pursuing its own educational mission, it can in fact contribute to the solution of that problem. Social mobility in the United States is very largely determined by education. Education is the gateway to the professions and, these days, to managerial jobs in business and other organizations as well. For the university to take special care where racial concerns are at issue, therefore, is not an effort to reach out beyond its capabilities but to do what it is meant to do and, in so doing, contribute to the well-being of the entire society.

PART IV

The Students

22 ▾ *The Joy of Teaching*

The special nature of eighteen- to twenty-year-olds and those who share their peculiar openness toward the world establish the delightful tone of the university. To be sure, our classes are much enriched by the many older students on campus, but the tone and tenor of the university are essentially that of a "youth culture," a world filled and defined by energy and enthusiasm. The students display an eagerness combined with vulnerability and a halfhearted (and therefore often belligerent) defensiveness. So many of them have just left the fascistic environment of high school, which no matter how overly "permissive" by some standards, releases the students into our classrooms full of pent-up frustration and ambition typically mixed with rebellious, raging, hormonal enthusiasm, which we can turn into intellectual curiosity and pursuit. (Luckily there is a welcome "blast" of a summer in between.)

Most of them are not yet tied to the anchors of marriage and mortgage. They have no children, and their parents are in good health. They may have time-consuming jobs to pay their way through school, but they are rarely wrapped up in them. In fact, most college jobs are notoriously mindless, and the students are free to think and feel and explore most of their time. And they really do think and feel and explore. In the average eighteen-year-old, there is an energy and a malleability virtually unmatched by any creature on earth and unappreciated by almost every American institution except the military. Full of themselves but full of self-doubt as well, these students want to be on top of things even if they do not always know which end is up.

They are ready to learn. Their brains are physiologically all geared up for it. But whether they get interested or not depends on whether one taps into that natural pool of frustrated and timid inquisitiveness. Their own insecurities, their uncertainty about the future, is a secure tap into their souls, and anything that can make use of (but not rub in) their own embarrassment about their ignorance has a pretty good chance of succeeding. Their natural sense of humor goes a long way, too, and certainly one of the banes of American education is the prejudice that favors seriousness rather than humor as a goad to learning (our German and Jesuit university heritage).

A little bit of eroticism goes a long way, of course, but it is essential that it never become obvious as sexuality, which gets them off the track (and onto another, already well worn) faster than anything else. Freed of its threatening sexual suggestions, this is to say simply that education and learning must be *motivated,* not by external rewards and promises but by tapping into the student's own reservoir of passion. We tend to confuse passion with appetite and think of emotion as primitive and uncultured. But culture *is* cultivated passion, and it is *eros,* not the authority of the faculty or the pressure of grades and career, that motivates students to learn.

Few of our colleagues are innocent of complaining about the "level" of interest or intellectual acumen in their classes, typically in the third or fourth week of classes, after the nervous honeymoon of the first week and the "down to business" hyperseriousness of the second. "The students are unprepared," we hear again and again, as if that is not the reason why they are in the university in the first place. "The students don't seem interested," they say, as if a teacher is supposed to be merely a waiter, bringing food to the gourmet diner. "The students don't seem interesting," we hear, too, as if it is not our business to make them not only interested but interesting. In fact, our colleagues sometimes marvel at how the same dull faces they see in the classroom become bright and enthusiastic immediately outside the building, as if it is no reflection on them. The best comeback we've heard comes from Steven Cahn, who compares such complaints on the part of the faculty to the analogous complaint of a surgeon—that all of his patients are sick.

Much depends, therefore, on how we see the students—as adolescent "Deltas" in *Animal House* or as adults, future colleagues, and members of Congress; as impositions on our precious research time or as the very heart of our mission in life. But this perception is not something we discover after several years (or weeks!) of teaching; it is something we bring to our teaching with us, the ultimate lesson plan.

All of the options are there before us, and if one looks for "Deltas," one will find them. It is a self-fulfilling perception. With this notion of a self-fulfilling prophecy in mind, one should think candidly about those university metaphors, according to which our students are to be treated like

- ▼ Children
- ▼ Raw materials for industry and the professions
- ▼ Protoprofessionals, already launched on (the first step of) their careers
- ▼ The leaders and citizens of tomorrow
- ▼ Potential scholars, new professors
- ▼ Consumers whose sovereignty consists not only in the free choice of which schools they want to patronize but also which classes they want and what they want out of them
- ▼ Customers who have paid for a quality class and fully expect and deserve to get one
- ▼ Welfare recipients, supported by taxpayers' money, deserving only whatever we deign to give them, for which they should be grateful
- ▼ Social baggage, a temporary danger to society, to be kept off the streets and out of trouble.
- ▼ Mere numbers, costing so much per head

We mentioned the depiction of college students in the popular media. It is anything but flattering. This may provide comic release for the students who watch it, but it is all too often mistaken for a genuine representation of campus life. One rarely sees a student going to class or to the library except as momentary filler, and a student expressing interest in an academic subject is probably a setup for a crude joke to come. One could easily walk away thinking that all college students are either frat-rats, jocks, jerks, nerds, or bimbos. But no more than a small number of the students in a large state university are anything like those stereotypes, and even those are not altogether hopeless.

During the sixty or so hours that make up the student workweek, they are ready and willing to be challenged, to be inspired, to become interested, and they genuinely hope, even hunger, to do something meaningful with their lives. Their hormones are percolating, but the direction in which that energy will get channeled is up to us. Bad teaching from us, bad advice from their parents, a mandatory, often boring curriculum from the university together with halfhearted but occasionally brutal discipline understandably turn them off, convince them early on that college is just a continuation of high school, that life, like school, is ultimately a bore.

Inspired teaching, on the other hand—with some enlightened advice and an interesting, flexible curriculum—should make education the ultimate fun, and the occasional beer or beach party will then be nothing other than what it should be—a break from the intensity of doing what one really wants to be doing.

23 ▾ *Treat Students as Adults*

When one of our (older-than-average) students was asked, "Are students children or adults?," she wisely replied, "They are adults but not grown up." Intellectually, most of our students are children. They do not know what is available, so they cannot really know what they want nor what they ought to study. Most of them, if pressed, do not know the meaning of the titles of their courses when they begin the term. And yet our students are also adults, not just in their physical maturity but in their social sympathies and political sensibilities (to be distinguished from political *sense,* which requires study and deliberation and is demonstrably absent in a clear majority of the populace of every country). They are *smart.* In terms of sheer brainpower, there is no match for a twenty-year-old, an appalling waste when one thinks of how little we feed those brains when they are at their hungriest.

There is perennial debate about the political wisdom of undergraduates, particularly when they go into the streets to demonstrate against public policies. Their "idealism" is ridiculed as immaturity or, worse, political gullibility. (The charge of "communist dupes" ran through the sixties to the eighties. With the worldwide collapse of communism, it will be curious to see how this spurious charge is continued in other dress into the nineties.) True, eighteen-year-olds are particularly susceptible to "brainwashing," which they insist they have been subjected to all their lives. Religious cults find a continuous source of new recruits in our college students. These not-grown-up adults are fertile ground for implanting new ideas, which quickly take hold, and one can only say that if professors fail to provide those ideas, then someone else will.

It was only two decades ago that American eighteen-year-olds were allowed to vote, although they have been invited to kill and die for their country since the beginning of time. But there is good argument that it is the idealistic eighteen-year-old and not the wizened devotee of *realpolitik* whose goals and priorities should be trusted. Of course, we should be very careful about overromanticizing the young and their idealism, but what is at stake here is not the tendency to radicalism but the enfranchisement of students at a critical age at which they are inexperienced, yes, but ready to make choices and take the consequences. Guglielmo Ferraro got it right when he commented, "What makes good judgment? —experience. What makes experience? —bad judgment."

Eighteen-year-olds have just emerged from a cocoon of authority. Most of them have never had their own bank account. Many of them have never had to make their bed, much less their own living arrangements. High school may have included one or two hobby group "electives" in addition to such traditional time wasters as "homeroom" and "study hall," but the idea of a voluntary, flexible schedule has seen the light of day in very few secondary schools, in which "education" means training and obedience. These students are just now breaking out into adult life. They can no longer be treated as children, but they are bursting with that energy and curiosity which it is the purpose of an education to feed, guide, and nourish.

24 ▾ The New Generation of Students

With no more embarrassment than an old professor,
Spring was turning the pages.

—Tom Robbins, *Even Cowgirls Get the Blues*

One of the aspects of teaching in a university that makes it so refreshing is the continuing turnover of students. There is a new crop every year, a complete rotation every four or five years. They are changing all the time, in fascinating ways. They are the cultural barometer of our society and the world. It is sometimes said, and we think rightly so, that a "generation" these days is about four years. Life changes so quickly— new technology, new geopolitical friends and enemies, new music, and new fashions—that the old biological yardstick, in which a generation equals the time between birth and parenthood, is woefully outmoded. Today, the language gap and the mutual incomprehension between generations, not to mention the differences in values, require a new outlook. Who are these new students? What do they want, and what are their values? Are they like us? Or could they be so different that we could not possibly understand them?

What we read in the press about these students is rarely faithful to the original. Typically, the caricature is a generation behind, a product of the memories of just-graduated seniors (now working in many of those newsrooms as junior reporters) and already out of touch with the new turn of consciousness on campus. Just about the time when reporters and commentators were lamenting the loudest the turn of the narcissistic "me" generation of the seventies, the turn into the Reagan eighties had buried that narcissism under a mountain of money. Investment bankers and not California-Indian gurus were the local heroes, and business school, not consciousness raising, was the place to be. And just as the press was getting around to excoriating the "materialism" of those two generations, youth took a turn into the nineties. Today we have an upsurge of students who tell us they want to be teachers and social workers, who think that thirty or forty thousand dollars a year is a reasonable living, who say that they "want to do something meaningful" and "make some contribution to humanity."

Not that these students form a battalion of saints. They remain desperately concerned with "having a good time," converting the word *party* into a verb. They have trouble taking their studies seriously or seeing the point of an argument. They are morally dogmatic (for example, about such matters as abortion) while at the same time pronouncing a strictly subjectivist stance in ethics ("What's right for me might not be right for her . . ."—an older generation's "Different strokes for different folks"). Purely academic concerns tend to bore them, and they take a Gordian knot approach to brainteasers and other intellectual problems. But they are, nevertheless, serious. They want to learn. They just do not know, as we once did not know, what to learn. What they really want is to be "turned on" (our generation's metaphor), to be excited by books and questions that they have not encountered before.

Students today face threats and fears that would seem to be all but unknown to earlier generations—horrible addictive and debilitating drugs, an unusually deadly venereal disease, a trillion-dollar federal deficit, and an extremely tight job market. But a moment's thought reveals that most of these novel horrors are but variations on ancient themes, and though the severity of the threat in question may vary with time and circumstances, life goes on.

Some basic human aims, however denied in theory by extreme relativists and multiculturalists, do not change—to live and live well, to live a meaningful life filled with friends and family, and to do something meaningful and rewarding along the way. The quest for meaning is the ultimate educational motive. It is a force with which a good teacher in *any* subject can work wonders. The new generation is different from the last, but much the same as well. They want to grow up and live well. They want to help create a decent world to live in.

25 ▾ Students Helping Students: Getting Students to Run the University

Students are social animals, and they often learn better in groups. Why, then, do we put such excessive emphasis on individual—even isolated—study? There is real truth behind the observation that students ultimately teach themselves—and each other. On most university campuses these days, small groups of Vietnamese, Chinese, Korean, or Japanese students sit studiously together, their collective minds intent on their schoolwork. This is their social life. They enjoy each other's company, and need we say, they carry some of the highest grade point averages in the school. One need not raise any racist issues to make the point that such cooperative work and focus is what the university is, or should be, all about. One need not overemphasize differences in background or culture or family pressures to suggest that, were most students to adopt a similar shared attitude toward their classwork, instead of viewing it as an annoyance that interferes with one's social life, there would be very little talk about how "higher education is failing our youth."

Such group activity can be encouraged and partially structured by the university. One suggestion, which we will develop in the following pages, is the employment of students in the process of education itself. This would be particularly important and helpful in large state schools where anonymity is a problem and it is not always easy to find help. Many schools have small programs of this sort already, usually on a volunteer basis or for special situations—for example, a tutorial system for athletic students, who often miss classes and need extra personal help with their studies. But we propose a universal "big brother/big sister" system, much like many fraternities and sororities have for their pledges. We propose a universal tutoring system that involves all the students. It is often said (and it is common knowledge among teachers) that the best way to learn is to teach. Why not give students that opportunity? It would be especially valuable where remedial studies are required, which these days includes about half the incoming freshmen.

Giving students responsibility not only for their own studies but for others as well would be perhaps the single most positive factor in the conversion of the campus into a more democratic participatory community. It would give them all a taste of teaching, a valuable experience in any case, and a sense of doing good for others. It would also provide an income for students who proved to be good at it and needed extra money to pay for school—perhaps through tuition reduction and waivers. But though it is a plan that would help students financially as well as educationally, it should not be introduced merely or primarily as a financial aid strategy. Even the wealthiest students, who have no need for a bit of extra cash and would treat such employment as unnecessary and demeaning, should participate. You could also give credit for it and have evaluations by the tutees. For real problem cases, you need real professionals, of course, and they should be treated fairly, not as fringe hirelings who deal with problems faculty refuse to recognize.

The most important thing is to change peer contempt to peer concern. It is perhaps the most essential lesson in good citizenship the university can provide, and it will open up the joys of teaching to thousands who otherwise might never have even thought of it. And it will help tens of thousands of students who otherwise might never have been able to discover the joys of learning, making the promise of a college education for everyone who really wants one a reality instead of merely a rhetorical flourish for administrators and politicians.

26 ▾ Telling Them Where to Go: Advising and Orientation

Take one of these young students from a small-town high school and plop her or him in the middle of a state university with forty thousand students, and what do you get? If you're lucky, a few happy chance encounters, one or two high-quality classes, a decent dorm room with a somewhat sane roommate and a minimum of substance abuse on the floor. For many of the students who show up on campus, there are at best a few fellow high school classmates to keep one another afloat.

But good fortune is not always with us. For those lone freshmen without such support, fraternities and sororities beckon as one obvious place to find friends and an instant community. Long before the newcomers ever get to receive our hard-earned wisdom and personal attention, they learn that their tender egos will be nourished only off campus, that good and interesting classes are at best a matter of luck and only occasionally the result of planning or interest or hard work.

They get little advice, and most of it is useless or worse. University advisers rarely know particular professors or specific courses and are wedded to the official requirements instead of the students' needs and interests. Professors have proved themselves notoriously inadequate for the job. They are often ignorant of courses and quality even within their own department—and in the name of "professional courtesy" they will often not tell the truth anyway. They are typically ignorant altogether of what goes on across campus. Teacher/student ratios are not a significant measure of the quality of the university. But the ratio of students to their advisers is very significant, and the ideal ratio is 1:1. The current ratio at many schools, in the range of one adviser to three hundred students, is clearly inadequate.

So we suggest the obvious: student advisers. Older students know their way around the university. Unfortunately, in the current situation it is often too late to benefit themselves, for it often takes two or three years just to learn how to find the best classes and the interesting programs as well as how to avoid bad teaching and get around pointless requirements. Why shouldn't older students convey that wisdom to the incoming students, so that they do not have to go through the same trial-and-error learning themselves? And as for living arrangements, socializing, and entertainment, students know far better than most of the faculty and staff how to get along and how to live well in a college town. As for minor drug and alcohol problems, psychological and sexual quandaries, why not have a student network to handle such situations as well?

To put so much emphasis on the students, their mutual support, and their responsibilities does not mean that professors, staff, and administrators are off the hook and free from their own responsibilities. To say that the university is a community is precisely to say that all this activity is best organized collectively, in groups of faculty, staff, and administrators as well as students, sharing their wisdom and experience. Indeed, it would do some professors a great deal of good to hear how students candidly discuss their classes and what they want and need that they are not getting. It would do some administrators a great deal of good to hear how their mandates are resisted or resented or abused by the faculty and the students, and it would do most students a great deal of good to hear how teachers react to their classes and what students can do to make those classes better. Most faculty, like most students, are actually hungry for advice and support, but too proud or timid to ask for it.

A campus should be organized so that everyone has a place to go for advice. Student advisers and counselors should always be available, but an even better suggestion is that every professor have a group of fifteen to twenty students, for whom he or she will act as faculty mentor for as long as five years—until the students leave the university. In their freshman year, the professor may teach them a course, but from then on, they will reconvene periodically for routine meetings and discussions.

This need not be particularly labor intensive for the professor, and in any case, it would be much more rewarding than the assorted hodge-podge of miscellaneous one-time students showing up for advice during office hours. As it now happens, the fact that there is no possibility of getting to know one's students or getting a sense of their long-range plans is one of the more serious disincentives to professorial involvement with them, for there is nothing that inspires good teaching and good faculty-student relations like a long-term relationship in which the professor gets to watch the students grow.

27 ▾ The Answer to Financial Need: Hire the Students

At the College of the Ozarks, a small but first-rate liberal arts school, the majority of students are from poor (and often very poor) families. They are not on scholarship, and they do not waste their time flipping burgers at Wendy's or MacDonald's for minimum wage. They work for the college. Of course, every university has some of its staff slots filled by students, but the difference at the College of the Ozarks is that this is built right into the college budget and the students' plans.

A state university the size of Texas or Arizona has a staff of ten thousand. Students care about the campus. Give them the jobs—janitorial, clerical, caretaker, but especially para-academic jobs, working the laboratories, staffing the offices, tutoring and advising, working in the library, helping with research and course preparation. One of the virtues of thinking of the university as a community is that students are then not mere customers, coming and going, but full-fledged members and participants, giving as well as taking.

When the students think of the university as *their* campus community, they will have every reason to make it thrive. In the face of so much moaning about the miserliness of the legislature and the administration, it is time to take back the finances of the university, starting not with the supply but the demand side of the equation. How much of the running of the university can we do ourselves?

Tutoring and advising are especially valuable student activities. They not only build community but extend the educational reach of the university into the lives of individual students. We should pay the students for such activities, and we can afford to be generous. Most remedial work involves focus and encouragement rather than expertise as such. You can pay a student six dollars an hour to provide this for another student, or you can pay a professor or a professional fifty to two hundred dollars an hour to do the same job no better and possibly less effectively. Students learn by teaching, and their enthusiasm is infectious.

The university is a community. In that sense, we want to go back to the old feudal system—not the hierarchy of lords and serfs, of course, but rather the monkish communities of friendship, shared responsibilities, and scholarship that dotted Europe and paved the way for the first universities. Students who feel that they participate in the running of the university are going to contribute much more than students who see themselves as victims of an impersonal bureaucracy and an inattentive faculty. In theory, this is the function of fraternities and sororities on campus—mutual support and help as well as shared enjoyment and camaraderie. In practice, this is how good student co-ops work on campus, providing advice and tutoring on a regular basis; sponsoring lectures and discussions by faculty, visitors, and students; providing friendship and community to fellow students who would otherwise have lost their way.

In their desperate search for funds from the legislature, the taxpayers, and the corporations, and in their now-routine insistence on the need to raise tuition, university administrators continuously ignore the fact that much of the university could well run itself. Of course, the faculty resist the extra work (unless it carries with it the honorific title of a "university committee"), and the administration would just as soon ignore it because it all too readily suggests that their jobs are superfluous, but it is in the interest of the students to make the university their own. Free tuition in exchange for useful, educational work would provide welcome relief for a good many hard-put students and their families these days, and a campus run by as well as for students would put the emphasis and attention of the university right back where it belongs.

28 ▾ Expand Fraternities and Sororities

We have already recognized that undergraduates are social animals. They need companionship; indeed, they are often obsessive about it. They also understand group responsibility, even if they sometimes employ it as an excuse. Most sororities and a good number of fraternities are good, responsible groups. It is extremely unfortunate that faculty, administrators, and local communities as well as the students themselves—not to mention television—tend to stereotype fraternities and sororities and reduce them all to the slovenly or giggling collectives on "Saturday Night Live." On a large university campus, fraternities and sororities provide the only elegant social setting for a great many students. They provide the best possible support system. They provide the healthiest outlet for fun and enthusiasm, although admittedly, besotted adolescents in groups of a hundred or more may be an inconvenience for the neighborhood and get a bit unruly, even dangerous.

The problem is not the fraternity and sorority system. The problem is the unfortunate value system endemic to *some* of these establishments combined with the fact that the university turns out to have very little control over them. Some fraternities, especially, maintain values and select new members solely on the basis of marginally social or even criminal proclivities. The tendency to abuse alcohol and other drugs, sexual aggression, contempt for other groups or nonmembers in general, a celebration of the extremes of human vulgarity—when these become the values that hold a system together rather than occasional missteps in a social organization, nothing could be more of an embarrassment to the university community.

It is a mistake, however, to launch a general attack on fraternities and sororities. The basic principles of the fraternity-sorority ("Greek") system would seem to be simply the provisions of the First Amendment, the right to peaceable assembly and all that our culture presupposes in terms of the right to choose our own friends and living quarters. There is no justification in our society for prohibiting exclusive groups, so long as they do not carry with them any special privileges. Indeed, the same argument for voluntary segregation that defends the importance of women's colleges (like Smith and Mount Holyoke) and all-black colleges (like Tuskegee and Spelman) supports sororities and ethnic organizations within a campus as well.

But then, what about fraternities? It certainly seems to be the case that fraternities engender unhealthy attitudes toward women. Does it matter that all-female groups may encourage hostile attitudes toward men? But here the question seems to be whether the presumption of privilege is so strong that there cannot be a fraternity system that is not inherently discriminatory. Exclusive male fraternities provide their members with both privileges and unhealthy attitudes toward women and other non-members. So perhaps the somewhat odd conclusion is that sororities and ethnic organizations are OK, but fraternities as such are not. But this is an absurd conclusion, and it means that the very idea of a fraternity ought to be reconsidered.

There are French-speaking houses and Russian-speaking houses and Chinese-speaking houses, which serve both as educational and social contexts as well as provide a comfortable home for French, Russian, and Chinese visitors to the university. There are astronomy clubs and chess clubs and history clubs and philosophy clubs, and all of these provide a home within the university for students who might otherwise find themselves alone. The university should encourage such groups; faculty and staff should welcome the opportunity to participate, too; and as educational organizations get more successful and visible, the marginal "party barns," those that have not yet earned the distinction of being eliminated, may start to get themselves into shape as well.

As in every other aspect of the university, it is the sense of community and shared purpose that should provide the most powerful vehicle for shaping university policy. It is the social well-being and mutual peer pressure of the students that will make a university great or not so great, fun or dull, inspiring or merely an ordeal to be gotten through. "Man is a social animal," wrote Aristotle, providing what is probably still the best defense of the "Greek" system and other organizations on campus. They are not a problem but rather the solution to a problem. Why not encourage them? Why not use them? Why not shape them into educational communities, at pain of exclusion?

Ideally, perhaps, every university would work on the college system, a flexible but well-organized network of stable communities, overlapping interests, and mutual support. The best-known examples are Oxford and Cambridge in England, Yale and Santa Cruz in this country, and of course, many of our small liberal arts colleges constitute such a system by virtue of their own small size. But as attractive as that system may be, it is out of reach for the majority of students and faculty in America today. They have to commute. They work full- or part-time jobs. Their hours are too irregular. They have families. The system is too expensive. Nevertheless, we should not lose sight of the tremendous advantages of such a system, and the practical ideal is to incorporate as much as possible of it, in more flexible and democratic terms, in even the largest state universities. The total enrollment may be huge, but the everyday context of life for the students may nevertheless be humane and intimate. We need more community among our students and our faculty and administrators, too. And if the age-old ideal of "fraternity" serves that purpose, then let's have more fraternities and sororities by all means.

29 ▾ *Once a Student: The Alumni*

If you have received something from an institution or a person, you have an obligation to do something in return. The university changed my life. It took a hayseed from Fort Worth and opened my eyes to a whole new world that impacted the rest of my life.

—Morton Meyerson, University of Texas, class of 1961

An undergraduate education marks neither an end nor a beginning but continues the ongoing process of a lifelong education. Accordingly, many of the more valuable students in and around the university are the alumni and alumnae, who should not be considered "ex-students," much less merely a valued source of donations and support for the football team, but the subjects of serious interest and concern by the faculty and the university as a whole.

University graduates seem to fall into three fuzzily distinguished categories. The largest group, naturally, are all of the indifferent graduates, who are off and running in their careers or absorbed in their families, who may pick up a book once in a while and have a nostalgic chat with an old classmate or two, but whose thoughts of the university are limited to a mixture of annoyance and muted generosity when they receive the annual appeal for donations.

The most valuable group of graduates are only formally "graduates" at all. They still keep the university alive within themselves, still live the life that they learned there, to the best of their time and abilities. Their graduation was just a stepping-stone along their educational way, not a milestone, much less a conclusion. Not infrequently they can be found on various boards and committees concerned with the university. Cynics might comment that they thereby betray a certain immaturity and incurable nostalgia, but we would argue, on the contrary, that they are a demonstration of the university's success. To the university's benefit, their appreciation and accumlated wisdom concerning the importance of a good education, not to mention their success, can be invaluable not just to the current crop of students but to the faculty and administration as well. We should do much more for them (and not just so that they will give much more to us). We should have more "continuing education" courses, weekend study retreats, plus the generous opportunity for further study within the established structure of the university.

The third category of alumnus also shows a continuing interest in the university. Unfortunately, this interest has very little to do with the actual mission of the university and is virtually oblivious to the meaning, much less the nature, of education. These are the graduates for whom their degree is the only evidence of an education, who are so often involved behind the scenes in the well-publicized scandals surrounding college sports and the political pressures that threaten the university. Some of them, to be sure, are extremely generous, but the pressure and advice to which they subject the university in return too often reflect the ignorance of academic life that they never tried to overcome while they were students. Unfortunately, the university as it is presently constituted remains beholden to them and dependent on their continuing largess.

The alumni question is much worse for private colleges, of course, but in state universities the phenomenon of the alumni legislator can be just as serious. The answer to this alumni problem is obvious, but it is rarely pursued in practice. The university's obligations and attention to the alumni should be exactly proportional to their appreciation and understanding of the university. When the alumni support and further the mission of the university, all doors are open to them. When alumni who never understood what the university is all about threaten the integrity of the academic community, the answer is "Just say no."

We have to appeal to a different sort of alumni and, most important, appeal to them while they are still students. Passing students through years of red tape and mediocre courses will not breed loyal and generous alumni, but giving students real opportunities and transforming their lives—as the best academic programs do almost routinely—leave the alumni grateful for their education and ecstatic in their memories of the university. It is not surprising that many such alumni are very successful and will continue to appreciate and support education. There is no excuse for the university to be selling out in the solicitation of grants and gifts when, if it were simply to pursue its mission, expressions of gratitude would be steadily forthcoming.

PART V

Students in the Open University

30 ▾ Admissions: Let Them All In

The only sensible admissions policy is an "open," nonrestrictive admissions policy. Let them all in. There are no good predictors for university performance, nor are there any noncontroversial standards for "success." The criteria used today—SAT scores, high school grade point averages—are only self-fulfilling; they prove that people who do well on tests before they begin university tend to do well on tests in the university as well. There are no good tests for readiness and willingness, no computer-graded exams to measure enthusiasm or creativity or intellectual curiosity. There is no way to tell which students are late bloomers, which ones are merely rebellious, and which ones may make great discoveries in one field but remain indifferent to all the others. The only sure test for college preparedness is college.

As it is, admissions criteria are profoundly biased, and in exactly the wrong direction. They are geared mainly to this year's high school graduates. Older students are discouraged, placed at a disadvantage, and in many cases, disqualified. Students who drop out or take a few years off from school are effectively penalized. Too many high school students go on to college just because they are expected to, because they have not even tried to think of any other possibilities, because it is thirteenth grade, and they nominally succeed just because they are conditioned to take tests. Nevertheless, they may be indifferent to the opportunities around them and utterly oblivious to the all-important differences between high school and college, apart from the easier hours and the freer social life. They are, whatever their high school qualifications, not yet ready for college.

Opening up admissions will let in the riffraff along with the neglected. But the riffraff will be quickly discouraged or marginalized. We do not need to run the sadistic "weed-out" courses that some departments notoriously inflict on their students to eliminate the unpromising enthusiast. It is enough that the culture of the university stays focused on education, so those who are not interested will soon find themselves with no point in being there. Flunking grades point to the door, but poor grades by themselves do not indicate failure, just the need for much more work. The sole requirement for study at the university should be interest and dedication, and those get tested only in the actual process of education.

Will the university be overrun with interested students? It would be delightful if that were to occur, but the truth is that once the university is made more voluntary and less mandatory, many of the current students will be just as happy to stay away and perhaps do something useful for a few years. They will come back when they are ready, at a time when they will actually appreciate what the university can do for them. Until then, their presence is a waste of time and resources. At the present moment, probably half the eighteen- to nineteen-year-old students at the university should not be there.

Is there room for new admissions? The prospect makes administrators gasp because of the problem of sheer space. But the truth is that we make terrible use of our university systems as they now exist. Not everyone has to go to the main campus of a state university system. Not everyone has to start out at "the university." There can and should be much more interplay between the university and the dozens of satellite schools that inevitably surround it. Branch campuses and statewide college systems are often underutilized. The University of California has long had a system (actually, three full systems) in which students who do not qualifiy for some campuses (say, Berkeley or UCLA) may well be quite happy on others. The University of Texas has incredible potential in its branch schools, whereas the main university in Austin is continually overcrowded. If a student really wants to be at the central campus, "where the action is," he or she should have to work to get there.

We should also spread "the action" around to a lot more campuses. Why should a student in Brownsville or Sierra Vista not have the same quality classes available to a student in Austin or Tucson? For serious advanced study, the central campus may be the only option, but for good, solid courses in a wide range of disciplines, one does not need a Nobel Prize–winning research faculty. We need to have more appreciation for our community colleges, and these should work in closer cooperation with the university. In fact, many of the students at the university already fill some of their basic requirements—particularly where classes are routinely unavailable or badly taught—at the local community college, and there is no reason (other than snobbishness) why the two could not work together to solve their mutual problems. Students who are not yet ready for a full-time university career ought to be able to go to a community college *and* take a course or two at the university.

Campuses are underutilized. There should be more night classes, more weekend classes, more summer courses, more utilization of an expensive physical plant that for many hours of the day and days of the year sits largely unused. Between the hours of ten in the morning and two in the afternoon, there is precious little seating (or parking) to be found, but in the early morning and late afternoon and evening, not to mention on Saturdays and Sundays and during most of May, December, January, July, and August, there are unused facilities galore. An exciting class could be filled even at midnight. As for faculty to teach those courses, if the "regular" faculty will not do it, there are many others, equally well qualified, who will. Overcrowding is not a problem at the university. Poor utilization of resources is the problem, together with Procrustean requirements that herd all the students in the same direction.

We should encourage older people to come back to the university— parents whose children have gone off to school, retirees, people with time off or evenings free. Give two-week "continuing education" courses in the summer to coincide with vacations. Work in cooperation with major corporations and government agencies to provide on-site classes, correlative studies, submersion in other languages and cultures, month-long multidisciplinary as well as job-related programs. There should be much more community-aimed effort, more evening courses, more "informal" nondegree courses, more of a nonexclusive social life, more cooperation between "town and gown." The old picture of the elitist university in the midst of the proletarian community is, or should be, entirely out of date. "Reach-out" programs, other than football, should be made available to everyone. Community courses, with or without credit, in subjects of interest to everyone—contemporary history and international politics, practical economics and government, other languages, great books, other cultures—should be readily available as well. *How much would our primary and secondary education improve if more parents went to school as an example for their kids?*

People are always interested in getting interested, and with good teaching and the right sort of marketing, the university could perform an invaluable community service that too many universities still think of as "beneath" them. In fact, opening up the university to the public will bring in a healthy critical perspective and flush out some of the effete and merely self-serving nonsense. The public will also bring in some of that much-needed income and political support that administrators are so feverishly scrounging for. An open university will discover renewed support among the local taxpayers, who would now find that the university has something to offer them as well.

We should give everyone a chance at a university education, a chance to improve themselves. But what do we do if they show that they cannot make it or do not have the skills or intelligence or preparation? Well, the first line of response is to give them the skills and the preparation, cultivate that intelligence, and create students out of those who would otherwise be failures. We can do it, and again, it is the neglect of the resources we have—including the other students—that makes such a mission seem impossible. What we need not do is to "flunk out" those who fail. Why put an indelible stigma on those who may simply not be ready? Rather, send them away for a few years.

Of course, there will always be students who should be disciplined and failed, and open admissions should not be an invitation to "anything goes." But we have accumulated a curious record of graduating mediocrities and not graduating geniuses that ought to make us think twice about our traditional standards of success and failure in school. A student who learns a great deal in one or two subjects, ignores the others, and leaves school without a degree to make waves in the world is by no means a failure, and those students who "satisfactorily" complete all of our scavenger-hunt requirements and qualify for a ho-hum job in which they will lead perennially bored lives are by no means paradigms of success. Why, then, should the university not encourage and nourish the kind of education that cannot be contained in a traditional curriculum or standard degree program?

Admissions should not be an obstacle to getting a college education. Let's give students the opportunity if and when they want it, and then let's do all we can to see that they get the most out of it.

31 ▾ Stop Sending "Kids" to College

One of the problems of university education—we are almost tempted to say *the* problem regarding the students—is that so many of them are not ready for college. By this we do not mean that they are ill prepared or undereducated. The problem is that many of them do not *want* to be at the university, whether or not they would rather be anywhere or doing anything else.

This is not to take anything away from our praise of eighteen-year-olds, who really are a marvel to teach. But they should be taught when they are ready, not just because our arbitrary system of career advancement and keeping kids off the streets happens to dictate "college at eighteen." There are many students, of course, who are quite ready for college, who have been treating their last years of high school as if they were already in college—doing extra reading, formulating favorite ideas, stretching their imaginations, and challenging themselves. They enter into freshman life with the demeanor and attitudes of a fish thrown back into the water. If they are not turned off by horrid courses taught by pompous incompetents, they are already into the swim of things a few weeks into their first semester. But too many students take to their classes more like a cat to a bath, because they do not have the *craving* for school.

College is not a privilege, much less a right. It is a blessing, a golden moment in life in which the life of the mind and the spirit can be explored to the fullest. Many students fresh out of high school are not ready for such a "blessing." They would be much better off hitting the road or getting a job or getting married. The same students, when they walk back onto campus three or ten or twenty years later, become some of the very best students of all.

We suggest that most seventeen-year-olds be *dis*couraged from going straight to college. Send them off to work. Suggest to them the Peace Corps, Teach America, or any of the two-year public services that are crying for intelligent, energetic young people to get involved. Encourage them to get involved in causes. Wish them farewell as they sail off into that recurrent American fantasy, the timeless cross-country or round-the-world trip, meeting people, learning new cultures, being on their own, "finding themselves."

We should encourage—and in some cases even demand—that high

school graduates do "something else" for two years before they begin college. Give students time to look forward to the university, and get rid of the types who should not be there (yet or at all). We would get much better students, face less wasted time and fewer student obsessions with narrow-minded careers. We would also find fewer students who start to "get it" only in the last year of their student careers, when the opportunities of college are just about coming to an end. Our celebration of the virtues of eighteen-year-olds notwithstanding, we need more of the "young at heart" and fewer of the merely immature.

Two years of mandated "national service," a not-so-radical suggestion that has been around at least since the days of the Vietnam War, has been recommended by social thinkers on both the Left and the Right. It has been standard fare in any number of societies and religions (notably, the Mormons, for whom two years of missionary work is mandated for all young people). The idea of mandatory devotion to the well-being of one's society is eminently defensible, and for those students who feel fully ready and anxious to continue to college right after high school, the obligation of two years' service might well be postponed. Indeed, those two years of service could serve much the same purpose for those college graduates, who might then be unsure what to do with themselves.

Most of these young people will discover new and more meaningful significance to the idea of an education. They will discover on their own—not from being force-fed and examined by high school sergeants—great books, great ideas, great problems. They will realize the importance of their basic but still incompetent writing and rhetorical skills and the importance of language and history and other intangibles, too. And then they will enter college, ready and willing, and most of the current student problems—with discipline and cheating, with abuse and misbehavior—will probably disappear as well.

32 ▾ SOTA (Students Older Than Average)

When Sarah enrolled at the University of Texas, her first and foremost feeling was that she "didn't belong." She had been a student here once before—a quarter of a century ago. She had performed passably in her classes but earned her "Mrs." degree by the end of her freshman year, when she married the graduating senior whom she had been dating since early in high school. But now, in her late forties, the last of her three children off to college, surrounded by students her children's age, she could only feel "out of it." She entered class as inconspicuously as possible; she sat in that anonymous midsection of the room, where all the faces begin to blur together. She was afraid to open her mouth, and after each class, she nervously double-checked the assignment, as if she alone must have missed something essential.

Sarah was a "special student," a student older than average (SOTA). She was officially "special," unfortunately not because she was better motivated and more experienced than most of her classmates but because, in the eyes of the registrar and the administration, she had entered with an out-of-date record and nonstandard, if not dubious, qualifications. She was, accordingly, put on probation, subject to a trial period before admission to a regular degree program.

In fact, many such students are not interested in degrees. They are here at the university for self-improvement, for stimulation, enjoying themselves immensely. But Sarah and the other "special students" are "special" in another sense, too. They are some of our best students. They work harder, think more, and enjoy their work more than the vast majority of their younger colleagues. They have a wealth of experience to draw upon, and most important, they have that hunger for learning that is the essence of a good education.

Sarah was not expected to go to college, and so she felt, mistakenly, that the younger students viewed her with some resentment. One brash coed, a friend of her daughter's from high school, had greeted her the first day of registration with "My God, what are *you* doing here?!" And that seemed to sum up her first few weeks. But by the end of the term, she had become the most popular and outspoken student in the class. She said what the other students could not say. She showed them that college can be something more than an extension of high school, a rebirth, even exhilaration. She was thrilled with it, if that is not too shrill a term for such a solemn subject. And everyone around her felt it, too.

Sarah is a member of a new and growing class of students. They tend to be in their mid- to late forties or older; most, but by no means all, of them are women. With the waning of the baby boom, they will fill an increasing number of places in our higher education systems. In fact, as enrollments drop, such students are more and more in demand, and some are even being recruited by the university. Some educators predict that, within the next ten years, nearly half of some college populations will consist of these older students. The quality of education will change, as will the nature of the curriculum. Older folks will not put up with the nonsense that is too often imposed on eighteen-year-olds, and they will properly respond to bad teaching with a complaint, a well-directed letter, or perhaps even a lawsuit.

We too often assume that the warriors of ideas are the young and open-minded, whereas their elders tend to be reactionary and anti-intellectual. Just the opposite is true: The older college students are more receptive and more willing to give up prejudices—or at least consider the other side. At the same time they have had more time to develop their convictions and more experience to support them. For example, in a weighty class called "existentialism," we were discussing no less a topic than "the meaning of life," and the general attitude among the twenty-year-olds was that life was "absurd" and "meaningless." It was then that Sarah, with her twenty-eight-year advantage and three grown children, turned them inside out, making them see that their profundities were just popular platitudes, and while they listened uncomfortably, she lectured them—brilliantly—on the meaning of life as she knew it.

Older students are making a difference. They are excited about the culture they are discovering. They see reading as an adventure and thinking as a challenge. They can appreciate the whole, rich tapestry of human experience because they have already lived so much of it, and now they are ready to examine it, understand it, and enrich it still further. Socrates once said, "The unexamined life is not worth living." He was already seventy-one, and his best student, Plato, was already "older than average."[1]

Stop Passing the Buck
33 ▾ (To Secondary Schools): "Remedial" Education

The university is not an extension of high school, but what is possible in the open university depends on what students have learned in high school, and all too often, they have learned exactly the wrong habits and attitudes. What most students learn in high school is that education is synonymous with imprisonment or, in career-minded families, that learning is their "job." In neither case is education made out to be fun or inspiring or an exciting challenge. A gifted high school teacher can make all the difference, of course, and there are a great many of them despite appalling pay, poor working conditions, and lack of status in American society. But even where the teachers are spectacular, the tendency of "dumbing down" that seems to rule so much of American adolescence and the oppressive if not culturally suicidal environment of most American high schools make this educational enthusiasm unlikely. And so the university has to make up the educational deficit. This is not an obstacle to our teaching. It is rather our obligation.

The university is supposed to be "higher" education, so why must it redo the job that was supposedly completed in high school? This question betrays a dangerous attitude that readily leads to predictable finger pointing. The high schools blame the middle schools, the middle schools the elementary schools, the elementary schools the preschools and the parents, and everyone can blame it on television. But in the midst of all this finger pointing, nothing gets done, except more political speech making and one more visit to some suburban classroom by the politicians.

The only principle that makes any sense, if we are not simply to abandon one or more generations of students, is that *we work with what we've got*. The university must play what it grudgingly calls a "remedial" role, teaching basic writing and reading skills and elementary math and history. But *remedial* is already a value-laden and offensive term. What is important is that students *now* learn to read, write, express themselves, think clearly and critically. That they are learning this two or five or seven years late, according to someone else's timetable, is not of importance. Of course, it would be superb if they could all learn the basics by the fourth grade—in effect doubling many of their intellectual lives. But this is just not happening, so there is no point in wishing it were. Giving students the basic educational tools they need must therefore become an acknowledged part of the university's responsibilities to its students and to the community as a whole.

Our first step is to convince the often conservative and understandably resistant professoriat to lower their sights and address the real problems of the students. Students have to learn "how to read," and whatever else it may be, teaching is reading *with* students, not just assigning exemplary readings. It is necessary to get them to write—journals, study questions, marginal commentary, anything, so long as they set pen and ideas to paper or fingertips to word processor. A professor may be limited by time as well as by patience and training, but the biggest obstacle to such elementary teaching responsibilities is the fact that so many people with a Ph.D. find such tasks utterly beneath them. To be sure, there is no way a professor, even with assistance, can read through hundreds of pages a week. But the mistake is to think that the professor has to do everything, that all written work requires professional grading and commentary. Get the students to help one another, read one another, criticize and correct and even "grade" one another, so long as the professors do not use this as an excuse to neglect their own responsibilities. The important thing is that students should read and write and learn to enjoy reading, writing, and thinking, and the limitations on the part of the professor should not be assumed to be restrictions on the students. Professors can and should do much more, but students can do still more to help themselves.

Raising college admissions standards is not the answer to the problem of unpreparedness. The obstacle to be overcome is a refusal to face our own responsibilities. Affirmative action in this regard is cruel, wasteful, and unfair if there is no mechanism for "bringing kids up to speed" and giving them a chance to succeed. But remedial resources need not and should not be in any way restricted to race or group affiliation. They should be open to everyone who is willing to work at learning. Effort, attitude, and personal progress should be the sole criteria for continuance. In the long run, of course, such remedial work pays for itself in the elimination of illiteracy from society. It is the most important investment in the long-term future that any culture can make. If we fail to give our students the skills and attitudes they need to succeed, it is not just the failure of the schools. It is the failure of our entire culture.[2]

34 ▾ In Loco Parentis

Eighteen-year-old students now have had experiences and pressures virtually unknown to the generation in their forties and fifties. They do not, as we did, simply assume that American industry and the American economy are unique in the world. They begin their sex lives in their early teens, and in junior high school they already face the threats of drugs and AIDS. Many of our undergraduates are painfully aware of the fragile state of the economy and the bleak prospects that exist for many of them. They have become all too aware of corruption in high places. They are cynics at a young age, pessimists before their time, and the combination of wisdom, naïveté, and youthful enthusiasm makes a strange brew indeed.

The issue here is *paternalism*—the university acting as a parent (*in loco parentis*). Should the university allow eighteen-year-olds who have never been out on their own to make their own decisions? Or should it "control" them with restrictions and requirements? But why (again) such a harsh "either/or"? A concerned faculty and administration and a good peer advising system operated by fellow students and a few good professionals provide a balanced solution. Students readily make the distinction between "university assistance" and "university interference." They want to make their own decisions. They want responsibility. They need help, not paternalism. Why won't the university listen to them? Because they are "only kids"?

When the topic of student responsibility comes up, the journalistic imagination leaps to the topics of drugs, alcohol, and sex. In fact, the vast majority of our students seem to be quite clear about the dangers of alcohol and the horrors of drugs, and their eighteen-year-old awareness of the complexities of sex exceeds the knowledge of many of their parents. College students do not need chaperones. They need to exercise their own sense of responsibility. And when that sense of responsibility fails, they should have to face the consequences like anyone else.[3]

Many "new" social problems are new only in the attention that is finally being given to them. The much-publicized crime of "date rape" has been a feature of American life since the advent of "dating." What has changed is young women's realization that they do not have to accept this as one more abuse to be excused under the "boys will be boys" philosophy. And of course, the shotgun wedding has long gone out of style. To be sure, such questions are confused considerably due to the rapidly changing expectations and standards of sexual behavior of the past twenty years, but to see this as a crisis demanding a paramilitary invasion of the university rather than a situation demanding (and getting) careful attention by the students themselves is to make matters much worse rather than better.

The real problems of responsibility lie not in these dark and sexy alcoves but in the halls of academe as such, especially in routine and such journalistically uninteresting questions as what students should study, where they should live, and how they should eat (at least at mealtime). Questions about course content attracted virtually no media attention whatever until the campus war over the "core curriculum" started up again recently, and then the media focus, as always, was on the irresponsible extremes. But the answer to such questions is not a "what" so much as a "who"—namely, *who* should decide what courses students should take? The answer is, in short, the students themselves.

To say that students should take responsibility for themselves does not preclude the availability and recommendation of various structures, schedules, plans, and arrangements by the university. Perhaps it is the illusion of freedom rather than freedom itself that is most important here, but it is essential that students have both adequate guidance *and* the sense of choosing their own path. Most important, of course, is the question of curriculum, a question we will return to again and again. But to begin with, take as an example the more mundane question of where to live. We assumed, before we raised the question with several dozen students, that undergraduates deplore living in dorms and yearn for the day when they can break free and have their own off-campus apartments. Off campus they would be free from rules, free from supervision, and free from the obnoxious roommate. But when we talked to students, we found remarkable agreement: Students should be *required* to live on campus for the first two years!

In their living arrangements students experience dorm life not as a continuation of life at home with their parents but as more akin to summer camp. It is an incredible freedom for most of them, and for many of them already more than they can handle. They welcome the camaraderie, the ready availability of help and advice, and they thrive on the collegiality and social experience of being surrounded by other students morning to (and through the) night. There are practical considerations, too: Most students do not have the money for a decent apartment. Moreover, college campuses can be dangerous places at night, especially for women, and surely one of the great virtues of on-campus housing is the ability to monitor and mitigate such dangers.

Does the requirement of living on campus violate the students' autonomy? Well, no, one might say; it rather anticipates their needs. But this, of course, is the backbone of all claims to paternalism, and with reference to on-campus living, too, we would suggest that a voluntary choice is always better than a mandate. The duty of the university is to make on-campus living available and attractive enough so that students can and will want to be there. It is no paradox or contradiction to suggest that students will gladly choose to do what you think they ought to do, so long as you do not make them do it. Make it the best alternative. Students generally know what is good for them—unless, of course, requirements and their natural sense of resistance get in the way.

So, too, students complain about dorm and cafeteria food but are equally forthright in confessing that, without such a regimen, they tend to live on an irregular schedule of Snickers bars and fast-food burgers. They are health conscious enough to be bothered by this, but harried enough and perpetually hungry enough to ignore it. One could imagine an overly conscientious college administrator attempting to enforce a nutritionally and politically correct diet for all students, but in such a context we would like to have first option on a fast-food franchise just across the street.

35 ▾ *The Problem of Authority*

The university should be a model of democracy as well as a training ground for democracy. This means that the students, in particular, should decide how they will act and how they will live and what they will study. They should have a say in how the university is run. How can the university be the training ground for democracy when the students themselves are denied a voice? How can you have open inquiry and an environment that encourages freedom of thought and freedom of speech when the university structure presents only obstacles and requirements?

Within the classroom the same democratic principles should be respected. It is well known that the professors who *need* authority and rely on it are typically disastrous teachers, whereas the best teachers' students would attempt to walk on water if they thought it expected of them. This is not to say, of course, that there are not excellent authoritarian teachers or that there are not subjects (some introductory language courses and technical skills, for example) that require something more than inspiration. But the tendency to substitute requirements and authority—in a short word, *force*—where in fact there ought to be encouragement, inspiration, and motivation is one of the continuing failures of the university.

In a well-run university that is defined by its excellent teaching, the practice of education itself does the organizing. We might note, however, that to reject the authoritarian notion of education is not to insist on egalitarianism in the university, the sometimes-absurd suggestion that the faculty has no special role. There will, inevitably, be classes and privileges, and the very existence of grades and evaluation of one group by another (senior professors of junior professors as well as instructors and students) guarantees an asymmetric inequality. Grading establishes an authority figure, but this need not be oppressive and abused, as it so often is in everything from force-feeding students inappropriate material with the threat, "You will be tested on this," to the moral outrage of sexual harassment.

Students learn fast that authority, as such, need have nothing to do with superior knowledge of either the subject or the world, and it takes only a few professors who exemplify authority rather than inspired teaching to convince many students that the point is simply to "play the game," give the teacher back whatever he or she wants, get the grades, and forget the education. Legitimate authority in the classroom is established by proven superiority in the field and excellent teaching. Teachers who know their field and teach it brilliantly do not need official authority at all. A good teacher only needs enough initial respect and attention to have a chance to affect even the most arrogant students, and most will become respectful and, ultimately, grateful.

The shared sentiment of conservative defenders of the "canon" of classics and the liberal to radical advocates of multiculturalism is that the student should be force-fed certain books and ideas. This violates the most basic principle of education—that it is responsibility and not resentment that we want to encourage. Even as children, we loved to read. But for many years we were revolted by the "great books" because we were *forced* to read them. It was only later, and in some instances only now, that we have come to appreciate what wonderful experiences were being ruined for us. If students are forced to read books by and about African-Americans, Latinos, and native Americans, will this assure multicultural appreciation and familiarity? Or will it breed further resentment and racism?

Our suggestion is to take every plausible step to *make the university voluntary.* That means eliminating required courses in favor of various forms of peer pressure, word of mouth, "guidance," and intellectual seduction. Some required courses will always be necessary, perhaps, but most of the courses required are nothing more than wholly inadequate compensation for the lack of good, exciting courses, adequate guidance, and a communicative campus culture. We would like to think that there is no need to require courses even in such rigorous curricula as engineering or nursing. Just let it be known loudly and clearly that one cannot become an engineer or a nurse without them. The distinction between "must" and "ought to" may seem nominal to those who fail to distinguish between externally imposed requirements and self-realization, but to students, it makes all the difference.

So, too, for matters outside the curriculum, from the basics of living away from their parents—finding a place to live and foraging for food for themselves—to social behavior and the actual running of the university. What the university needs is more support, encouragement, and guidance for the students and fewer directives. Imposed rules inspire rebellion in an eighteen-year-old. Responsibilities inspire—responsibility. *Choice* is the key word in our philosophy of education; excellence will follow.

36 ▾ *Sabbaticals for Everyone*

Sometimes in life there is nothing of more importance than time off. Too many people save this simple fact of life for their retirement—which may never come; or they cram it into two action-packed weeks of vacation—which end up being as exhausting and mind clogging as their job back home. Academics are often criticized for their two- or three-month summer vacations (and as much as a month at Christmas), but the truth is that virtually everyone in our society should have a similar advantage. Americans have some of the fullest working schedules and the shortest vacations in the industrialized world. What we lack is educational leisure. Productivity would increase, not decrease, not to mention the increase in our collective sense of health and well-being. And the great advantage to the university would be an appreciative flow of the very best students.

Americans are not for the most part educated in their use of leisure time, and their love of sports and recreation, however appropriate for weekends and two-week vacations, would soon betray a certain lack of substance. Leisure time—or what Bertrand Russell ironically defended as "idleness"—is not just time "off" but time "on," time to retool and re-examine one's life, time to train and learn new skills and fields, too, looking ahead and enriching one's life as well as taking a "break" from it. There are some signs that our more enlightened captains of industry are beginning to see the advantages of such a scheme, but for the time being, it will be reserved for the lucky few, or rather the enlightened few, for the secret of life as a learning experience is not just for those who fall into it but for those who seek it out as well.

We urge sabbaticals and summer vacations for everyone. Our work force is large enough. We have enough professionals, and there are many more to come. It is not, as some Japanese politicians have been saying, that Americans do not work hard enough. They work too hard, and like the Japanese, they too often "work themselves to death." What is wrong with our free market is that it is not free enough. It does not let people explore and enrich themselves, except in the too-limited terms of careers and commerce.

Work and professional life should not be a never-ending grindstone. It must be punctuated and spurred on by new challenges and opportunities. Executives and workers alike would do well to go back to school, not just to update and improve their job skills but to upgrade and improve their lives.

The university is a cultural oasis, and we should give everyone a semester for learning, enriching, finding out about life. Productivity would increase. People wouldn't feel trapped in the tracks of their careers. And they wouldn't feel such horror toward the end of them. We can and should make a special effort to help people prepare for a new life, often more rewarding than the life they have pursued in their careers. Japanese corporate preretirement seminars begin as much as fifteen years before retirement. Instead of just encouraging people to build financial "nest eggs" for themselves in preparation for retirement, why don't we help them give some content to those years as well?

Actual American life as experienced by most people is so boring, uniform and devoid of significant soul, so isolated from traditions of the past and the resonances of European culture, that it demands to be praised and misrepresented as something wonderful. BAD [not just bad but pretentious] thus becomes an understandable reaction to the national emptiness and dullness.

——Paul Fussell, *BAD: Or, the Dumbing of America*

---

37 ▾ Dropping Out

How long should a student stay in college? Once it was simply assumed that a college education would last four years. But now that some professional programs insist on five years and some schools combine college and professional training, not to mention the embarrassment of the five-year fraud, this needs to be reconsidered. For a great many students, four continuous years of college may be excessive. They find, after their first or second year, that they really need a break, or they want to try something else, or they are just not capable of the concentration that their studies require. Why should they be trapped in an opportunity that they can no longer take advantage of? Why not come back in a few years when they are once again ready?

The phenomenon of "dropping out" may still horrify parents, but it is sometimes the wisest decision a young adult can make. Some students realize, even in their first year, that they have made the wrong decision. Universities should be wide open for students coming and going, perhaps over the better part of a decade, and if the administrative procedures for accounting for such "irregular" students are too complicated, then those procedures should be simplified. For some students, two or three years is an ideal amount of time for university study, and then restlessness or impatience will prod them on to the next stage in life. It is only our obsession with degrees as the "end" of an education that makes this suggestion sound implausible, but as our emphasis shifts from degrees and credentials to the education itself, it becomes perfectly obvious that four years is an utterly arbitrary specification for higher education.

Ideally, education should be so desirable, so rewarding, and so much fun that it will continue throughout life, long after retirement, and according to some eschatological theories, even after death as well. For some of us, the thesis of continuing education has become so obvious, so irresistible that we have decided never to leave the university campus. The luckiest of us are called "professor"—but we are really just students all the same.

PART VI

Students
and Their
Careers

38 ▼ *The University Is Not a Trade School, But . . .*

One of the most often-heard complaints about the university today, from both the Right and the Left, is that the university has prostituted its mission and become a mere "trade school," a training ground for the professions instead of a bastion of learning. Liberal arts professors, who find their subjects marginalized, lament their subjects' being categorized as "service" courses or simply dismissed as "useless." Their resentment is mirrored, of course, by accounting and engineering professors who find their subjects and themselves dismissed as "nonacademic." There is clearly a confused antipathy between academia and the professions, another fallacious "either/or" argument that serves only polemics and not understanding. There is no contradiction, we suggest, between education and learning to make a living.

The current antagonism between liberal arts and professional programs depends on a misconception about the history of the university. The university has always been a professional training ground. It is the professions, not the mission of the university, that have changed. University students are perfectly entitled to be concerned about what they will be doing for the rest of their lives, but it is doing them no favors to tell them they should avoid subjects that are "of no real use to them." The liberal arts are of enormous value to them and to their careers. Morton H. Meyerson, an extremely successful Texas entrepreneur, puts it succinctly: "People who come from a liberal arts background have a broader outlook on life and make better businesspeople because they are not niche specialists."

> Today, more than ever, purely utilitarian aims happen to coincide with the highest humanistic and civic purposes of schooling, such as promoting a more just and harmonious society, creating an informed citizenry, and teaching our children to understand and appreciate the worlds of nature, culture and history.
> ——E. D. Hirsch, Jr., *New York Review of Books*

What a good education provides is the facility for imagination and thinking for oneself as well as the material to feed imagination and thought. More basically, the university teaches and refines the most fundamental skills—reading, writing, and calculating—which can be both precious and pedestrian. One can appreciate the joy of mathematical puzzles and games, whether they involve parlor-room numerology or trying to prove the latest equivalent of the Goldbach conjecture, but one will also undoubtedly use those same skills to balance checkbooks and calculate expense accounts, income taxes, and repair bills. One reads for pleasure, but one also reads for news and information, and one reads warnings on medicine bottles, memos from the boss, contracts from the realtor, and technical treatises, from how-to books to the stuff of one's profession.

Professional training is not just training. There are, to be sure, those professions that involve purely technical skills, but why should they be excluded from the university? The only argument is that the university can only do so much, and although air-conditioning repair and plumbing may be essential skills in our society and a fascinating practical elective for many university students, the resources and facilities of any campus are limited. The bad argument, however, is the snobbish rejection of such skills as menial. We suspect that much of the training excluded from the university has more to do with *class* than with educational resources.

The exclusion of certain skills and subjects from the university curriculum ought to be determined by time and space limitations only, not by class or tradition. Much of the career training that is now farmed out to "colleges" should be included at the university—along with a healthy dose of the liberal arts. Why should so many working-class students be abandoned to fly-by-night operations that neither train nor educate? Future plumbers and air-conditioning specialists have just as much to gain from college as do potential lawyers and engineers. Even now, universities give courses in such practical matters as cooking and car repair on an "informal" basis. But since we reject the distinction between formal and informal, credit and noncredit courses as well, the question of what should be taught in a university remains for us an open one.

Professionals have not only a right to, but a special need for, the kinds of thinking that "useless" liberal arts courses can provide. This is becoming increasingly evident, for example, in the number of professional ethics courses that are now being added on a required basis for medical, law, business, and engineering students. *Ethics* is a code word for a healthy introduction of the liberal arts—history and philosophy as well as a little sensitivity training through literature—into what have become, in the past few decades, overly technical and technocratic courses of study.

> **For those who end up in the corporate world, or in the world of work, it is a liberating experience to learn to think, to write well, to speak well. A liberal arts education opens rather than closes, and I'm concerned that with corporate leaders, and our government and even some of our educators increasingly calling for these well-trained people, . . . we may not get well-educated people.**
> **——Johnnetta Cole, president, Spelman College, Atlanta**

As the introduction of ethics becomes more established, what is increasingly clear is that a few "add-on"–type courses or electives are not enough. In business schools, for example, new programs are making the

attempt to introduce ethics into *all* the courses of the curriculum—
in other words, to integrate education and professional training, just as
they were before our age of hypertechnology. The divide between professional training and the liberal arts is breaking down, and that is just
as it should be.

39 ▾ Two Cultures, 1992: Business and the Humanities

At Harvard University the business school is separated
from the rest of the university by the Charles River. The symbolism of this
separation is unmistakable. There are many voices within the university
insisting that business schools do not belong on the campus at all and that
business courses do not belong in the undergraduate curriculum. Meanwhile, enrollments in business schools continue to multiply to near-
bursting capacity.

The increase in the number of undergraduate students majoring in
business nationwide has been largely at the expense of the liberal arts.
Some liberal arts departments have simply pretended that nothing has
happened, but they have then lost touch with a great many of their
students. Others, to maintain their enrollments, have become service
organs of the business school. This has fostered not cooperation and
exchange but resentment. Ironically, the liberal arts have become the
"dumping ground" for the business school, the last resort for those students not bright enough, not conscientious enough, or not adequately
prepared for business courses.

The effect of this has been destructive on both sides: It endangers the
integrity of the liberal arts department, and it turns the business school,
as well as the university, into a glorified job shop—the very antithesis of
a university. Administrators fight for turf and warm bodies. Business
students graduate without even being exposed to the classics of their own
culture. Liberal arts students leave the university with contempt for business, despite the fact that most of them will end up in the business world
one way or the other.

We think that the business school and business courses belong on
campus, but the idea of a predominantly business undergraduate major
is a travesty for both the students and the people who hire them. What
smart employers know but business schools are not telling is that most

of what gets learned in business school is outdated by the time the students get to their first job, where they will in any case be trained in the practices of the particular firm. Business schools act primarily as human resource departments, weeding out the truly incompetent, giving gold stars to the best performers (in classwork, anyway). And when so many students attend business school only because their parents insist on it or because they have been told throughout high school that they ought to prepare for a career, the results are disastrous. Students put little effort into nonbusiness courses because they are not interested, poison their future career possibilities, and squander the valuable years they have in college. This is not career preparation but a preliminary to a wasted life.

Too many students in the liberal arts graduate with the regret that they have not had even a glimpse of practical preparation. Too many students who believe they are "forced" into business feel that they have wasted their years at the university. They find out too late that they could have gotten the same job and also satisfied their interests in liberal arts subjects. They find out too late that they would have had a *better* chance at the best graduate schools with a major other than business. (At Harvard more than 80 percent of the first-year MBA students are nonbusiness majors.)

What is to be done? First, there needs to be more integration and cooperation at the university level, encouraging mutual programs and concerns and discouraging competition between the colleges. It is incumbent on both the liberal arts college and the business school to get to know each other and to encourage their students to do so as well. It also means that the business school should encourage its students to take more electives outside of the business school, especially language, culture, science, and literature courses.

Much of the task falls on business itself: Employers can encourage well-rounded students by expanding their own searches, recruiting campuswide instead of just in the business school, and having the foresight to hire students who can quickly learn the business as well as those who have had a textbook introduction to it. Indeed, insofar as business schools operate to select and train future corporate managers and executives, why not have the corporations themselves sponsor the business schools? Business schools may belong in the university, but only so long as they share the mission of the university and are not just the unpaid servants of the business community.

40 ▾ *The Career Athlete*

The most visible and popular career program administered by most institutions of higher learning is the intercollegiate football program. Every autumnal Saturday, hundreds and hundreds of college campuses all across the country enjoy a day of (for the most part) amateur athletic competition. Across the country millions of television sets are tuned in to games televised locally, regionally, or nationally, and tens of thousands of phone lines are buzzing with bets and wagers. For three hours a quarter of the country is focused on the same activity. This goes on for eleven or twelve weeks every fall. Then comes the bowl season, and along the way basketball season begins.

There have been many marvelous moments and outstanding young individuals in "big-time" intercollegiate athletics. From the traditional Harvard-Yale and Army-Navy clashes to our nationally televised, mythical national championship game on New Year's Day, from Red Grange to Bo Jackson, icons of glory abound. Many students recall with fondness their intercollegiate athletic training. Discipline, physical development, camaraderie, strategy, and institutional representation are just some of the benefits derived from participating in intercollegiate athletics. For some, intercollegiate athletics provides scholarships that enable them to receive an otherwise barely affordable university education. But for others, the glory of college sports is just an illusion and a prelude to tragedy.

Big-time intercollegiate athletics has confronted the university with serious problems. Widely known are the host of academic scandals—namely, student athletes who cannot maintain even a "C" average in the easiest of courses, graduation rates that range far, far below 50 percent, and the criminal and gang element that has begun to creep into college athletic programs. Wholesale cheating in exams is commonplace, and faculty members are told in no uncertain terms that their "standards" do not apply when an athlete is in their class. But many of these student · athletes do not bother to show up for class at all. They are "students" in name only. It is a category of eligibility, not an expression of interest in studying.

Many of these young athletes could not attend class even if they wanted to. A football player has practice almost every afternoon, lifts weights three times a week, has to look at pre- and postgame films, attend team meetings and strategy sessions, and leave campus to attend away games at least five Thursdays or Fridays a semester. They are at a serious academic disadvantage. Accordingly, many football players take a lighter load of courses during the fall semester to meet the demands of such a schedule, but by the time their football eligibility is used up four years later, they have not amassed the number of credits required for graduation. Few of them continue long enough to graduate—more victims of the five-year fraud. Some successful athletes are drafted by the NFL or NBA or signed by major league baseball, but then their academic career comes to an abrupt halt. A few years and several million dollars later, they are hardly of a mind to finish their college degree, but they are the lucky ones.

"Student" athletes in general are ruthlessly exploited. Each year well over a billion dollars is spent on college football and basketball alone. Of this, the student athletes receive nothing, and the NCAA forbids them from receiving money or gifts or from holding additional employment. The student athlete is, stereotypically, a young man who spent too much of his time in high school working toward the single, difficult goal of being recruited by a top-ranked, highly visible intercollegiate athletic program so that at the end of his four years of eligibility, he might be drafted by a professional sports franchise and be paid hundreds of thousands, if not millions, of dollars. In between, he is given room and board, forty hours of practice, and almost incidentally, the opportunity to receive an education that is hardly an essential component of his career goals.

Meanwhile, his nonathlete friends drive sports cars and wear hundred-dollar athletic footwear and drive to California at midsemester to see some friends. He cannot afford such a trip, and indeed, he knows that if an alumnus or a coach were to give him 150 bucks to buy an airline ticket to fly home to visit his sick grandmother, he would bring an NCAA investigation down upon the entire program. He cannot work. He cannot take gifts. He cannot earn enough to live on—even assuming that he is not also trying to use his "good fortune" to support a family back home.

Intercollegiate student football and basketball players—just like library workers, laboratory assistants, and teaching aides—should receive a salary for the work they perform on behalf of the university; for the fame and visibility they bring to the university; and for the huge sums of alumni, community, and television money they raise for the university. The letter-sweater–bearing amateur athlete of the past—a noble image, to be sure—is an outmoded concept. Even the Pleistocene International Olympic Committee has come to this realization; we are now sending professional athletes to the Olympics. Athletics, like universities, has become big business, and those who do the work should be adequately compensated.

Perhaps the basic problem with intercollegiate athletics is that too much emphasis is placed on NCAA competition. A typical university athletic department budget these days is over ten million dollars. The same university's English department's budget is approximately two million dollars. In fact, at most universities you would have to add the budgets of the English, math, history, French, German, Russian, and Spanish departments to reach the sum of money that pours into the athletic department. Surely, there is an improper balance here, a disproportion that does not keep in focus the goal of higher education. And, in terms of equality, women's athletics suffer enormously by comparison. A talented, even brilliant, young female athlete cannot hope to get the same attention, training, or opportunities as her football-playing counterpart—or even her male colleagues in the same sport (such as basketball). The money goes where the money already is: where the boys are.

Ideally, perhaps, we should strictly maintain the amateur status of all student athletes and make sure that they are students first, athletes only secondarily. In the Ivy League, this ideal has survived for many years, however uncompetitive their teams may be against the virtually professionalized Big Ten or Southwest Conference. But our society has become too infatuated with college athletics to allow its importance to be diminished. Our universities must therefore adjust accordingly and distinguish between the money-making intercollegiate athletic programs and the more important educational mission of the university.

A few colleges might want to offer career athlete programs with an education on the side. A better way to separate professional sports and academics is to think of big-time college sports teams as campus affiliates. This is comparable to the way cities think of their sports teams. There is, for example, no pretension that a Bronco quarterback was born or even lives in Denver, nor is it assumed that he will loyally remain with the team however fortune beckons beyond. He plays for the team and the team "represents" the city, but the relationship between them is strictly contingent. So, too, let colleges recruit professional teams if they choose, but let's not then confuse that straightforward professional activity with college athletics. And of course, such teams would be strictly dependent on their own success. Although they would be expected to support the school that employs them, that financial expectation would not be reciprocated.

Of course, the most important perk for the college-affiliated professional athlete could be the opportunity to take courses and work for a degree. But this would be an option—as it is for most staff members—and not a prerequisite. Part of one's pay could come in course coupons, or chits, which could be "cashed in" as tuition, possibly at some future date after the season (or one's brief career) has ended. Such student athletes would indeed be welcome in our classes but as students, not as athletes, and they, in return, would get what they paid for rather than being exploited by the illusion of college for free.

Even without examining a university's budget, the interested reader can calculate how much money a stadium filled with fifty thousand people—each spending up to twenty-five dollars on admission, concessions, and parking—will bring into the athletic department's coffers, especially when the players, the band, and the opposition are provided at minimal cost. It is often argued by athletic directors that all that money pouring in from football and basketball only pays for other, less lucrative sports. That is indeed true, but like other businesses, intercollegiate athletic departments continually expand to meet the budget they produce. Volleyball teams fly to Wisconsin or California or New York for competition; the men's basketball team plays some exhibition games in Europe; ten or eleven coaches fly around the country recruiting players for next year's squad. Successful coaches receive well over five hundred thousand dollars (including what they earn from their television, advertising, personal appearance, and endorsement contracts), and the stadium and training facilities are state of the art, even if two hundred yards away stands an overcrowded, ill-equipped classroom building. Within a constrained university budget, such expenses are grossly out of proportion. Pulitzer Prize–winning authors earn a fraction of the salary of a football or basketball coach, and we have seen athletic department offices that rival the president's or the governor's office in plushness.

Universities will no doubt balk at the suggestion that they pay their football and basketball players and that these sports should in turn pay for themselves. But here is a partial solution to the question of resources: Have the professional leagues pay for part of the costs; after all, why should the university and tax dollars pay for football and basketball minor leagues? Also, limit recruitment. In fact, why should the university be stuck with athletic recruiting at all? Why not leave it to the professionals themselves? Professional athletics could be a boon to the university, but there is no excuse for its being an obsession, much less a drain on resources and a source of corruption.

41 ▼ Are Graduate Students Students? Five Modest Proposals

New graduate students are usually but three months out of undergraduate college, barely more sophisticated than an average senior. New graduate students often arrive without an adequate background in their chosen field of study. They are almost as confused as freshmen with their new surroundings and the new expectations thrust upon them. These beginning students are now expected to be junior colleagues, fellow professionals, with duties and obligations that were no part of undergraduate life. They are encouraged to adopt the worst professional pretenses and prejudices, which all too often they do with the piety of religious converts. Most important, many graduate students are expected to grade exams and teach classes, activities for which their only preparation has probably been from the other side of the desk. They are expected to display professional skills and knowledge of techniques almost from the beginning, and in any decent graduate department they will routinely be invited to hobnob with full faculty on something of a regular basis.

Are graduate students students? Faculty typically treat them with a kind of schizoid confusion, as both students and colleagues, whichever seems to be less appropriate at the time. Some professors routinely teach incoming graduate students their most advanced work—indeed, "They work on their book in class"—when, in fact, most graduate students need just about the same courses that undergraduate majors need. Many graduate students, even the best and most promising, did not study as undergraduates the subject they are now studying in graduate school. Faculty sometimes treat graduate students as fully paid colleagues in the most exploitative way, "asking" them to teach their courses and handing them more grading than they would conceivably require of themselves, if they did not have virtually slave labor to help them. Like student athletes, the graduate students are in a bind. They are honored and exploited by a system that gives them very little and promises them a great deal.

On the other hand, faculty sometimes treat graduate students as mere children, for whom the most important decisions are made without their approval or input and whose progress is measured in the most sophomoric fashion—scheduled tests, for example. But if undergraduates should be treated as adults and allowed to plan their own education, this goes double for graduate students. Graduate students should be overloaded with opportunities but unburdened of requirements that would interfere with their exploration and progress. Indeed, the real problem with many graduate students is that, in the name of professional advancement, too many of them bypass the all-important exploration of the material itself and ask instead to be taught "the tricks of the trade." They get narrow just when they have the opportunity to broaden themselves.

Graduate school is not a training ground for effete pretentiousness. It is a rare opportunity to concentrate on what one loves and finds fascinating, and if one maintains one's enthusiasm and has the ability, it provides the opportunity and the training to teach. It is, more than anything else, a place to share and enjoy the riches of education, and the fact that it is a "professional school" should never allow us to forget that it is above all a joy and a privilege.

1. **Graduate School—for Love, Not Money.** The availability of jobs in academia is problematic. Just a year or two ago, the demographics promised a surge in retirements and openings for younger scholars in the mid-1990s. But then the Reagan-Bush recession did its damage, and the result for the foreseeable future is still hard to discern but not promising. It is immoral, we think, to attract and invite graduate students to study under the illusion that they will get a job when they have finished. There are not nearly that many positions available.

What we suggest, accordingly, is that much more emphasis be put on graduate school as a place not for protoprofessionals but for students who love a subject and want to study. Graduate school should be for fun, not eventual profit. For those who insist on a credential to "show" what they have been doing, we can offer more terminal master's degrees, not as a booby prize for those who have failed to get a Ph.D. but as a certificate of accomplishment. We should have programs for people who just love a particular subject and want to spend another year or two concentrating on it.

We should limit Ph.D.'s, and we should put much less emphasis on them. As a measure of personal wisdom, worth, or intelligence, the degree has no value. For this reason, schools such as Princeton follow an old English custom and insist on addressing all professors as "Mister" or "Ms." To emphasize a Ph.D.—on letterhead or on a business card—is pretty much to admit that you haven't got much else of interest to say. To have spent a few years devoted to something you love, on the other hand—that says a good deal about you.

2. **Teach Them How to Teach.** Those who do intend to get a Ph.D. should never forget that it is—whatever else it might be—a license to teach. In education schools it is often pointed out that students are taught how to teach but not what to teach. In graduate schools the problem is that students are taught what to teach but not how to teach. Every graduate student should have the opportunity—as beginning elementary teachers do—to practice their new craft in front of an experienced teacher, not once but many times. They should be taught teaching strategies, how to cope with difficult cases, how to entertain as well as convey information and answer questions. Instead, some graduate students never get a clue that they will ever have to teach, or they are told that if they are good enough, they will never see a classroom. If they have to teach to justify what would otherwise be a research fellowship, they may do so with the mixed resentment and gratitude that they will, with luck, never have to do it again.

Such an attitude not only does the poor undergraduates in their classes no good, but it also does a disservice to the graduate students. To treat teaching as an inconvenience or a degradation is to rob intellectual life of at least half its flavor. In the humanities and the social sciences, teaching is the heart of academic life, no matter how exciting the findings and fads that punctuate the slow progress of those sometimes ancient fields. Even in the sciences, where nonteaching research positions are much more common, teaching is an exercise in presentation and clarity, valuable tools for scientists who will inevitably have to explain and justify their work and their findings to the nonscientists who sponsor and may use that research. It is doing graduate students no favor to make them specialists in teeny, tiny subjects and otherwise illiterate, both in their own fields and in the life of the intellect and the spirit. Teaching them to teach is at the same time teaching them to be continuous learners and interesting human beings who will have a contribution to make to society whether or not their research dreams ever amount to anything.

3. **Stop Exploitation.** Graduate students are self-supporting adults, often with families. They are not and should not be slave labor, even in return for laudatory recommendations and a few precious hours of a distinguished professor's time. They should be adequately compensated for what they do, and it should not be taken away with the other hand, as is often done, by raising tuition or requiring that they be "enrolled as a full-time student the semester one receives the degree." Graduate students should not be placed in teaching positions and situations they cannot possibly handle. Graduate students and advanced graduate teach-

ing associates provide the most cost-effective means of teaching lower-level discussion classes, but they should not be used to teach lecture courses, and they should not be expected to regularly "fill in" for a professor at his or her convenience.

General complaints about the use of graduate-student teachers are typically unfair as well as counterproductive. Some graduate students are already brilliant teachers, and they are well employed to conduct small, multiple discussion sections that could not possibly be handled by the faculty alone. (A large lecture class of 240 students, for example, should have at least twelve and ideally sixteen discussion sections.) But they should also be paid fairly for what they do.

4. **Stop Killing Creativity.** We should stop teaching graduate students to be petty professionals if that means that they are going to forget why they are there in the first place—because they love the subject. A graduate student in English once said (to a large colloquium filled with the country's leading English literature scholars), "As far as I can tell, the main aim in graduate school has been to teach me to despise literature." He received a standing ovation for his comment, and the ominous scowls of his professors.

How do we teach graduate students to despise their subject?

▼ By showing them all the mistakes that preceded them and underemphasizing the insights and joy of discovery

▼ By ideologizing and dehistoricizing the past so that a fifth- or fifteenth-century genius gets dismissed for views that are politically incorrect (by today's standards)

▼ By teaching methods and theory to the exclusion of substance

▼ By subjecting them to degradations that force anyone with any pride to drop out and dismiss the subject

▼ By making graduate school an obstacle course instead of an opportunity

▼ By teaching advanced research seminars without any regard for the background or interests of the students

▼ By failing to teach the basics of the field on the self-serving assumption that students can learn such material on their own

▼ By reducing the field to a trivium so that fascination and imagination are no longer possible

▼ By presenting professors as role models of petty power-mongering, mutual resentment, and prejudice to all fields and approaches other than their own

▼ By forcing students barely involved in the field to spend years doing servile scut work represented as "original research."

5. **End the Requirement of Ph.D. Dissertations.** Among the outstanding reasons for the failure of graduate schools to produce well-rounded, productive scholars, particularly in the humanities, is the antiquated doctoral dissertation, that grand culminating project, several hundred pages of professional-level research and study constituting an "original contribution to the discipline." The project usually takes a couple of years, although a few candidates complete it in a year or less, and a great many more take as long as five to ten years. Others never finish the project at all, sometimes wasting a full decade or more of their lives.

Needless to say, it is very rare for a graduate student to produce an "original contribution to the discipline." At best, a good graduate student can give a slightly new twist to work that is already going on, unearth some documents in a field already swimming in such intellectual flotsam, add some confirming data to an already partially confirmed hypothesis. An articulate graduate student can sometimes clarify and present the work of his or her mentor, and every once in a while a graduate student may turn up some truly striking or shocking evidence that more seasoned scholars may have ignored. But in general, the contribution is minimal, the effort is monumental.

What good are doctoral dissertations? As contributions to the field, they are premature. Real insight, depth, and understanding take years of simmering and exposure to a field (except, perhaps, some of the more technical fields of mathematics, physics, and logic). As evidence of scholarly potential, they are excessive. One does not test students' ability to build a skyscraper by making them build a skyscraper. Nor are tests preparation for professional success. Success in most academic fields is determined by articles and scholarly publications, not tiresome reviews of the literature and three-hundred-page monstrosities. On the other hand, if what is intended is a bibliographical survey of the literature, why not just require that? Or a few substantial papers. Why encourage what looks like a life's work to please a picky committee of four?

Dropping the dissertation requirement might allow most graduate students to get a life before they get a Ph.D. There are too many ten-year dissertations—projects whose only real consequence is the resolution on the part of the new "doctor" never to write anything again. It is worth noting that most Ph.D.'s junk their dissertation as soon as they get their degree, perhaps milking it for one or two articles only because of the desperate pressure of an impending tenure decision. But many tenure committees will not accept a dissertation, even a dissertation revised, as scholarly work. Thus they admit in one role what they will not admit in another—namely, that after all that nonsense, the dissertation does not really count at all. We tell our students, "It's not your first professional work, much less your *magnum opus*. It's your last student work." Indeed, why should it be required at all?

PART VII

Teach as If Education Counts

42 ▾ The Good, the Bad, and the Barely Competent

The mission of the university is to teach undergraduates. We know some spectacular teachers, people who change students' lives, inspire them, and inspire them to do great things. We know teachers who can turn a potentially dull, tedious course (Latin or German grammar, statistics, set theory) into the experience of a lifetime. We know teachers who live for their students, give them sixty, seventy hours a week. We know teachers whose dedication to their subject is second only to their dedication to the students who will carry that subject into the future.

And yet it is fair to say that virtually no other institution or organization, public or private, has as bad a record for neglecting, ignoring, or denying its basic mission. People hired to teach are selected on the basis of nonteaching credentials, sometimes even in the face of the knowledge that they are horrible teachers. People hired to teach are unabashedly tenured, promoted, and continued on the basis of nonteaching accomplishments, again, even in the face of accumulated evidence that they have proved themselves to be incompetent or uncaring in the classroom. In any large institution one expects there to be "a few bad apples," a few incompetents who slipped through the seniority system and whose incompetence has to be finessed by their superiors or compensated for by younger faculty. But the proportion of bad teaching in most large universities is, by any measure, appalling.

Individual colleges and departments within the universities vary widely as to their commitment to staffing classes with good teachers. We not infrequently meet intelligent, conscientious, but disenchanted and even bitter students in various fields who tell us that they have had only one or two "decent" courses in their entire university experience. The teaching evaluation accolade, "Best course I ever had," must be taken with a proper pinch of humility. We know that the competition is in too many instances none too keen.

43 ▾ *The Future of the Mind*

We get outraged every time we meet a recent graduate who tells us that he or she had an introductory course in one of our favorite subjects, "but I hated it and never took another one." How much immeasurable damage is done to the liberal arts by such irresponsible staffing of basic courses, often with the attitude, "The students are required to take it anyway," or worse, "This will keep the riffraff out of the more advanced courses"? Some of the sciences, much to their credit, have committed themselves to the very best undergraduate teaching. Will the humanities make the same commitment before their subjects so dry up that they are simply blown away?

Teaching is not just an addendum to research. It is not an obligation that comes along with the job. Teaching is the continuation of a culture, the continuity of what we have done and known, and the sustenance of our intellectual life. Professors often act as if their research topics were eternal verities, independent of fashion or context or the enthusiasm that can be sparked in the next generation. But the truth is that many of the "disciplines" as we now know and categorize them in the university curriculum are already dead, of no interest or relevance to today's students. They are only propped up by tenured professors who will not give up what they once learned in graduate school. But what kills a subject matter is not its age or origins. Ancient Greece and Egypt are both still very much alive, whereas some of the latest fashions in the social sciences and literary theory are disintegrating before they are fully formed. What kills a subject is the lack of good teaching, the inability to communicate whatever once gave it vitality. What keeps a subject alive is enthusiasm and new ideas.

> Teachers usually have no way of knowing that they have made a difference in a child's life, even when they have made a dramatic one. . . . There is an innocence that conspires to hold humanity together, and it is made of people who can never fully know the good that they have done.
> —Tracy Kidder, *Among Schoolchildren*

44 ▾ *Liking the Students, Loving the Material*

We have served on search committees to hire teachers, we have served on promotion and tenure committees to evaluate teachers, and we have served as well on teaching award committees to evaluate the very best teachers. We have helped draft departmental, college, and university guidelines for quality teaching, and we have ourselves won awards that labeled us "outstanding" or "distinguished" teachers. We have seen thousands of student evaluations of ourselves and our colleagues, and we have been teaching (between us) for forty years. What we have learned at the end of all this is that there are no unexceptional guidelines as to what constitutes good and effective teaching and no single quality that definitively characterizes a good teacher.

We have become convinced, however, that the right attitude toward the students and their education is the single most essential ingredient in teaching. Knowing one's material is assumed, of course. The ability to present that material well and clearly is obviously important. But the best teachers also make the students love the material as much as they do, they make them think, and they make them feel good about their learning and themselves.

This is not to say that a reprimand is never in order or that criticism is not one of the most important functions of a teacher. It is rather to insist that an education is first of all an appreciation of the value of learning and the motivation to go on learning. In a sense, the subject matter is secondary. Which courses are actually taken is almost beside the point. When a student learns to be excited about his or her own abilities and curiosity, an education will last a lifetime.[1]

A good teacher likes the students with a genuine affection. It is possible to fake one's way through a visiting lecture or an institutional dinner, but in the face-to-face intimacy of a fifteen-week term, nothing emerges so clearly as contempt or lack of respect for the students. This attitude is often reciprocated, needless to say. As in any sort of relationship, affection can be nurturing, or it might be rough. It can be solicitous, but it might be threatening. Nevertheless, we have never seen or met a good teacher who did not ultimately care for the students. A good teacher constantly pays attention to the students to see how they are reacting, whether they are "getting it." It is not just the delivery of the material that counts. It is the caring.

Some of the poorest teachers, by contrast, give "excellent" lectures. The material is perfectly organized and presented, but the students do not understand a word of it. The focus of attention should always be the students, and an alert teacher constantly monitors their progress, even in the largest classes. One student with a puzzled look or a frown may be a barometer for others in the class. Without being tedious, the alert teacher asks repeatedly, "Are there any questions?" or "Do you understand this?" and will not take awkward, fearful silence or a meek "yes" for an answer. Paying attention to the students, obvious as it may sound, has to be the first rule of good teaching.

A good teacher is a role model. His or her enthusiasm for the subject is infectious. His or her attitude toward the students is exemplary. Whether the approach is that of a sixties liberal or that of a marine sergeant, what is taught is also what is shown, and the attitude that the teacher demonstrates in front of the class is itself the main lesson in what that subject is about. Teaching is first of all a relationship, not just between the students and the material but between each student and the professor. A good, effective teacher is a seducer, an enchantress, a stand-up comic, a conversationalist, a good buddy. But in the final analysis, a good teacher is a good example. A teacher ultimately teaches, "Be like me."

Nevertheless, good teaching is not determined by the characteristics of the teacher or the techniques of the teaching but rather by its effects. Thus it is said, rightly but misleadingly, that the main measure of teaching is learning. The very best classes are not those in which you convince students how brilliant you are but those in which you convince them how good they are. And when they end up learning even more than you teach them, then that is a job well done.

45 ▾ *The Heart-to-Heart*

A teacher is human, and the fate of a class is determined by much, much more than the teacher's knowledge. There is the personality of the students, the "chemistry" of the class, the subject matter, the state of the world, the weather. Sometimes a class is not going well. The teacher knows it. The students know it. Halfway through the semester, the course seems to be going down the drain. The teacher works harder, tries a few tricks, gives a quiz, but nothing seems to succeed. What most of us do, given our authority and our professional pride, is slog our way through. It virtually never works. The momentum of the class is set, and it will take a special gesture to change direction.

This is the time for the old "heart-to-heart," dropping one's role as authority figure and teacher and sitting down to a long, initially awkward but ultimately effective talk with the students. "What is wrong with this class?" is not an admission of defeat but an expression of concern, and students are remarkably forthright and insightful in providing the answer. After all, they are currently involved in more different classroom settings than we are, and they have a keen interest in getting things right as well as the proper perspective for doing so.

Sometimes there is nothing that needs to be done. Indeed, the heart-to-heart itself has broken the ice, dissolved the distance, opened up the class to a new kind of relationship, a new experience. The teacher may never again have quite the same authority in the classroom, but the good news is that he or she will not need it.

46 ▾ *Naming Names*

Nothing is more expressive of a teacher's concern and attention to the students than the simple effort to learn their names. Not only will the students feel more attended to and cared about, but the teacher is more likely to see and think of them as individuals rather than just a nameless, even faceless classroom mass.

Even in a large class, a teacher should attempt to learn as many names as possible. In any class larger than twenty students or so, we ask for photographs (last year's picture ID, a casual snapshot), or we bring in a camera and make our own "flash cards." Trying to learn names during the bustle of class time is both frustrating and disruptive, but in an hour or so out of class, one can learn most of the class. It is a small investment of time and money, but nothing sets a class up as much as this bit of familiarity.

47 ▾ Saying "Hello"

At the very least, teachers should be willing and even delighted to talk to students outside the classroom, not only in their designated office hours but casually along the way. Students will often pretend not to see or recognize a professor in public, not because they despise the class but because they are so certain that they will not be recognized in return. A simple "hello" can be a fine surprise (and with a name attached to it, so much the better). A brief chat before or after class, in one's office, or in the student union can make all the difference between an impersonal, almost anonymous relationship in a class and one that is personal and encouraging. And as teachers, we find the kinds of questions our students ask outside class to be very informative and inspirational; they often reveal what some or many of the students are thinking as well as their personalities, backgrounds, and educational agenda. Sometimes talking with students helps us rethink the direction of a lecture or the entire course; sometimes it simply helps us appreciate what kinds of people we are teaching and what they expect from us.

We meet the products of impoverished, dysfunctional families who have to drop out for financial or personal reasons; we meet the first scion of a family to go to college who is struggling to succeed at any cost; we meet young people who have plans for starting up their own business, those who have no idea what they are going to do with their lives, and offspring of corporate executives who have more money than Croesus and would just as soon buy an "A" or bullshit the professor as read a book. In every case, learning about these students, and sharing with them some nonacademic thoughts, can, among other things, teach the students a most important lesson—that an education can make someone a more understanding and widely perceptive person than many people they have encountered in their lives. Or, at least, it makes it clear that one cares.

48 ▾ *Does a Teacher Need "Charisma"? Teaching as Entertainment*

Some excellent teachers come into a classroom and immediately command interest, attention, and eagerness. They have what is sometimes called "presence" or, in old religious language, "charisma." This is not to say that a hush falls over the room. In fact, a much better sign of an exciting class is a boisterous roar simmering down just as class begins. A generation ago one's professorial status alone might have been sufficient to snap a class to attention, but in the nineties this is no longer the case. The teacher needs some sort of charisma to gain and hold the students' attention. But this is often misunderstood.

Charisma is not the same as flashiness. It does not require a personality that will light up a room, a voice that will inspire the troops, or the robust humor of a borscht-belt comedian. What it does mean is that a good teacher must be inspiring. Stephen Hawking is charismatic in a classroom despite his physical disabilities. Arnold Schwarzenegger was only a tolerable kindergarten teacher.

Celebrity is good for momentary charisma, but authority and even world-historical importance are not enough for classroom charisma. The president of the United States could certainly hold the attention of an introductory Western civilization lecture, but by the second week he or she would be like anyone else. Charisma is more than just grabbing the students' attention; it is inspiring them and establishing their confidence, not only in you but in themselves. If a teacher is merely entertaining or even mesmerizing the class, that is not the same as teaching. But then again, if you do not reach them, you do not teach them.

49 ▾ *The Techniques of Teaching:*
From the Chalkboard to TV

The stereotype of the teacher is the lone figure in front of the class, droning on. Indeed, the minimalism of the classroom has become something of a challenge, to see what one can do with nothing but a podium and a captive audience. But the truth is that even the slightest addendum to the linear stream of professorial verbiage helps the students enormously. An outline on the board, a photocopied or mimeographed handout, or even some verbal guidelines at the beginning, middle, or end of a class help the students not only organize but concentrate on what they are learning. So does repeating the main points made during class. Repeating oneself may be offensive in standard academic prose, but it is a welcome gesture in class. It is the refrain that reminds the students where they have been and what they are hearing. Even if they think, "I already understand that," students appreciate hearing something they are confident they understand, and they are even more appreciative when they rehear something they did not quite understand. An outline or a handout is a nondisruptive way of doing that all the way through the lecture.

A generation of students who have been raised on television will quickly fix its gaze on any illuminated surface. Overhead projections, slides, and videos guarantee close attention and, if well used, can make an otherwise only sonorous lecture more memorable. The representation at stake need not be subject to extensive analysis. Indeed, it need not even be directly relevant to the topic at hand. But if it can fix the students' attention and establish dramatic associations with the material, it has more than served its purpose.

The coming of video and cable TV made possible new techniques that were all but unthinkable just a few years ago. Live broadcast of current events can be used in class. Internationally known experts can be brought in to "teach." Film clips can be used to punctuate or illustrate the lecture, and an original Monty Python skit can be employed to add humor to a class.

The advent of TV also invites new abuses in the classroom. Showing a film on class time is not the same as teaching, and piping a lecture into a classroom on closed circuit television is no substitute for standing up in front of the class and talking to and with students. The new technology provides the opportunity to bring expertise into schools that could not afford their own specialists in a subject. It allows the discussion of film as well as the traditional analysis of books and pictures. It adds a dimension to the traditional lecture that only a conservative of the "technology corrupts" school would criticize, but it cannot replace the essential relationship between student and teacher. However terrific the movie, there is no substitute for a good conversation.

50 ▾ *Big Classes Are OK*

One of the most obstinate obsessions of both educators and students alike is the ideal of small class size. Small liberal arts colleges sell themselves on this, and most university faculty are horrified at the thought of a lecture class with four hundred students. But just because classes are small does not automatically mean they are good. (Indeed, they may be small just because they are the worst and the word has gotten around.) Conversely, many of the best are the biggest, and it is the large, even huge, classes that make the ideal of democratic education possible. Of course, this does not mean that every class should be large or that efficiency should be the measure of the university, and as a rule every large class should be coupled with at least one small discussion-type class. But as a way of making use of faculty talent and turning on hundreds and not just dozens of students at a time, the large lecture is to be recommended.

There are some subjects that are by their very nature interactive and require virtually one-on-one tutoring for their mastery. Mathematics and logic, although the basic material might be demonstrated *en masse*, require small, intimate work groups. Foreign languages, creative writing courses, and fine arts courses require active participation, individual critiques, and consequently, small groups and small teacher/student ratios. But if the instructor has need to lecture to such a small group, it is often awkward and typically inefficient. Frequently the same basic principles need to be promulgated to every one of hundreds of students. And the difference between lecturing and holding a conversation is such that a small class may breed discomfort and distance rather than the intimacy that was intended.

Lecturing, far from being awkward in a large classroom environment, is a skill that utilizes and flourishes in large groups. A good lecturer can make each student feel as if he or she were being personally talked to. A good lecture can so engross students' attention that they feel an almost totemic solidarity of involvement. Indeed, some students react to a lecture as if they had just enjoyed an individual consultation of the most extreme intensity.

For some students a lecture class that enrolls several hundred students may be just what the doctor ordered. Perhaps they do not like, and consequently do not work best in, an intimate, interactive situation. Perhaps their intellectual skills do not include thinking on their feet, and the pressures of reacting in a language lab or seminarlike atmosphere overwhelm their ability to learn or enjoy their learning. Students who otherwise prosper in a small classroom atmosphere might in certain subjects or at different levels of their college career enjoy the relative anonymity of a lecture class, or perhaps they want to take that "fun" course raved about by all their friends.

There are many reasons for taking a large lecture course. Perhaps a student needs three units to graduate and wants an interesting, low-pressure course. Some students are so fed up with the abuse they have experienced in some small classes that they prefer the anonymity of a large lecture. Perhaps a student is just one of hundreds or thousands who are interested in a subject so popular that the only way to study that subject at the university is to take the large lecture class. Some courses become large just because students flock to a class that their friends tell them is good. (Ideally, the university should be filled with them.) That is fine with us. The more the merrier. What is essential is that no one should think that such anonymous spectatorship on the part of the students constitutes an education, no matter how good the courses and no matter how much they learn. But it is equally important that democratic education not be sacrificed to the current fixation on small classes and S/T ratios.

Students and many educators charge that large classes are the root of poor education. They are wrong. But there are too many large lecture classes that are not taught by inspired, dedicated, experienced lecturers but by faculty who feel that the course and the students are beneath them. Instead of being flattered or challenged, they resent the great numbers of students interested in their subject.

Some teachers are brilliant in a small class but terrified or ineffective in a large lecture. Why, then, are they forced to be there? It is often because of faculty politics or simple neglect, but in any case it is without regard for the best interests of either the students or the teacher. Good lecturers should be hired as specialists (instead of, "We need another medievalist"). Large lectures require special care and attention. But even high-quality lectures must be coupled with small, hands-on discussion classes so that students get a chance to "talk back," to respond with questions and try out their own formulations and views. It is not that large lectures are bad, but bad teaching and the absence of supplementary opportunities for conversation give large lectures a bad name.

In most state universities enrollment pressures have become very intense. During the last decade, many state universities have held faculty positions to a minimum while simultaneously increasing undergraduate enrollments, building lecture halls, laboratory and administrative buildings. This means that the majority of courses a student takes are large, lecture-format classes. We have talked to seniors majoring in political science, business, and history, and in their five years at the university, they have never had a class smaller than fifty students! This is poor planning and a poor excuse for education. We have to figure out a better way to use (and not abuse) our faculty to allow more intimate contact and small discussion classes for all students while at the same time opening our doors to all students who are interested in what we are doing. That means, inevitably, more large lecture classes, but preferably with better teachers and better planning and more contact with students.

51 ▾ Survey Courses: In Praise of Superficiality

One of the primary roles for large lecture classes is the introductory survey course—the course that gets students interested in a subject while also giving them an introduction to the scope and diversity of the world. Professors too often poo-poo such courses as "superficial" and shy away from them in favor of their own narrow areas of specialization. But perhaps no courses are more important in the overall education of most undergraduate students than these survey courses. Although we do not think they should be required, we do believe that they should be the best-taught, and consequently the most widely popular, courses in the university.

Very few educators would disagree that a university undergraduate education is not today what it was twenty or forty years ago. It seems more and more that students with high school diplomas cannot locate Mesopotamia or Guatemala on a map or Napoleon or Michelangelo on a time line. The writings of Hamilton and Madison are unfamiliar to them, as is Plato's *Republic*. They have never heard of writers from the rest of the world. There is a need for basic courses that inform students about the history and distribution of the human race and the most influential components of earlier periods of our culture (and other cultures) as well as the wonders of nature and the basic rudiments of the sciences.

In an educational world that has vastly—but only with a great, internal political struggle—expanded its cultural and social parameters, it is equally necessary to inform students of the variety of cultural facets that comprise not just the world at large but the "melting-pot" population of the United States. Many state universities now require at least one semester of non-Western civilization, even if they do not require any semesters of Western civilization. Too few make readily available and attractive probing (not damning) courses on the complexities and conflicts within our society. Despite the fact that they made such courses requirements for graduation, university administrations and legislatures hardly provided any funding for teaching enough of these courses to accommodate the tens of thousands of undergraduates who will need to take them. The obvious answer is, again, to offer quality lecture courses.

A variety of introductory survey courses require large, lecture-format classes: introductory chemistry and earth science; introductory psychology, sociology, history, and anthropology; introduction to art history, music history, philosophy, economic history, political science, Greek mythology; and so on. These are alternately known as either (negatively) "service" courses or (slightly better) "feeder" courses. The former term designates an obligation to the university that pays the freight, as it were, for the faculty to be allowed to teach small, more specialized classes; the latter refers to the hope that students who enjoy the large introductory survey of the subject will want to take another course and perhaps another and ultimately major in the subject.

The truth is that these courses are vitally important in their own right, and the idea that small, specialized classes are the essence of education and faculty responsibility has the whole system ass-backward. What has to be "fed" are not the special interests of the departments but the curiosity and perspective of the students. And quite the contrary of the oft-repeated criticism of superficiality, we would insist that the best education is the broadest education. What is commonly called "depth" can come later.

52 ▾ *Lecturing as a Skill: It's Not "All in the Textbook"*

The key to success for any moderately large class is the quality of the lecture, which is not just an efflux of information and not just a verbal rendition of the textbook. The skill of lecturing is the rhetorical ability to move and inspire people. It is the talent to render personally and persuasively that which may be by its very nature abstract, technical, and impersonal. A good lecture requires more than careful planning and a script spelled out in advance. It should seem almost spontaneous, as it sometimes has to be. After years of experience, a good lecturer, like any professional, knows what to do and can salvage even the most disastrous lecture. Sometimes the result can even be dazzling. Some of our best lectures have been those that did not proceed at all as planned. That is where the lecture extends beyond—and improves upon—the textbook. It makes the text come alive and invites the students to not only read their books but to join in making them their own.

There is nothing inherently wrong with having the students use a textbook. Many textbooks are competent. They are often written by another professor who teaches the same subject. Textbooks often help a lecturer in presenting in an orderly, graphic fashion material that might be deadly to present in a lecture. But one hopes that the lecturer knows more than the textbook and supplements the textbook material, explains it differently, gives insight to the class, and answers their questions. It is too much of a temptation for poor lecturers simply to repeat what the textbook has said or for ambitious lecturers to assume that the students have assimilated everything in the textbook and then lecture on a much higher plane, one that the students are not ready to explore. As we have stated more than once, what is most vital is to pay attention and always ask what the students are learning.

It doesn't matter how many there are. In fact, the more of them, the more one has to pay attention. A large lecture does not have to be a "mass class" in the derogatory sense.[2] Lecturing is a skill that can be taught and learned, and the best way of teaching it is to show a skilled lecturer in action, provide a role model. A professor is sometimes praised as "a gold mine of information," someone with whom much digging is necessary. How much better that he or she be a fountain of wisdom, affecting all who come near.

53 ▾ Remember Who They Are, What They Carry Away with Them

Just over two thousand years ago Cicero remarked to his friends and colleagues in the Roman Senate that their society was becoming less moral and less educated. Considering the civil strife under which Cicero lived, he was no doubt speaking the truth. But it is quite common for members of one generation to think that the younger generation is inferior, less moral, and less educated. We ourselves have often remarked to colleagues how amazed we were that our students had never read Nietzsche or had never even heard of Aeschylus. But it is important to be fair and to put matters into historical perspective.

When we were college undergraduates, there were plenty of great books we had not yet read. We probably would have struggled to locate Sri Lanka or Laos on a map, and we certainly were not aware of all the profound ideas discovered centuries before by great thinkers whose works and ideas we now discuss on a daily basis. To say to a friend, with respect to whom one has no educational purpose, "I can't believe you've never heard of Aeschylus or Nietzsche!" would be insulting. To react that way to students is not only insulting; it is counterproductive. Our goal is to inspire the students to become interested in Aeschylus and Nietzsche so they will want to read them. The point is not to embarrass them.

There is another side of this point, and that is that not everything we teach our students is going to remain in their active memories. It may be that less than 10 percent of what we teach them will be remembered for a few months, let alone a few years. Students have often forgotten most of the material from the fall semester by the time Christmas break is over. Father Guido Sarducci tells us that he remembers his college education: "Economics? Supply and Demand! Spanish? ¿Cómo está usted?" So what we teach them, ultimately, is not the material but the discipline, the love of learning. It is not a failing of the human brain or the students if they cannot remember all the details, the names and dates, the specific theories and procedures that we may or may not have taught them, as some educators currently complain. What is really important is that they know how to look them up and are motivated to do so when they need to—or even when they do not.

54 ▾ *Teaching Is Hard Work*

Teaching, even if it comes naturally, is hard work. One can only teach so many courses well. People who do not teach just do not seem to understand the intensity of standing in front of a lecture hall of two hundred students or corralling a conversation of fifteen lively and argumentative students or stimulating a conversation with a number of shy students. Pop psychologists tell us that "speaking in public" heads the list of things most people fear. Well, imagine yourself giving a public lecture, and think of the pressure that builds up around that. Now do it two or three times a day three days a week. You really don't "get used to it." (One of our old colleagues, one of the world's great teachers, told us the year before she finally retired that she had never gotten over the "butterflies" before class and would have known it was time to quit the profession if she had.)

State legislators, indignant about the small number of hours most professors seem to work and furious about the obvious "inefficiency" of the university, have been pushing for years to increase the teaching load and get more teachers into more classes with more students. With the current budget cutbacks, the appeal of squeezing yet more work out of the faculty is all the more attractive. But it is a classic case of sacrificing quality for mere quantity. A single class can take up to twenty hours of preparation, and the exertion of a large lecture class can be the physical equivalent of running a short marathon. Good students are demanding, and there is an inevitable parade of them after virtually every lecture or seminar as well as during office hours and beyond.

Professors complain that more teaching would seriously cut into their research time, but this is not the real argument. The fact is that more teaching would seriously cut into the quality of the teaching. "Efficiency" is not a virtue in education. We must insist on quality and opportunity. Good teaching is hard work, and although some of us might gladly take on more of it, the fact is that most young professors are already pushed to their limit. Those who have not done it or have not done it well have no idea what is involved.

PART VIII

Good Teaching, Bad Teaching

55 ▾ Good Teaching, Awful Teaching

Teaching has always been considered a suspect and subversive activity, in part because the students are so often viewed as "victims" of the process. But students are the active element in the learning process. They allow themselves to get involved, or they refuse to listen. They get themselves excited, or they resign themselves to another boring semester. They learn by doing, by reading, by thinking, by listening, by criticizing. No matter how magical the lecture or accomplished the lecturer, it is the students who make the class. Of course, the teacher is not incidental, and it is irresponsible to declare simply that the students teach themselves. But nevertheless, students are not just passive receptacles, no matter how receptive they may be, and this idea shakes up that old fashioned conception of education. A good teacher, accordingly, is one who teaches the students to teach themselves.

A good teacher is a catalyst. A good teacher gives direction, but without seeming to do so. Sending the students off to "write a term paper" or "read something on the subject" is an abandonment of the role and almost always a hopeless failure, but overly strict insistence on narrow topics or uninspired assignments will kill both a course and the students' interest in the subject. The role of the catalyst is much more understated.

A good teacher is also a social synthesizer. In the emphasis on the relationship between teacher and student, we all too easily forget that the primary relationships are for the most part between students and students. They like to work together. Students are personally much more concerned with the opinions of their classmates than the official judgment of the professor. Accordingly, a good teacher gets students to work together. Collaborative group research has been tragically ignored in the name of "working independently" and may be far more educational than anything a student can do alone.

A good teacher can be only so effective, and ultimately the teacher's function may be limited to that of a facilitator. Contemporary learning theory and everyday observation concur in this. No one can "make" a student learn something. The student must be active as well as receptive, willing, and disposed to learn. The stereotype of the turned-off student usually applies to those students who just have not been invited into the process of learning.

We have stated that the problem in most universities, more rarely in colleges, is not so much the lack of excellent teaching as the ever-presence of bad, too often horrible, teaching. Some—usually teachers who do not want their teaching evaluated at all—object that teaching cannot really be evaluated, especially by students who are ignorant of the subject and apt to make evaluation a popularity contest. But rooting out bad and horrible teaching does not take much experience, much less an expert. Almost any student, present or former, can identify the following for you:

1. Teachers who hate students, who pay no attention to them in class, who do not tolerate questions in class, who are forever inaccessible, who make their contempt fully palpable. We know one teacher who boldly announced to a class on the very first day that since he was tenured, he did not care about the class and would delight only in signing his paycheck every two weeks! Too many times have we heard faculty members refer to students as "little bastards" or "stupid, little shits."

2. Teachers who insult and humiliate their students in class. We do not refer here to teachers who use the Socratic method and ask pointed, repeated questions of an unprepared student to elicit a thoughtful conclusion to the lesson. We refer to rude, haughty academics who abuse their power and privilege as an authority figure, virtual sadists.

3. Teachers who refuse to recognize that their students have not yet

mastered the material before taking the course—presumably why they are taking the course in the first place.

4. Teachers who use the classroom as a forum for their own brilliance and relegate the students to serve merely as an audience. At best what they learn is only the professor's individual ideas. Of course, for a few professors and some students this may be exhilarating. But for the majority of self-proclaimed authorities and to most students it is just a matter of showing off, not teaching.

5. Teachers who have become bored with the material, so bored that they fail to present it as anything other than boring and dull to the class. This is particularly unwelcome in required introductory courses, where interest and inspiration are the keys to students' success. We know professors who ridicule the material before it has even been introduced.

6. Teachers who have such a narrow vision of the field that they know only their own research area and cannot provide any perspective, much less motivation, for students to grasp the material. When one of us was an undergraduate, he had a basic biology course in "vertebrate anatomy and physiology" that spent the entire term on a few experiments concerning the neural development of the frog fetus, the special interest of the professor.

7. Teachers who have to figure out their own problems in class, often wasting entire class periods doing so. They waste the students' time and energy doing what they should have done the week before as their preparation.

8. Teachers who have no visible organization and provide no way for students to follow along. Nor do they care.

9. Teachers who consistently arrive late and unprepared for class. Once they have arrived, they have already sacrificed 15 percent of the semester, and have wasted most of the rest.

10. Teachers who never look at their students. We have seen some below-average teachers give good performances, energetic and full of the right information, dramatically presented, but they never bothered to get their bearings with the students and monitor what was actually happening in the class. We know of one professor who, like Miles Davis at his most disdainful, lectures with his back to the class. Genius perhaps, but not good teaching.

11. Teachers who give no feedback whatsoever; take too long grading and giving back tests (sometimes not until after the students have already taken the next one). There are teachers, of course, who do not grade at all, handing back tests and papers with arbitrary grades in the expectation that their authority will not be challenged.

56 ▾ *Who Should Evaluate Teaching?*

Who is to say whether a teacher is a good teacher? The evaluation of teaching has to rest mainly in the hands of the students. Peers can evaluate the quality and accuracy of the material and the "competence" of the presentation, but teaching is primarily a relationship between the teacher and the students, and it is the students who are in the best position to evaluate this relationship.

Of course, they can get it wrong, but that in itself means that the teacher is not getting through to them. And they can be vindictive. It is rare not to find in a large class at least one or two resentful students who will be vituperative and vicious in the anonymity of unsigned course evaluations. But against a great many of our colleagues who insist that the students are not sufficiently "experienced" to gauge what they have learned, much less the competency of the professor, we want to argue that it is *only* the students who are in this position. They are the ones who are giving their time and paying their money for the experience. If they are not satisfied with the class or the teaching, then the class is not satisfactory. If the teaching process in the classroom is not working, the students will certainly recognize it.

The most often-suggested alternative to student evaluation is teachers evaluating teachers, which is always a risky business. Teachers rarely have the patience to sit in on each other's classes, and when they do, they are often a disruptive force. Given the bitter competitive and political atmosphere of the university and the dramatic differences in styles and approaches, not to mention ideological differences concerning the same subject matter, "peer review" is a notoriously undependable form of evaluation. If the students are thought to be immature, at least they are generally open and unbiased.

Peer review does not take into account the development of a class over the course of the semester, and it lacks the engagement that makes much of the procedural part of the conversation meaningful. The sudden presence of a strange professor (sometimes very strange, indeed) in the middle of an ongoing class may come as a shock and is often intimidating to the students, and in a class whose main virtue is dialogue and debate, the talents of the professor may remain wholly hidden as the conversation is undermined. When the evaluating teacher is a tenured professor and the evaluee an assistant professor, of course, the situation may be much worse, and the accuracy of the evaluation may be on a par with the analysis of traffic behavior by uniformed police officers: Their very presence assures that it will be abnormal.

The evaluation itself is bound to be suspect as well. Quite a common scenario is to evaluate a colleague through comparison with one's own teaching methods. This, of course, makes for a very subjective evaluation. Indeed, as often as not, the considerable weaknesses of the evaluating professor become the main criteria for evaluating the strengths of the teacher evaluated, and in our experience it is often the worst teachers who give their peers the worst evaluations.

Professors, unfortunately, also tend to be particularly dogmatic about their own teaching styles, elevating personal preferences and idiosyncracies to the level of pedagogical theory. A dynamic Socratic lecturer of the "Paper Chase" school will find considerable fault with a sensitive but unassertive teacher who is much better suited to roundtable discussions. A professor who cringes at the thought of a knockdown, drag-out argument will find the professor who believes that the teacher should be the devil's advocate a downright bully. Some professors have nothing but contempt for the so-called seminar, which they consider as just an excuse to let the students do all the work. Others recognize themselves as nothing but facilitators and have little but scorn for the show-off professor who turns teaching into a slightly intellectualized version of the "Tonight" show monologue. Socrates himself would surely receive poor grades in teaching effectiveness from an Aristotelian. And how can a professor be considered to "teach well" when his or her evaluating colleague thinks that the subject should not be taught at all?

There are a great many arguments circulating against student evaluations, almost all of them fraudulent and self-serving. First and foremost is the argument that students are in no position to recognize the quality of teaching. We reject this argument completely. Spotting bad or horrible teaching, recognizing that fraud has been perpetrated by the university in the assignment of the wrong teacher to the wrong class, is well within the capacity of any student who comes to class more than a few times.

It is often argued that students evaluate teachers on the basis of popularity. If they think a professor is funny or "cool," only then will they give positive evaluations. Although humor and the ability to relate to young people are often qualities that help endear a faculty member to students, they will take a class only so far. The content has to be solid, and the humor or contemporaneity only punctuates many sober moments. Even the cinematic Indiana Jones lecturing to a room filled with goggle-eyed coeds speaks quite seriously about the excavation at

Naucratis by Sir Flinders Petrie. In fact, we have seen numerous teaching evaluations of "popular" professors that criticized them either for wasting class time with irrelevant material or for being "goofy."

The problem in most universities is not so much the lack of excellent teachers as it is the fostering of an environment in which good teaching is an incredible accomplishment. Overcrowded classes, stupid or politically mandated required courses, bad advising, overworked or administratively hassled teachers, lack of attention to teachers' talents and abilities all contribute to what will, inevitably, appear to be the teachers' own failure.

Moreover, the problem in most universities is not so much the lack of excellent teaching as it is the ubiquitous and unabashed presence of bad and even horrible teaching. A teacher enters the class after a two-martini lunch and forgets what he was going to say. A teacher berates the students for being uneducated and stupid. A teacher misses her office hours and offers no apology. A teacher waits more than a month before grading midterm exams and then passes them out, harshly graded, without a comment. Students can certainly tell the difference between a bad teacher and a decent one.

Faculty rarely give students credit for appreciating a tough teacher, but some of the award-winning faculty we have known were also some of the toughest teachers. The students feared them and often dreaded going to class, and yet long before the end of the semester, the students felt great satisfaction in how hard they had worked, how much they had learned, and how fair and honest, albeit demanding, the teacher had been with them.

57 ▾ *How to Use Teaching Evaluations*

Teachers who do not want their teaching evaluated often object that teaching cannot be evaluated. We agree. Teaching cannot be evaluated in the sense that evaluations are quantified, as most administrators would prefer, and most of the "measures" and percentiles employed for this purpose are useless.

What is needed in universities is basic pedagogical competence in *every* faculty member. To this end, students are more than capable of evaluating faculty, and their evaluations are the most powerful tool for the elimination of bad teaching. Given the sacrosanct aura of privacy that surrounds the classroom, too many horrible teachers get away with it for years. In fact, most faculty already know through unofficial channels who these horrible teachers are. Large, introductory lecture classes contain so many students that word quickly gets around campus as to the abilities and attitude of the professor. Students drop the course a month into the term or beg the chairperson for a "drop" pass at midterm. Introductory classes are evaluated by the same students who continue into more advanced courses. The more honest ones will without inhibition reveal how they feel about their earlier education, and their performance will often give an indication of how well they have been taught and how dependable their views are.

Advanced students who have already taken a number of courses in the subject can give the most informed and direct evaluations. In fact, departments would be well served to run teaching surveys among their majors and minors before they graduate from the university. Student evaluations should then be used to reform or get rid of bad teachers. Not to take them seriously is not to take teaching seriously, whatever the official publications may declare.

In some universities student-sponsored evaluation booklets are distributed free of charge every semester just before registration. University administrations, at the insistence of the faculty, consistently balk at this suggestion. They, too, have little respect for the student body's opinion and at most consider student evaluations as a mere concession to the paying "customers." They claim that the distribution of student evaluation booklets is too expensive, costing tens of thousands of dollars each semester, but the university could print up only a few hundred copies, to be housed in the library, the union, departmental offices, advising offices, and Greek houses. Or they could be sold at cost. In our experience, the students consider this cost a bargain if it means they are saved from a dog of a course next term. And it means they can enjoy their fellow students' comments on that course they hated last semester.

Some teachers will be offended. That is the price of a profession in which public performance is the main event. But what happens now is that such productions are kept conveniently inaccessible, or they are issued primarily in computer printout, as unattractive and clinical as can be, or the evaluations are too quantified and confusing to be meaningful. Perhaps course evaluations could be limited to three categories—outstanding, satisfactory, and unsatisfactory—or just to student comments. Students deserve to know what kind of teacher they are getting, and they deserve the opportunity to tell others about what sort of teachers they have gotten.

58 ▾ *Teaching Awards*

When teachers work hard to "wow" and win over the students, everyone emerges a winner. The students get great courses, the faculty feel challenged and enjoy their teaching, and the university genuinely deserves the reputation it has claimed for itself. But the competition becomes pathological when it leaves the realm of teaching and enters the arena of administrative handouts and privileges. Teaching awards are supposed to encourage good teaching. What they do instead is encourage faculty resentment.

Virtually every university recognizes its "best" teachers with teaching awards. We have each won several, and we would be lying if we denied that the kudos felt good and that it was nice to have a little extra spending money. But ultimately they also made us feel very uncomfortable. One of them came during what one of us thought was our worst semester in years. The disturbing thought that we were teaching for money (which is in a sense perfectly true) was never quite so clear-cut. Our colleagues hardly looked upon such fortune kindly, and our reputations as "good" teachers were confused with being "popular." There was also the assumption that because we were honored teachers, our scholarly abilities must be second-rate. At best, we hoped our reputations were not too seriously jeopardized or besmirched by such an "honor."

There should be no teaching awards. To insist on excellence in teaching is not the same thing as encouraging competition in teaching, much less creating one more forum for scrounging before the administration and begging for recognition. Teaching is not a competitive sport, and arguments between students about who is a better teacher tend to be pointless. But like so many childish ideas about excellence, this one is happily seized upon by the administration, not only as a way of "rewarding good teaching" but as a mode of publicity. In the newspaper there will be a full-body shot of the president and the blessed teacher(s). The subtext of the caption reads, "See, we really do care about teaching excellence here." (The administration has been known to deny the same teacher tenure the following year.)

Too often, that is all the university does to encourage good teaching—offer teaching awards each year to a dozen professors (out of a faculty of several thousand). We think the very concept of a teaching "reward" is wrongheaded. Good teaching, to be trite, is its own reward, and isolated financial rewards undermine the very shift in emphasis and reallocation of resources we are trying to encourage, excusing a devastated teaching budget in the name of a few fancy awards. They are often political, and no one is surprised when a "teaching award" goes to the dean's favorite ally or a defender of the current policy. Typically, the same professors win them year after year, and that must be devastating to all those who rightly see themselves as also doing a superb job.

Teaching awards are divisive and can even bring ridicule on the winners. We would rather see the money allotted for teaching awards go to equipping classrooms; stocking the library, media resources, and classrooms with pedagogical aids; and assisting in the teaching of large classes. Or, let's be really radical: what about actually paying people to teach well, not as a supererogatory performance but as simply what they have been hired to do?

59 ▾ How to Encourage Good Teaching

In place of teaching rewards, the university must make clear that good teaching should be not just a criterion but *the* criterion for teaching positions. The university should finally get honest about its very reason for using tax dollars to hire professors. The job is teaching, and the salary, benefits, and work schedule are generally adequate as compensation for the job. What the university needs to do is hire the right people for the job.

First, universities must hire faculty on the basis of their teaching ability and their teaching record. This does not mean that someone's publication record and areas of scholarly and research interests should be ignored or even downplayed; it simply means that teaching ability should always be the *sine qua non* of hiring. We know many, many fine teachers who happen to be excellent and prolific scholars as well, whereas we know only a small number of faculty who are fine scholars and technicians but perform miserably for students. But we have met more professors than we like to remember who have been, at best, mediocre and pretentious scholars and cruel or boring teachers. They did not get that way; they were always like that. They were hired and got tenure for their "scholarly potential," and when they failed to live up to that promise, they took it out on the students.

Second, the universities often find the wrong people for the wrong positions. In hiring each other, faculty members almost always insist on hiring someone with a scholarly specialization in particular areas of study. Why do they not hire them specifically for their specialization in certain types of teaching? Some people are brilliant in small classes—some in introductory classes, others in upper-division classes—and others are completely comfortable in large lecture halls. Why hire a blacksmith when you really need a cobbler? Why not hire people to do what they can do or learn to do? In many cases the problem is not lack of energy, effort, or excellence; it is miscasting.

Third, universities need to get rid of the caste system inherent in teaching assignments. In many departments teaching graduate students is now considered a right for full professors and a great privilege for junior faculty; it carries with it a tinge of honor. By comparison, teaching undergraduates is considered one's duty, and lower-division courses an obligation. How do you staff the required introductory nonmajor undergraduate courses with the very best people—that is, those best qualified to serve the students and the department in that capacity—without at the same time "penalizing" them with the perceived stigma that they have been demoted to teaching undergraduate survey courses? Simultaneously, do you "reward" those whose teaching is so bad that they cannot be let loose on the general undergraduate population by assigning them to the "plum" graduate courses?

We can start by eliminating the perks that go to teaching faculty for their research despite their bad teaching. Professors do not care about teaching their students because they are constantly rewarded for paying attention only to their research. Winning grants and publishing lead to a bigger paycheck and better perks, and given the tax-dollar-supported university's relatively limited financial resources, the easiest perk to award a star researcher is a light teaching load—one or at most two courses a year! This must stop. It throws the whole balance of emphasis among the faculty out of whack. We all immediately think, "If he or she does not *have* to teach as much as I do and gets paid *more* than I do, then obviously teaching equals less money and research equals more." Teaching is relegated to a secondary tier, and in the extreme, teaching is hardly even considered part of one's job.

Above all, do not reward bad teaching with a reduced teaching load. If a professor should not be in the classroom, then unless the individual is a research genius, he or she should not be in the university.

60 ▾ *Show a Commitment*

There is no lack of words or speeches on behalf of undergraduate education, from the president of the university to the president of the United States. The students listen. The students guffaw. The hard part is letting it be known that the university means business. For decades universities claimed to believe in racial and sexual equality, for example, but it was only after years of pontificating that they actually began to show a firm commitment to affirmative action. They conducted searches, created positions, paid careful attention to promotions. How much of this was show and how much may be hypocrisy is not the point. When the university really decides to do something, it does something. How can the university show its commitment to undergraduate education? Here's a start:

▾ Base faculty hiring and firing on teaching.

▾ Base faculty promotions and tenure on teaching.

▾ Base faculty merit raises on teaching.

▾ Give substantial support to course innovation, development, aids, and materials.

▾ Distribute course evaluations broadly at registration time.

▾ Establish equitable teaching loads for all faculty, including senior faculty and research faculty; encourage faculty to do more than expected and required.

▾ Make sure that there are excellent classes for students to take, fully staffed and not overcrowded.

▾ Assign large lecture classes to the very best lecturers in the university.

▼ Celebrate student scholars—with something more than the usual commencement-week photograph in the *Campus News.*

▼ Tolerate no student organization that does not encourage and support education (including fraternities, sororities, and the football team).

▼ Use all types of university income to help support undergraduate teaching.

▼ Have administrators teach. (They are often terrific and it will keep their minds focused on classroom concerns.)

PART IX

The Open Classroom

61 ▾ *The Open Classroom*

The classroom is the home base of teaching and learning. Excursions to the library, reading alone, writing a paper, and study with friends may provide the bulk of one's education, but it is in the classroom that all this gets put together. Our hope is that the classroom will more consistently become a place where students learn by doing and participating, a source of delightful surprises.

There is no reason why the classroom should not be an open one— open to visitors and auditors, who can catch what they can and plant a seed of interest for the future. There is no reason why one's classroom presence should be merely a means to pass exams or get a degree. It should also be an end in itself, a thoroughly enjoyable, enriching experience that may at the same time prepare and excite one for more advanced studies in the same field.

The open classroom is a festival of learning, not a preparatory prison. It invites novelty and newness. It welcomes outsiders, not just friends of students and interested auditors but even "outside lecturers." Handing a class over to an outside lecturer is strongly disapproved of by university administrators ("That's what the professor is being paid for!"), but an interesting outside lecturer can not only enliven the class but inspire the professor as well. A different voice is always welcome, and the argument that this breaks down the "intimacy" of the classroom may indicate that there may have been no real intimacy—only intimidation.

The key to the open classroom is a new trust of the students, a renewed emphasis on good teaching by the faculty, and a ruthless slashing of requirements and mandated courses. A good education should be there for the taking. It will be up to the students, as it has always been, to take what they will.

62 ▾ *In Place of Requirements . . .*

We have argued that requirements encourage bad teaching and bad learning attitudes. Standing in front of a required class filled with resentful but captive students, teachers are understandably hesitant to put their egos on the line by reaching out and caring. It is much easier to present the material in a professionally competent manner, hold one's office hour, and go home. As for the students, when they feel forced to take a course, they seize on the slightest flaw—the textbook is too expensive, the classroom is too far away from their last class, the professor is a real eccentric—and rather than make the best of it, dismiss the course as an unfortunate necessity. They might study for the exam, but chances are they will not develop any interest in the subject being taught.

Fixed requirements represent the worst of bureaucratized university chaos. Many schools now have such voluminous requirements and such an understaffed advising system that many students do not even know whether they have fulfilled the right requirements. They may need to have an elaborate "degree check," which in some institutions can take as long as six months—long enough for students to waste an entire year before they find out they need one more required course.

Putting required courses on the books involves a good deal of intellectual gerrymandering. Departments are funded according to the number of students they serve, so a single mandated course can make the budget for a whole semester. The philosophy department needs more students, so it gets the accounting department to add an ethics requirement. Requirements are also a means of delegation. The business school has too many students, so it requires them to take a liberal arts course.

We want to get rid of requirements. That does not mean that nothing should be required, but such courses should be rare and subject to the most rigorous, ruthless evaluation. For every required course, the burden of proof should be on the requirement: Is this really a course that *every* student should be *forced* to take?

Students should be allowed to take anything they want, as long as this freedom does not exist in a vacuum. There is no pressure on an under-graduate student so powerful as peer pressure ("If you don't take so-and-so's course, you're really missing out"), and it is one of the great failings of our larger institutions that they ignore this wonderful source of mutual educational inspiration in favor of the purely bureaucratic relationship between the student and the registrar. *Students will take the important courses because they are told by friends and friendly mentors that they ought to. Students will take the important courses because those courses are well taught.* Where education is already exciting, there is no need for requirements.

It is as if a secret committee, now lost to history, had made a study of children and, having figured out what the greatest number were least disposed to do, declared that all of them should do it.

—Tracy Kidder, *Among Schoolchildren*

For the intellectually timid and unadventurous, there can be suggested "tracks," even a whole set curriculum, not as requirements for graduation but to serve as a guide. Such students might be looked down upon, but the courses included in the "track" need not be so condemned. These courses are obviously important; therefore students will want to take them. One hopes students will also learn to explore and experiment. And, needless to say, those strongly recommended courses should be the best taught courses in the school.

63 ▾ *The Curriculum as a Marketplace*

The first law of the marketplace of ideas should be supply and demand. If the students clamor for more Asian and African history and express their half-informed opinion that "Western" history is oppressive, then this is an argument that deserves to be answered, not by vituperative faculty debate or more required courses but by a dramatic improvement and opening up of courses.

The marketplace of ideas is where students learn to determine what they want and what they ought to want, and this is where they help the faculty learn where the future is going. If the students moan their way through *Moby Dick,* perhaps they are telling us something about the current state of literature rather than simply expressing their ignorance. Not every book remains part of the curriculum forever.

Most eighteen- to twenty-year-olds are not in a position to determine what is important and what is not. But they are seasoned shoppers, and what they are shopping around for in college is a subject that will interest them, something that is at the same time important and useful and will make their lives that much more meaningful. If such courses are offered, they will be taken. If they are not offered, they will be demanded. Here is where advertising begins to mean something, not just by way of informing students that a course on Shakespeare's histories is available but by way of persuading them that they really need to take more Shakespeare, that they really want to take more Shakespeare, that they will really be missing something if they do not take more Shakespeare. But what too many universities offer instead of interesting, accessible courses is a catalog of their own requirements based on the politics of the faculty. Courses are not advertised because they are required; and because they need no marketing, they are often of poor quality. Students will choose wisely if there are wise choices put before them, and they will choose what is worthwhile, obviously, only if it is available to them.

The underprovision of teachers, classes, and classrooms, however, makes it a seller's market: One can fill virtually any damn course, no matter how irrelevant it is or how badly it is taught, just because there are not enough courses for students to choose from. And students will continue to take such a course, even when it gains its well-deserved reputation for tediousness and irrelevancy, because they have no alternative. Add up enough such courses and you have a critical mass that smothers all intellectual curiosity and interest. Open up the market to new courses competing for student interest, eliminating the requirements that get in the way, and you have a recipe for an inspired student body.

When we say the curriculum should be determined by student demand, this does not mean, as those who insist on seeing the undergraduates as irresponsible children will say, that we will have a curriculum full of trendy pop-culture courses on Madonna and vampire bisexuality in late medieval Romania. In the open university, students will receive useful, frequent, and ample advice and leadership from faculty and student mentors, and they will be taught not only what is available but what is considered valuable and rewarding. They will be given public promotional lectures, as entertaining as movies, as inspiring as a pregame pep rally. They will be given more and better introductory courses that provide a sampling of the subjects in a discipline so that turned-on students can recognize the areas they might like to pursue. Distasteful as it might sound, the faculty will need to be salespeople for their disciplines as well as fonts of information and learning. What they are selling, after all, is what makes their own lives worthwhile.

Ideally the biggest problem for students should be that there are so many exciting subjects and so many good courses that they have a hard time deciding among them. It does not matter that all the students will not take the same set of courses or that there will be "gaps" in their knowledge. There are gaps in the knowledge of even the most distinguished professor. What is essential is that students learn to make their own choices and learn to learn, and that the outcome of college is not accumulated information nor just grades and a degree but a continuing demand for what is interesting, inspiring, and important.

64 ▾ *The University Community: You Can Take It Over There*

For reasons that have much more to do with pride than with education, the best universities feel compelled to house top programs in every field within their own inevitably limited domain. This is not only inefficient; it is impossible. Accordingly, schools take the destructive way out, discrediting fields they do not cover and discouraging their students from taking any but the subjects they offer. Many universities, in their bid to build the world's best Sanskrit or astrophysics program, grievously neglect general undergraduate education. The argument, with which we agree, is that a student ought to be able to advance as far in any subject as is possible. The possessive posture, which we deplore, is the insistence that each and every university worthy of the name can do this by itself.

Every university ought to cover the basic fields of inquiry, and there are enough competent scholars and good teachers so that all of them should be covered. But the meaning of a "higher education" is precisely that it does not merely offer a basic set of courses but enables a student to proceed farther and farther—as far as he or she might want to go. Rarely can any one university do this on its own, and one of the reasons that so many great universities are having financial difficulties is that neurotic attempt to fill the "gaps" in every program. Not every university can have not only excellent survey courses in Western and world civilization but also a course on the *Iliad* or the *Tao Te Ching* as well as, for those few students who are ready for it, a course on the *Iliad* in Greek or the *Tao Te Ching* in Chinese. But why should every university be able to do this? It is enough that one school or other in every area of the country be able to fill this need, and students who are worthy and interested should be free to apply their tuition and time wherever they will get the most benefit.

We need more cooperation and less exclusiveness between neighboring universities and colleges, and if one university cannot support some specialized study, it should be able to arrange for a student to take a course or two at another school, often just down the road. So, too, the university and so-called junior and community colleges should drop their mutual pretensions and antagonism and pool their considerable resources. Universities should encourage educational mobility among their highly mobile undergraduates.[1]

65 ▾ *Education and Exams*

Bad teaching and required courses smother student interest, but what makes both bad teaching and required courses possible is that education is too often valued as a means, not an end in its own right. Courses, books, and intellectual curiosity may be instrumental in this regard, but they are ultimately beside the point. If a student has a 3.3 GPA (a B+ grade point average), a bachelor's degree, and evident career potential, it seems that no one cares whether he or she has the cultural sophistication, political acumen, or intellectual curiosity of a ground slug.

Testing is not in itself an evil. Indeed, broadly construed, it seems part and parcel of the biological makeup we share with a great many animals. We are *agonistic,* and students naturally compete with one another, just as schoolchildren race to see who gets to the water fountain first. More to the point, it is often difficult to know what one has learned until one has been forced to organize and articulate it, to test one's knowledge in the face of a challenge.

From the point of view of the teacher, announcing an exam is the surest way to assure that students will study the material, and grading their exams is an excellent way of finding out just how much the students have gleaned from the readings and lectures. But note here that every test is just as much a test of the professor as of the students. If the students do poorly, the professor is partly at fault. If they did not understand the material, the teacher must take some blame, no matter how brilliantly or elegantly the material was presented in class. If the textbook was inadequate, then the professor must accept responsibility for the poor choice, and if the students did not come to class or did not even try to study the material, then most likely the professor should have done more to inspire them, help them, and encourage them on their way. Testing is ultimately a test of both the class and the test—a measure of success not only for the students but for the teacher.

In the larger picture, student life is defined by exams. Students learn that doing well in exams is what education is all about. They learn this when they take the Iowa Skills Exam in the primary grades. Their secondary education is filled with exams, culminating in the infamous Scholastic Aptitude Test, which almost alone determines the future of a great many students. Indeed, the deficiencies and distortions of our entire educational system can be mapped in terms of the dreaded SAT. Where education fails, the tests take over. When bureaucracy takes over, exams are more meaningful than learning.

The SAT has been under fire for two decades. It has been demonstrated to be ethnically biased and irrelevant to some of the most essential skills involved in educational success—notably, creativity and attitude rather than aptitude, not to mention a sense of wit or prudence. But there are still very few institutions of higher learning that do not require an SAT and later a Graduate Record Exam score from every applicant. The message is unmistakable: To get into the university, you must be good at taking exams. To get beyond the university, you must be good at taking exams. And while you are in the university, you must be good at taking exams. And if you are good at taking exams, you will get good grades and a degree, the only official recognition that one has indeed received an education.

66 ▼ Testing the Tests

When a student asks, "Is that going to be on the test?" we know that we have somehow failed. "Do we have to know that?" Our visceral response is, what's the point? Why not give them a telephone book to memorize, with multiple-choice questions to follow? After all, if the test of education is to do well on exams then *what* is tested is of secondary importance. Tests are self-absorbing, and even when their purpose is clearly to measure knowledge of the material learned during the course, their ultimate effect is to focus all attention on themselves.

The problem does not begin with the university. After the students have weathered a twelve-year gamut of exams and the SAT, as soon as they enter the university, they are offered "placement" exams that allow them to skip introductory courses. This is, of course, a good idea. It saves time and avoids repetition as well as frees up space for those who really need the courses. But the message, unfortunately, is to reinforce in freshman minds the idea that college courses are just a matter of doing well on the tests, not learning anything new, much less enjoying a "learning experience," a good phrase that has become something of a joke.

As we have already said, tests do serve several important purposes. Besides giving students the opportunity to articulate what they have learned, tests also serve to measure minimal competence, a prerequisite for more advanced material. Tests also serve to reward those students whose commitment to a course is not always matched by their confidence and to eliminate those few students who really should not be taking the class in the first place.

We are therefore not suggesting that tests be eliminated but that their purpose be clarified both for the students who take them and for those who would use (and misuse) their results.

We have to create a course environment in which the student's engagement in the course material is in fact recognized and rewarded. There should be alternative forms of grading—projects, student presentations, papers, field trips, reports, and above all, explicit recognition for student participation. When there must be a test, it should be fun, a challenge. (This should not be confused with "trick questions," those quasi-sadistic brain twisters that professors use to trip up their students.)

In large classes, where individual discussions between professor and student are unavoidably rare, "objective" tests should not be the crux of the course. If they are helpful at all, they should be preparatory obstacles to be gotten out of the way before the serious business of the course proceeds. Teachers too often reinforce this distortion of focus by routinely referring to tests as a way of commanding students' attention. "This will be on the test, so you'd better learn it." But "objective" tests, or what we call "thought-free" tests, should always be supplemented by essay questions, independent essay topics, or critical reports that require thinking.

We find that take-home tests inspire thought. There is some increased danger of cheating, but collaboration as such is not cheating, and we elsewhere encourage cooperative, mutually inspiring intellectual activity. We always encourage our students to work together on take-home exams, the (enforceable) stipulation being that each test paper must be written by the student. The obvious fact is that students enjoy working together, learn more and faster, and supply for each other the critical edge that they may find difficult to achieve on their own.

A similar strategy is to give out a list of potential test questions before the exam. We sometimes do this as much as a month in advance or even at the beginning of the course. The obvious disadvantage is that it tends to focus the class on the test, but the same disadvantage becomes an advantage if it presents the students with a set of organizing principles throughout the course. The antidote to test obsession is to make sure the test questions are sufficiently broad in their scope. Eventually, the questions become a background structure that does not seem like a test at all, and the forced distortion of the class that usually comes from test anxiety relaxes into the natural contours of the class itself.

Book reports as such smack of high school, but giving students a substantial choice of books on an annotated reading list and requiring a thoughtful, critical review not only encourages critical reading but individualizes the course as well. Group projects and reports can be evaluated in a number of ways—giving the entire group the same grade, for example, or (somewhat more diabolical) grading only the group leader, who in turn grades all the others. (Student reaction to this can be vehement, but it teaches them an enormous amount about group dynamics and justice.) Such experiments should not determine a student's entire grade, of course.

Ideally, writing-intensive courses, in which creative essays and reports throughout the semester determine most of the grade, should proliferate. There is no education like articulation, and getting students to express themselves is not just a matter of testing and evaluation.

67 ▾ *Stop Emphasizing Grades*

At the end of every semester we hear from all those "C" students who think they deserve a "B" and from all those "B" students who think they deserve an "A." Only rarely do we see a student come in after the final exam to discuss further a point brought up during the course. Why should they? The tests are finished, the grades are in, the course is over. If the grade defines the course, then only the disputed grade survives the course. Indeed, on some occasions, students who came in to challenge their grade, when offered the opportunity to take a substitute exam, admitted that they had already sold their books back to the bookstore and destroyed their notes from the class!

We need not explain how demoralizing these experiences are and how they make us want to eliminate grading entirely, but if tests can be a positive experience, so can grades. A good grade for work well done rewards and inspires students. Caring, conscientious teachers naturally want all their students to do well, their students in general do well, and the teachers then give high grades. It is in part the increasing number of such teachers that has caused the so-called problem of grade inflation, where a "B" in the early 1990s is an average grade, whereas a generation ago it would have been a "C." Bad grades ("C" and lower) also send an important message. A kick-in-the-butt grade lets students know that their performance was not up to snuff, and when students occasionally thank us for shocking them into a new chapter of their educational career, we should perhaps not be quite so surprised.

Robert Paul Wolff nicely distinguishes between three quite different meanings of grading—criticism, evaluation, and ranking—and he rightly objects to the ranking function's eclipsing the other two.[2] There may be all sorts of reasons to rank students for certain purposes—admissions to a limited program in graduate or professional school, sorting out certain students for special honors or awards—but surely this cannot be the purpose to which all of the university's expertise and expense are dedicated.

If a student applies for admission to a specific program or profession, there are some much more accurate measures of his or her abilities (an interview, for example). For most jobs a brief conversation will prove far more than overall college performance. And for almost any program of any merit whatever, grade point ranking is surely a poor excuse for a decision procedure. We have known many students who played around during the first semester or two in college, came to life a little later, and suffered forever after because of their low grade point average (GPA). In a society in which the person with "the highest IQ in the world" is reduced to answering brainteasers and writing philosophical homilies in the Sunday newspaper, one would think that intellectual ranking alone would be in ill repute.

We would like to see a system in which official grades are simplified to "fail," "pass," and "excellent" and the GPA eliminated. Let the students come to the university and learn. Make grading more of a private affair, another part of the contract between student and teacher. By contrast, in this context grades would be much more fine-grained—not mere As and Bs but pluses and minuses and even double pluses and minuses. Nothing is more frustrating to a teacher or a student than a strong "B" that represents nearly excellent work, because some students will receive the same grade for work that is barely above average. For the student, the more grade information and precision the better. Let the corporations determine their own means of evaluating their future employees, not pass this business burden on to the university. Let the students get educated. Let the professional schools devise their own simplified scheme for determining aptitudes without swallowing the whole of a student's educational career. Let's let our future doctors and lawyers become something more than grade grubbers, for our sake as well as for theirs. Let's put the meaning of our courses into the substance of the class, not in the competitive ranking we assign at the end of the term.

If professors still think they need rank grading in order to keep control of their class, perhaps they should re-examine their teaching. If students still think they need rank grading in order to motivate them, perhaps they should reconsider their courses or even whether they are best serving themselves by being in the university. And if parents, administrators, and future employers suffer a moment of panic at the loss of their usual evaluation mechanism, the compensatory thought should soon set in that the students might actually learn something in the 1990s.

68 ▾ *Stop Emphasizing Degrees*

The idea of a university with deemphasized degrees may seem pointless to some, but this only shows how far we have wandered from the idea that a university degree signifies an education rather than *constitutes* an education. We do not question the value of credentials for various purposes or the sense of achievement that accompanies the completion of a hard-worked-after goal. As university professors, we would hardly argue that degrees should be eliminated. They have their place, and there are practical and cultural reasons for maintaining them. Many avenues of employment require a person to have a university degree, so universities need to issue them. Twice each year thousands of parents and other family members flock to commencements to convince themselves that so much time and money have after all been well spent, so most students want to receive them. Earning a degree is for most people an accomplishment of some significance. Accordingly, some standard has to be set to determine who should receive these coveted diplomas, so the universities need to maintain basic requirements for graduation. These requirements amount to earning a certain number of credit hours, and to earn these credit hours, students must pass a number of courses. But then courses become thought of not as an educational experience but as a means to an end.

The current atmosphere in the university, clearly reflected in the official categories, is that all students are assumed to be degree candidates except in very unusual circumstances, when they are, for example, "special" students on probation and awaiting admission to this or that degree program. Every once in a while, a student makes an important and dramatic gesture, although usually only the despairing parents pay attention. A week before graduation, the student "drops out." The message, unheeded and even unintelligible to some, is that one can get an education without getting a degree. Indeed, some of our most successful citizens are dropouts. They went to the university to get an education, and they got an education. They just never got the degree.

We need to pay more attention to nondegree students, to older students who come back to school just to learn something, to graduate students who simply love the subject but have no intention of doing professional work and no need for a degree. We should make much more room for casual auditors, including other professors and administrators, staff, and community personnel; including, for example, football players and other athletes playing for the school who just want to take some courses. We should open our arms to alumni, who will be in a much better position to support the university if they actually know what is going on there and enjoy it. In short, we should stop making distinctions between our students. If they get a degree, that's fine. If they get themselves an education, that's even better. We should give respect to those who learn rather than those who sport credentials.

69 ▼ Outside the Classroom: Beyond the Celebrity Culture

Once we have shifted the attention away from credit units, grades, and degrees, once we have opened the classrooms, the distinction between "in class" and "out of class" begins to break down. The teaching and learning environment of the open university is not limited to the classroom and the library. The overall atmosphere of the campus should encourage education. Fraternities and sororities should be places for students to learn as well as live and "party." Campus activities should be educational as well as entertaining. This is no argument against movies and football, of course, but it is to say that, whenever appropriate, education should be encouraged.

One of the most obvious roles in this continuing, ubiquitous education is filled by visiting speakers. These fall into two categories—celebrities brought in to address the entire campus and scholars brought in to lecture other scholars in a specific discipline. On any given day, there are usually a dozen such lectures on a single university campus. The celebrities brought in to address the university campus at large are the same lineup of entertainment and political personalities on virtually every university campus and on TV. They come parading through, highly paid and rarely with anything important or new to say. The sole advantage, perhaps, is that one can be more sexually explicit on campus, a boon to visiting comedians but hardly the key to higher education.

What are they doing here? Their role is to provoke thought and stimulate argument. But once the student association has invited these major figures from government or the arts, it finds that its twenty-five thousand dollars plus expenses, paid out of mandatory student fees, were spent on a one-hour speech repeating the same thing they heard on C-SPAN last week. We have heard authors give the same speech at the same university ten years running. We have seen debates that resemble tennis matches more than conversations. Except when there is a threat of violence—a Louis Farrakhan or Phyllis Schlafly talk, for example—little conversation follows. Indeed, even when there is a question-and-answer session (and there often is not), the questions are predictable, and the answers, equally routine, tend to be wisecracks. There is no serious discussion. There is very little that provokes thought. This is hardly education. It is at best a face-to-face confrontation with some celebrity who has been making news.

One of the scandals that occasionally puts an embarrassed university administration on the evening news is the shouting down of a visiting speaker by the students. In the media this is usually presented as a freedom of speech issue and perhaps as another mistaken charge about the violation of academic freedom. The truth is that it is really an issue of poor judgment on the part of the administration or the students— whoever invited the speaker in the first place. The topic is already established as controversial, but no allowance is made for an active debate, nor is even a little time provided for questions. It is hardly a forum for the exchange of ideas; indeed, the practicalities of security require that the opportunity for any such exchange be kept to a minimum. And so the students misbehave. In lieu of a chance for a real conversation, what is the point of the whole expensive business?

Such performances are inappropriate on a university campus. It is not that they should be excluded for their content. Indeed, they are just as valid as a lecture by Shirley MacLaine on her various incarnations or by Joe Namath on the high points of his football career. But in times of tight budgets they are unaffordable, and given the supposed emphasis on the importance of education, they should simply be a thing of the past. If celebrities are brought to campus, we should think of them as sporting events: Charge admission, and let the events pay for themselves. Don't use mandated student fees. Save those for speakers who are not so well known but have something to say and to teach.

The second type of speaker, the scholar visiting other scholars, is less heralded and less costly. Typically, the main consideration is the "old boy" tie with one of the senior members of the department. The talks tend to focus on specialized topics that are well beyond the comprehension or interests of undergraduates and many graduate students, too. Indeed, most of the faculty—if they attend at all—are often not fully conversant with the subject of the day, and there is little attempt to introduce the topic or bring everyone up to speed on the discussion. The point and purpose of such a lecture is not education and has little to do with the students. What could be an ideal opportunity to bring in a different perspective and build bridges between courses is squandered instead on a bit of wining and dining with the faculty. Little effort is ever made to give the students access to such visitors, and we have often seen them fly in and out—lecture, dinner, and run to the airport—without having said "boo" to a student.

For a thousand dollars or much less, it is possible to get any one of thousands of intellectual and cultural speakers who are delighted to talk about new, exciting ideas; who are more than happy to visit classes and spend time with students; who need no security guards. Many visiting academics will speak for free or can be funded by some national or regional council that supports a tour of such lectures. Departments can team up to invite interdisciplinary speakers who transcend narrow departmental specialization. Colleges and larger units of the university will also often have special funds for speakers. These should be used well—for education, not as personal perks.

PART X

Teaching Values

70 ▾ *Teaching Values (the Problem of Indoctrination)*

There are no "value-free" subjects. The values canonized and promulgated by the scientific method include the value of knowledge for its own sake, the importance and even the nobility of mere curiosity, the necessity of going after the truth. The very nature of intellectual life embodies the value of study and the importance of criticism and debate, the prohibitions against fudging results and stealing ideas, the contempt for claims that cannot be demonstrated, and the rejection of religious or political authority as the final court of appeal. Indeed, these are values that are basic not only to any scientific or scholarly discipline but to much of our American way of life. The university flourishes in the United States because it embodies many of those values that are most valued by us all.

Claims that the university should be "value neutral" or "apolitical" and that courses should be taught "objectively" and without bias are simply absurd. Indeed, objectivity is already a very important "bias," which dismisses certain ways of thinking from the outset. Quite the contrary of being "apolitical," the very nature of our education is defined by a set of political rights and principles—notably, the rights to freedom of speech and assembly and the liberty to raise questions frowned upon by the establishment. Paradoxically, this insistence on freedom of thought and speech coexists with speech that denies that same freedom. This has always been one of the dilemmas of university life, whether in the name of "piety" back in the twelfth century or in the name of "political correctness" today.

It is the mission of the university not only to uphold and protect these values but to teach them as well. This raises difficult questions about the importance of teaching values within the university curriculum. And yet not all values should be taught at the university.

Indoctrination is the term of abuse launched against unacceptable ideals or values. It refers to a rejection of the appropriateness of a certain teaching. Thus a sermon on original sin in a secular university is condemned as indoctrination but is perfectly in place at a Catholic university. A Marxist harangue is considered indoctrination in a political science class but might be perfectly acceptable in a course on Marx and Marxism. The difference lies in what one expects or should reasonably expect. If a person signs up for a course that has been entitled "The Role of Patriarchy in the Undermining of Womyn's Literature," there should be no cause for complaint if the teacher becomes "political." So, too, if one signs up for a course on "Homosexuality as an Alternative Life-Style" or "The Role of Western Imperialism in the Oppression of African Democracy."

If such courses were required or hidden under a more general rubric, however—notably, "English Composition" or "An Introduction to Sociology"—the student who has no other options would indeed have serious cause for complaint. So much more reason, therefore, to drop all but the most inescapable required courses and encourage explicit, honest advertising. Indoctrination is being forced to listen to ideas that you oppose. The alternative to indoctrination is not value neutrality but openness and honesty.

On the other hand, exposure to ideas is by no means indoctrination, and the prohibition of such exposure is not a viable alternative to indoctrination. No economist steps into the field without some strong opinions about the values of the free market and the nature of government "interference," and no political scientist or professor of government presents even the most technical or seemingly descriptive topic without some strong views about democracy and its alternatives. To teach such subjects without bias is all but impossible, even if the biases are often subtle. To make such biases explicit and open for class discussion is not only good teaching but essential to good research as well.

In the humanities the facade of objectivity drops as fast as the curtain in *The Wizard of Oz*. If one assigns Alice Walker's *The Color Purple* to a class, student minds are going to consider race and gender relations. One could, by contrast, pretend to put race and gender questions aside by assigning only white, male, conservative authors, but this ploy has now become so transparent that it is almost universally the subject of ridicule. It is much better to read the books and raise the questions. Let all views be aired and let the students think about them, whether or not they are willing, as will be one or two of their bolder classmates, to talk about them.

The presupposition of the indoctrination argument is that eighteen-year-olds are for the most part unopinionated and extremely vulnerable to seductive ideas. Students are not impressionable things lacking minds of their own. Most see and hear nonsense as nonsense, and if it does not jibe with what they already know and believe, then it is not at all likely that they will immediately adopt it as their own.

> It's not that our education system has failed. It's that it has succeeded beyond our wildest expectations. Having taught our kids to tuck in their wings, to narrow their range of vision and concerns, to jettison moral encumbrances and seek self-fulfillment in some narrow sphere of self-interest, we then want them to be inspired members of our work force and make that better and smaller computer chip. They won't.
> ——Steve Tesich

71 ▾ *Minimize Politics in the Classroom*

The obligation to teach values is often conflated with the license to indoctrinate the students instead of educating them. But the right to teach the justification of slavery in the antebellum South or the rise of nazism in Weimar Germany does not excuse the use of the professorial podium to promulgate controversial political themes. The difference? One is a discussion, the other a promotion. The first assumes a conversation of equals, the second a captive audience.

The teacher is granted a position of rare power. It is the power to stand in front of an audience that is bound to listen to you and respect what you say. To abuse that power is nothing less than unethical, as tempted as we all might be from time to time. (See Chapter 111, "Academic Freedom.") It is also unethical, not to mention pedagogically incorrect, to insist that your students not think for themselves but pander to the same "politically correct" viewpoint you have presented in class.

Similar criticism applies to those professors who hide behind the hypocritical notion that their ideas, because they are conservative, are not "political" at all. A refusal to take seriously a student's clumsy Marxism or feminism is just as much an abuse of professorial power as the professorial insistence on Marxist or feminist views. It is the nature of the conservative viewpoint that it does not need an agenda. All it has to do is react against whatever the opposition proposes. But that viewpoint is political, too.

The point is not that politics does not belong in the university, much less that "the university should not be politicized." The university is and always has been a hotbed of politics, and the university is by its very nature a political institution. The argument is that politics does not belong in the *classroom*, where the teacher has the power not only to direct or stifle the discussion but to punish those students who disagree.

There will always be those situations, both local and global, in which faculty members feel an overwhelming urge to speak out. If so, they should air their views in a public lecture, not in the classroom. And if they feel bound to initiate a discussion in class because of a momentous event, then it is their obligation to drop the role of professor. But this is not the usual situation. It is not the outbreak of war or the invasion of the campus by some controversial group that sparks most of the complaints about professorial abuse. It is the ordinary, everyday abuse of the forum.

It is often hard to make out the difference between advocating and talking about politics, particularly in a class in which politics is the legitimate topic of discussion. But despite certain glib political slogans, not all topics are political, and in most classes political discussions, as such, are inappropriate. Professors are only human. A great many subjects cannot be discussed without a professor's political orientation showing through. But an honest professor will conscientiously avoid such provocative political material on the exam and will avoid playing the double game of assuring "tolerance" and then grading by prejudice. But when politics and personal political views become the main content of a lecture on literature, psychology, or philosophy, it is almost certain that the professor is overstepping the bounds. In addition, promulgating politics in class is often counterproductive. Students readily take foolish professors as prototypes of views they have been taught to avoid, and the result of a political diatribe may well be the undermining not only of one's political position but of one's classroom credibility.

In classes where political discussion is unavoidable, there are still fair methods of presentation that do not involve resorting to blandness. One might invite a fellow faculty member who disagrees. Some of our colleagues team-teach a course involving controversial issues and argue with one another before the class, courtroom style. The students themselves can be recruited to hold debates and argue with one another, a role the best students often appreciate. It is essential that if a faculty member insists on advocating political positions, he or she still treat the students as equals, possibly even passing on the grading to someone else. The problem with politics in the classroom ultimately involves not controversy but fairness. It is the power of the professor, not his or her politics, that is the problem.

72 ▾ Teaching Students to Think for Themselves

As we have said, the entire process of higher education should be aimed at enabling students to think for themselves. This is often neglected in the heated debates over what students should be taught and learn, as if the students themselves were intellectually incompetent and mere empty vessels incapable of intelligently challenging the authority of their elders. Indeed, one of the most unfortunate symptoms of the current debate over multiculturalism and the canon is the emphasis from both sides on what the students ought to be forced to know in the absence of any consideration of what they might already think and learn for themselves.

Thinking for oneself (like learning) is a skill that is by no means wholly "natural." Some students come from articulate, argumentative families and have had practice in asserting and arguing their own opinions for years. But many others come from homes in which discussion is limited, argument is not of debate quality, and the voicing of one's own tentative opinions is either ignored or condemned. Television has killed much of what used to pass for public debate, and few local newspapers give much indication of "thinking for oneself" (as opposed to standing on a soapbox). Even the most articulate students need to learn a great deal by way of style and subtlety.

Most students need encouragement in formulating and expressing their own views. It is not that they do not have opinions, but insecurity with language (not always their first language), timidity long inculcated in them by their parents or peers, and fear of rejection or "put-down" are more than enough to keep some students quiet and unassertive, if sometimes sullen and resentful. How utterly destructive and inexcusable, therefore, the professorial disdain with which many courageous questions or comments are answered. And how much is sometimes achieved, without fanfare and evidenced only by a glimpse of a smile, when a slightly confused first-time question or comment is greeted with praise, helpfully reformulated, and then answered. Thinking for oneself is taught with simple encouragement and the corralling of one's own cultivated professorial combativeness.

In their classes, their readings, and their conversations, students are exposed to a variety of conservative and liberal opinions—Marxism and fascism, the New Deal and Reaganomics, feminism and male chauvinism, Western ethnocentrism and multiculturalism, and much else. All too often, though, they are presented with arguments for and against these alternatives simply as material to be mastered, not as lively debates. When a class discusses a live-wire subject such as abortion rights or capital punishment, the debate often amounts to no more than an exchange of gunfire in the darkness, as the students shout out their prejudices without listening to any of the other viewpoints. But it is in between memorization and the shouting match that the real process of learning

---

I am recommending the ancient tradition of making as big a fuss, as noisy a complaint about the world as humanly possible. . . . Let there be rowdyism.

—Salman Rushdie, *Imaginary Homelands*

---

to think and debate takes place. It consists of argument but not antagonism, criticism but not hostility, tough-mindedness but also humility. Teaching students to disagree is in this regard teaching them to respect one another.

Students have to be taught how to read in college, and part of that lesson is that good reading is active reading. Students now seem addicted to the fluorescent marker, that obnoxious instrument that turns white pages into yellow or pink wallpaper and often serves to trace where the students have gazed rather than where their attention has focused. Perhaps the first thing to do is to get students to throw away their fluorescent markers and replace them with good, old-fashioned pencils. A pencil can be used for underlining, but more important, it can be used for making question marks and raising queries; writing comments in the margin; and noting cross-references, possible conflicts, and contradictions. A well-read textbook should look like a battlefield, and the more the students write on the pages, the better they are reading. Students sometimes speak of "tackling" their textbooks. The truth is, they could not give themselves better advice.

And so, too, when students discuss a subject with their professor, it should not be assumed that they are only asking for clarification and not trying to establish a tentative position. Even in a large lecture, when responses are barely appropriate and a good argument is extremely rare even when it is encouraged, the idea is to get students to think, not just "digest the material." Rhetorical questions and dramatic pauses can work wonders.

Critical thinking should be the main aim of tests and papers as well. Although these are also implements for seeing "how much students have learned," how much they have learned is much better measured by the depth of their criticism, not the accuracy of their regurgitation. Anathema to thinking, of course, are most multiple-choice or so-called objective tests, which encourage guessing and emphasize the importance of recognition and first impressions.

Career training depends on the ability to think for oneself, to be flexible in changing circumstances. Students trained to think for themselves have a keen awareness of their strengths and weaknesses, their interests and preferences, and they have the ability to choose consciously what directions their life should take both professionally and personally. To be able to use one's leisure time fruitfully; to enjoy the opportunity to read, watch films, documentaries, or creative television shows; to have intelligent, witty discussions; to be able to articulate one's political, personal, or cultural dislikes; to understand personal success and depression is to be able to think one's way off of but also back onto the beaten path.

The key to thinking for oneself is wrestling *with oneself*, arguing not only against opposing opinions but against one's own. Accordingly, thinking critically is not a subject that is best taught in separate classes but in every class, and in the course of ordinary reading and conversation as well. Understanding is half of an education. Acknowledging conflict and contradiction and being willing and able to work one's way through confusion and ambiguity is the rest of it.

73 ▾ Teachers and Students: Students as Friends

The inevitable fact that the professor is often the most significant source of inspiration in a class raises a problematic concern. What is the proper relationship between teachers and students? Some have said that, as a strictly professional relationship, the teacher-student relationship should be one of utter impartiality. Friendships between teachers and students, it is argued, undermine that impartiality and inevitably give some students an advantage over others, not only come grading time—this, presumably, might be resisted by a conscientious professor—but in terms of time and attention.[1]

We utterly disagree. This is not to say that teachers should play favorites or grade on the basis of personal feelings, but teachers are not bureaucrats. Impartiality and impersonality are not professorial virtues but vices. Teachers are human beings, and the teacher-student relationship is one of the most human of relationships. It presumes personal knowledge, personal (and not just professional) trust, and rapport. Ideally, teachers should be "friends" with all their students. In practice, of course, some students are pointedly inaccessible, others make themselves pests or are simply indifferent, and teachers will inevitably have their personal preferences.

Students respond to attention and care. Most of them want to know that the teacher knows something about them. Some of the confessions and autobiographical revelations that emerge in essays and during office hours are truly remarkable and occasionally extremely awkward. To be sure, it is also necessary to "keep one's distance" in many instances. Lecturing to three or four hundred students in a class, one keeps up the front of friendship but of necessity protects oneself against massive reciprocation. But this is not to say that such friendship is false or fraudulent. It is, as many friendships are, just very limited and very well defined.

There are friendships with students that become much more than this.

Teachers and students often spend a good deal of time together, eating lunch, having a beer, and engaging in long conversations. In itself we see nothing wrong with this, but there are dangers that cannot be ignored. An unequal friendship always threatens the integrity of the less experienced party, and there is almost always a problem with the perception of favoritism. This is where critics have urged that professors simply abstain from any contact with students that is not strictly professional. But the same argument has been advanced concerning senior and junior professors as well as administrators and faculty, and here the argument becomes absurd. The university is a community, and its function is to foment intellectual relationships. Indeed, as we put less emphasis on competition and grading and academic jealousies, there will be less reason for resentment regarding relationships between teachers and students as well as between members of different status levels.

Professors should be willing to be friendly to their students, and this is no vice or breach of responsibility. It is, where and when appropriate, part of the job. The best teaching schools, small liberal arts colleges, make no secret of the fact that "getting to know your professors" and becoming friends with them is part of the attraction and the justification for that five-figure tuition bill. But this is not the case just in small liberal arts colleges. A professor in the university ought to be personally engaged, not only with the material but with the students. The notion of the "teacher's pet" belongs in elementary school. At the university, friendships should be the norm, not the exception.

74 ▾ Friends, Romance, and Sexual Harassment

There are relationships that go beyond the bounds of mere friendship. A student can develop an emotional attachment to a professor, a student "crush." And then a teacher-student relationship can also become sexual. The problem is not one of "moral turpitude," which pretends that intimate relations between nonequals are wrong as such, but of equity and fairness.

Barring romances on campus, however, is both a mistake and impossible. As so many of our standard love stories clearly show, no fruit is as attractive as a forbidden one. But casual sexual relations raise other issues, and although prohibition is a mistake, both professors and students would be well advised to avoid them. Some faculty members exploit their student lovers, and too often the "relationship" is one of extortion, not mutual attraction.

It is not always the professor who is the dominant partner, of course. Some students have shown themselves quite capable of wrapping professors around their proverbial little fingers. Nor is it always a woman who is at a disadvantage now that increasing numbers of faculty members are women, and homoerotic relationships can also cause problems of an equally threatening emotional nature.

It might seem that we are understating a serious problem when we insist that sex between teachers and students is primarily a problem of bad teaching and not a matter of morality. But a twenty- or twenty-two-year-old student is not a child; he or she has probably been sexually active for years and is sometimes more experienced than the professor. And between professors and their graduate students, who share interests and a life together, any official prohibition of romance is surely outside the university's authority. To be sure, there will be problems and complications, particularly when the graduate student comes up for a job. But to say that the situation is problematic and complicated is not to say that it is immoral.

None of this is intended to be even a partial defense of those sexual encounters between faculty and students that are in any way forced or humiliating to the student. There are limits to intimacy, and mutual consent is one of them. We have been assuming mutual consent, and although it is true that such relationships always carry with them the threat of force, undue influence, or domination, to assume that this is inevitably the case is to simply assume that students as such are naive and incapable of looking after themselves. To be aware of a danger is not the same as refusing to take a risk. But when force is quite clearly involved—as opposed to the more usual situation in which student admiration evolves into erotic interest—our argument reverses abruptly.

Sexual harassment is not a form of romance but a form of rape in which the explicit use of official power constitutes the crime. When a professor makes sexual submission by a student a condition for a grade or an academic opportunity of any kind, or when submission becomes a basis for evaluation or other academic decisions affecting a student, the professor should be fired, with due process, but then summarily. To trade sex for grades is extortion, nothing less, and the very least punishment appropriate is being fired from the profession one has betrayed.

Of course, the process by which such charges of sexual harassment can be proved is a matter of considerable dispute, but it seems clear since the

Anita Hill–Clarence Thomas hearings that the familiar mythology of "his word or hers" is by no means the end of the issue. There are, no doubt, casual comments and one-time propositions that are just as well forgotten. There are encounters that, however inappropriate or traumatic, are not subject to verification. But experience suggests that sexual harassers are compulsive repeaters and usually devoid of much sense of discretion. They are typically known to nearly everyone and are the talk of the campus. Dozens of students, not just one or two, are ultimately in a position to testify to the abuse. Exploited students and university grievance committees should take advantage of such numbers.

Harassment can take many forms, of course, from the instructor in California (since retired) who required his students to have sex with him to fulfill the requirements of a human sexuality course to more "innocent" jokes about sex or sexual orientation in class. But sexual harassment, for all the attention it is getting, is not the only form of harassment. A professor has an incredible license to muck with students' minds while they are a captive audience in his or her class. To abuse that license is harassment, even if all that is touched is their self-esteem.

PART XI

Books

75 ▾ *Why Read Books?*

At the center of every university is the library, the very heart of the university, and books are its blood. The love of books has always been the key to the life of the mind, even if nearly thirty years ago Marshall McLuhan and other latter-day prophets were circulating the message that books were passé. Ironically, this thesis was read and accepted by hundreds of thousands of readers, who read McLuhan's book instead of watching television, a "hot" medium. And today, more than ever before, professors are writing that books are on their way out. Unfortunately, too many of the students agree with them, without reading the books, of course.

Most college professors we know would fall over backward if they caught more than a handful of their students doing extra reading (let alone their assigned reading). Illiteracy is an established part of American life—not just the obviously tragic illiteracy of those who cannot read at all but the more subtly tragic illiteracy of those many students who can read quite well. They may read all the time, but it is the personals section of the school newspaper, the sports page, the front page of the *National Enquirer* at the checkout counter, a few articles in *Time* in a waiting room, and an occasional *People* magazine that they read. Most of them do not read books unless they have to and even then they do not always read them.

Education involves many things, not least among them diverse camaraderie, intelligent conversation, a variety of experiences, and a wide range of lectures, films, and so on, but the material core of a college education is still a stack of books: textbooks, classic novels and plays, political tracts, the Bible—everything a student can get his or her hands on—and the mission of the university might just as well be stated as teaching people to read and to love reading.

The library is with good reason thought to be the architectural centerpiece of almost every university campus, no matter how overtowering the nearby sports stadium. It is not inappropriately dressed, if only superficially, like a Gothic cathedral or a Greek temple, and although its practical purpose often seems to be a mixture of meeting place, study hall, and denatured singles bar, even the most casual interloper is usually moved to pick up a book or two. Browsing in the library is one of the great discoveries of undergraduate life, and the joy of collecting a dozen learned volumes on the topic of one's five-page assignment signals a flush of accomplishment, even if it is poorly matched by the writing of the paper itself. Whatever else they may be, whatever new technologies may come along to help out, books remain the basis of education in our society.

Reading is a skill. It takes practice. It is, to begin with, a lot of work. When one has been taught to do the work but not at the same time taught the value of books, reading continues to be a chore, an assignment, not an adventure or a joy. But we professors too often treat the assignments we give our students as chores to be done before class (or before the test). We insist on the assignment, but we do too little by way of promotion, to make the students look forward to reading and spark their curiosity.

It is sometimes said that books unjustifiably ignore what is called the "oral" tradition in literature, and there is much to be said for the virtue of sharing and speaking together. Oral cultures preserve the social aspects of their stories in a way that we do not, but the correct response to this observation is not to condemn books as instruments of cultural imperialism or overromanticize oral culture. It is rather to take our books more seriously, turn reading into a social activity, and think of books, as many of us were first taught as children, as wonderful experiences to be shared.

So why read books? College presidents may puff up on commencement day exclaiming that books make better human beings—unaware perhaps that Nero and Mussolini were both well read—but there are three better answers.

First, despite the pervasiveness of television, books remain the primary vehicle of our culture, the source of our concepts and our ideals.

Second, books are an important source for communicating experiences as well as a means of understanding other people's experiences and providing a perspective for those experiences.

Third and most important, the activity of reading books requires an exercise of the imagination and the use of a critical faculty that is forcibly suspended through the continuous onslaught of TV programming or, for that matter, through the continuous onslaught of words and images from almost any source that forces our attention rather than inviting our critical and imaginative participation.

It is sometimes said that books are an instrument or a conspiracy of the dominant culture. To the contrary, books have always been the best weapon of the subversive, the rebel, the oppressed. Books are powerful media for developing a message, and they are inexpensive to produce, easy to distribute, and very portable. They are, accordingly, the friends of the embittered and oppressed as well as the bored, the fed-up, and the curious. But politics aside, reading is too often unappreciated as the key to independent thinking and an inexpensive essential in a rich, meaningful life.

76 ▾ *Three Kinds of Literacy*

It is with books in mind that we can define what we mean by *literacy*. There are three kinds. The first is the ability to read and write. This is "functional" literacy. The practical importance of functional literacy is unquestionable.

The second is "literacy" in a more snobbish sense, meaning "well read." It is the sort of literacy that is represented in the pages of the *New York Review of Books*. It is having read not only *Moby Dick* but also *Typee*, being familiar with Nietzsche and Stendhal as well as contemporary fiction. Such literacy is unabashedly elitist, often competitive, and it is taken as a mark of social superiority, which is not, we hasten to add, an argument against it. Since the aim of a university education is to foster the urge to read everything, to leave no page unturned, this second type of literacy could be considered an ideal. But this type of literacy is too often motivated not by the love of books or reading but by the need to show off. It may be appropriate for certain cocktail parties, but it is not the concern of the university. We need to teach enthusiasm, not pretentiousness.

The third kind of literacy includes familiarity with other arts and the variety of life's experiences. It can come from having conversations on the street, viewing films and art exhibits, attending lectures and political rallies, but it still revolves around the printed word. It creates familiarity with a variety of human experiences even if we do not actually experience them ourselves.

Reading Einstein or Darwin or the *Iliad* is not just getting knowledge. It is sharing intellectual struggles and adventures that lie at the heart of civilization. In this sense literacy is participation in the intellectual, artistic, and political development of the human race. It is being familiar with and part of society's fabric, its myths and legends as well as its theories and self-images, and today's expanded literacy includes the

---

"Apes don't read Nietzsche."
"Yes they do, they just don't understand him."
——*A Fish Called Wanda*

---

myths, legends, theories, and self-images of all peoples. Familiarity breeds curiosity, and literacy and multicultural ethics are not two different disciplines but one, both contained in good books.

There is a clearly practical problem of functional literacy in our schools, but there is also a cultural problem of fragmentation and ignorance. Students with high school diplomas cannot date the Civil War or the world wars, and they do not know the names of great writers, artists, or powerful politicians past or present. Many people, even college graduates, treat reading books as an unpleasant necessity in school and then as something of a dispensable luxury for the rest of their life.

To label such people "illiterate" is not necessarily to say that they *cannot read;* it is, much more often, to say that they *have not read and will not read.* What they miss is the experience that only literature can provide, but force-fed education supplies only the literature, not the excitement. What is so beautiful about books is that we can both share them and at the same time foster the illusion that we each discover our favorites alone. It is the mission of the university to instill this sense of literacy as well as the functional literacy that is its prerequisite.

77 ▾ Shooting "the Canon": The Great-Book Debate

Is there a canonical collection of literature worthy of the epithet "great books," or is the quality of any work dependent on the specific culture or reader and thus purely "subjective"? As is so often the case, the choice is bogus and the truth lies somewhere in between. It takes very little historical research to remind ourselves that many of the books we consider "classics" were ignored or condemned in their own times. Even the works of white male Americans that are now the subject of so much disdain did not make it onto the list of required, canonical readings until a few decades ago. Now they have made it onto the list, but it is not because chauvinist American professors insist on teaching some of their own culture; it is because those works and authors have earned the academy's attention, as African, Asian, Native American, and South American authors are earning our attention today.

Too much of the rejection of the "great books" is a reaction to the treatment of the classics as one-dimensional masterpieces that are to be admired like sacred objects, totems of "our" particular culture. But there are a great many ways to read a book—for its place in history; for its influence on subsequent events; for its influence on other writers; for its information about the times and place; for its insight into the mind of its author or the author's politics, class, sexuality, or gender; for the author's use of language or metaphor, as a target for criticism or abuse, as a set of ideas or visions, as a sequence of demonstrations or arguments; not to mention for sheer enjoyment of the characters or story line.

Some books are important because they seem to express some important truth, whereas some, palpably untrue, seem rather to express the perspective of the times or the prejudices of a particular group or the personality of the author or authors. What certainly should not be simply assumed is that a book is an expression or a confession of its author or that the words of an author are expressions of his or her race, class, or gender. Frederick Douglass is not just a "black" author but a great author, and Sappho is not just a woman poet but a superbly skilled artisan in the craft of poetry. It is for certain purposes important to know that Douglass was black and Sappho a woman, but it need not be because it is by a black person or by a woman that their literature is valuable. One reads a book because it is worth reading. There are many reasons why this might be so.

Books assigned in most university courses have a straightforward instrumental function. They are tools for analysis. They may be appropriate books at some stage of language learning for translation or reading aloud or vocabulary building. They may consist of arguments to be dissected and countered. They may provide problems in a particular discipline and the techniques for solving them. They may simply supply information for digestion and synthesis in class. A book that is considered a classic may be employed in any number of these tasks, though rarely all of them and not all at once.

Plato's *Republic,* to name one widely recognized "great book," might be read in the "I've got a secret" mode suggested by Allan Bloom in his *Closing of the American Mind,* but more often it is read as a superb example of philosophical creativity and argumentation, as an obstacle course for students whose ideas are too pat and naively confident, as a trial test for those learning to recognize arguments and fallacies, as a vision of a possible society against which students in a democratic society are expected to react with some horror, or as a vision of a possible society in which women are promised genuine intellectual equality. There is no one way to read the *Republic,* even within philosophy. And when that book becomes a text in an ancient history course, a Western civilization course, a political science course, a feminism course, or a reading course in ancient Greek, we should expect that any singular sense of the book as simply one of the canonical classics will quickly recede into the background.

The problem with the concept of the "canon" is that it denotes holy books whose words are gospel truth. But even real holy books—the Torah, the New Testament, or the Koran—are subject to interpretation, critical examination, and provocative questioning. We should not confuse the need to get students motivated and appreciative, which is our job, with the tendency to promote reverence and uncritical devotion, which is not. To take an extreme example, one might get students to appreciate the crude rhetoric of *Mein Kampf* without revering either the book or its author, much less its message. Indeed, exposing students to such hate-filled rhetoric is the best possible inoculation against it, although parents and alumni sometimes do not understand.

We have to get over the idea that the aim of the curriculum is primarily to teach "what's most important" and remind ourselves that the more important thing is to teach well. Of course, one cannot teach well without teaching substance, but substance varies enormously from time to time and context to context and cannot be readily limited to a "canon," no matter how inclusive. Indeed, what is so rewarding about "great books" is that there are so many of them and that there are always more coming.

Not even the most voracious reader can ever read them all. It is a wonderful thought that on a rainy Saturday one will never run out of "great books" to read. But in the university, faculties and semesters are limited in size and duration, and what gets taught is going to be limited, too. What will be taught well is what the faculty are excited about teaching and the students are excited about reading.

We should beware of turning academic politics into a curriculum unto itself. Gerald Graff, a superb teacher of English at Northwestern University, suggests that instead of either the "canon" or the new multicultural lists, we should "teach the conflict." But this meta-level debate will be all but meaningless to students who have not read a substantial body of literature from any culture. Of course, a few students might be thrilled to be brought into the action of the latest academic war, but for students who know the literature on neither side of the divide and lack the motivation to read at all, the redirection of literature departments away from the straightforward presentation of literature would be a real deprivation. There is plenty of room for teaching the theory of literature, but not such that it eclipses the activity it attempts to help students understand. Contrary to current belief, literary theory is not by itself literacy; poorly presented, one can discourage the other.

78 ▾ *The Place of Primary Texts*

Books are beautiful. In such a tiny package the brilliant thoughts and words of a writer many years or centuries dead still live. Whole worlds are contained between those two pieces of cardboard. Imagination and subversion can be smuggled in a purse or a pants pocket, passed on quietly from person to person, or carried on a plane or out into the field. One of the most persuasive arguments against the replacement of books by any electronic medium, at least for the foreseeable future, is the physical aspects, the *feel* of a book.

It is an important part of a literary education to grapple with a book as a whole, getting the feel of it, becoming familiar with its parts. This is one of several serious problems with the proliferation of used books. It is not just that used books do not really save the students much money. One of our colleagues in French recently checked the shelves of the university bookstore before classes began and discovered that every single book was used, or rather abused, the best of the lot marred only by compulsive fluorescent marking (in pink) throughout the entire text. How can students come to respect and love books when what they buy are dirty discards?

Given the finances of book publishing, the price of books, and the red tape involved in reprinting parts of books, it has become almost impossible to order all primary texts and individual books for a course. In a single survey course, one may well cover two dozen readings, all of them from different books. For the sake of the students' pocketbooks, therefore, it is often necessary to settle for anthologies—that is, books designed specifically for classroom use that include selections from up to a hundred or more different books. There are also single-author texts, a summary and elementary survey of a subject, particularly appropriate in the sciences, where it is the system of ideas rather than particular writings that are of primary importance. These are extremely important teaching tools, and we feel that faculty who so readily demean them are being, among other things, snobs. But the use of textbooks means that, except for an occasional quotation or two, students might never read an original text in the field. They will think of books merely as tools, to be sold as soon as possible after the course has ended and not to be treasured, looked back on, lived with. To that end, an original book or two is an invaluable part of a student's education.

The appreciation of books is not to be confused with the uncritical worship of books, however. Moreover it is not enough to simply encourage students to read. They should be encouraged to *devour* the classic texts in question. That gustatory term suggests more than study. It means chewing and digesting, making the texts one's own. Too often we assume (without warrant) that our students are ready and receptive when in fact they are hesitant and resisting. Too often we bring the books to them without also bringing them to the books.

One of the latest and most important literary theories goes by the name of "reader response theory." Despite its often one-sided theoretical bias, it is a welcome corrective to the old "pour it in" vision of reading assignments and spit-back exams. RRT defends the thesis that reading is an active process, and if students are not energized by the process, passive receptivity is not enough. Moreover, different students from different backgrounds, cultures, and socioeconomic classes will respond differently to different novels and theories (consider the variety of reactions one would expect in a mixed class to, say, *The Great Gatsby* or Franz Fanon's *Wretched of the Earth*). As a dynamic activity, reading has to be taught, not in special classes but in every class, each with its own approach, with consideration for the differences and unique interests that mark every student. To think that "exposure" to great books is enough to educate our students is to condemn them to reading as a boring ritual and thought and life as something unliterary. Books should be made part of their lives, and that means that we first of all have to let them give their own life to their books.

79 ▾ The Used-Book Industry: A Conspiracy against Students

Parents and students are rightly concerned about the high price of textbooks, most of which now cost between $35 and $100 each (× four courses per semester × four, five, or more years = thousands of dollars). This is just one of the scandalous aspects of the inflated costs of education, so it is important to understand the real problem, which is an odd variant of the "gray-market economy." This gray market is the marketing of used textbooks in place of new ones. In itself this is an innocent economic activity, and no one complained when the used-textbook market was merely fraternities and sororities raising a bit of extra cash in the spring.

The used-textbook market is now a nationally syndicated, computerized industry run by aggressive companies that have captured such a large proportion of the college book market that it is becoming more and more remarkable that any books are published at all. After the semester is over, students sell back their $50 textbook for perhaps $15. The next semester the retailers sell that same textbook to another student for more than $30. The author and publisher are deprived of a return on these secondary book sales, and as used-textbook sales increase, the publisher makes less and less on new books, even as the book becomes more popular and more widely used in classes. As a result, the price of textbooks goes up, double or even triple, because what was once assumed to be a three-year income for the publisher now becomes a one-year income. Some textbooks now cost $150 each.

Making matters worse is that the bookstore gets to sell the used textbooks first and then return unpurchased new books for free—the publisher pays the freight. It is not uncommon to find only used books on the bookstore shelves while new books are kept in the basement. A bookstore may sell three hundred copies of a textbook that is two years old, yet the publisher will not see a single cent on the deal. As a further complication, excellent books aimed at small markets cannot find a publisher, since publishers become less and less willing to take risks with their already marginal profits.

To recoup some of the lost profits, the publisher persuades the author to prepare a "new edition" of the book, usually only four years or so after it (or the previous edition) has appeared. Students complain, for their previously used book becomes worthless (assuming, of course, that a book's only value is its worth as a commodity). Authors complain, for although one might welcome a second edition as an opportunity to make those few inevitable changes or additions thought of after publication, the demand for a substantially revised book is more of an insult than an opportunity. One would like to assume that he or she got it basically right the first time. And by the time the order comes for the fourth or fifth edition, ideas for "improvement" are stretched thin indeed.

What can be done about this? It would be unfair to ask or demand that undergraduates stop buying used books. But it is only in the short run that it is cheaper for students to buy used textbooks, if they are willing to tolerate the inevitable fluorescent marking and dog-eared pages. In doing so, they support an underground market that in the long run multiplies book costs and undermines publishing. Some professors, we should add, are unscrupulous and sell their free desk copies on the same market. (The used-book syndicate actually sends purchasing agents around to faculty offices, soliciting such sales.) For a few extra dollars, they are ultimately stealing from their students and from their colleagues as well. But there are possible solutions.

The most complete solution would be court or congressional action guaranteeing authors their contracted royalties on every sale of their book, whether the book in question be new, used, or merely copied. A much-publicized court decision against Kinko's copying service a few years ago made some progress in that direction, but it was an excessive ruling that now adds mercilessly to the cost the average student pays for photocopied required readings and creates mountains of needless paperwork. Now a student must pay a substantial royalty for thirty photocopied pages of a three-hundred-page book the professor would not have ordered for purchase in the first place!

It is the *substitution* of used textbooks and photocopies for the sale of new books that is in question. In light of the Kinko's decision, which says that one cannot photocopy without paying the publisher appropriate permission fees, there ought to be a case against the used-book syndicate and bookstores to force them to pay fair royalties on every used book sold.

Although it does not solve the real problem, another effort is now being made by a small number of publishers. The price of a textbook is reduced annually in subsequent years after publication, thereby enabling new books to compete with used books in price and making the slight savings not worth the drawbacks of a badly marked used book. This salvages some sales for the publisher, but the financial crunch remains just around the corner. The necessity for new editions continues, and the price of the new book does not ultimately come down. Thus this is one of the few instances in which we are willing to appeal to the legislature to help solve a university problem, for both the used-book syndicate and the problem have gotten much larger than any single group of students and faculty can handle. If authors and publishers got rewarded for their risks and efforts as the free market supposes, students and parents would find the cost of textbooks a much smaller portion of their university expenses. There would also be many more books available and a much greater choice of books, a substantial boon.

80 ▾ *Books in Translation*

Teaching a book is not just analyzing its plot, characters, theme, and style. A book has a place—in history, in a culture, in a genre, in an author's life, in a sequence of books, some by the same author and some by other authors. To teach a book is to place it in its larger landscape, to appreciate its language and the importance of that language in the determination of thought and experience of an entire culture. But all this derives its meaning from the language in which one reads the book, and on these grounds scholars are very quick to insist that one cannot really grasp a text on the basis of a translation.

Reading a translation of a text is already reading an interpretation of the text and not the text itself. Upon picking up several translations of the *Tao Te Ching*, for example, one is struck by the thought that these could not conceivably be translations of the same Chinese characters. The shock is milder but still substantial upon picking up a work translated from German, French, Greek, or Russian, and even when the meaning stays more or less constant, the style can be very different indeed. Two recent translations of Camus's novel *L'Étranger,* one brand new and very

American and one older and British, are quite different books. No student who reads Homer in translation can get the full flavor and clever word-play of the original Greek, even though many of the translations are very well done.

But—and this is a big "but"—it is an enormous mistake to limit the reading of such books to those fluent in the original language. That would deprive millions of readers of a great source of inspiration, sec-ondhand though it may be, and even those students who do become fluent in the language in question will be at a disadvantage compared to a cultured native speaker. Indeed, the conscious linguistic accomplish-ment and effort may distort the easy flow of a conscientiously un-reflective text. Every student should be able to read works in another language, and every student should be encouraged to do so. But to get on a high horse and, for example, resist teaching or refuse to teach "works in translation" courses in literature departments is robbing most of the students of their only opportunity to make contact with some of the best products of a culture.

We should remember how long literary and even religious studies were kept as the exclusive property of an elite by virtue of the lack of widely available translations. The translation of the Bible into modern vernac-ular languages has often been considered a revolutionary act. Popular translations of the *Odyssey* and *Iliad* were not readily available to most students until the past few centuries. Even if translations inevitably dis-tort a classic text, it is far better, we believe, to offer the students a half-decent translation than nothing at all.

Later in this book we address the problems created when some depart-ments of the university appropriate texts translated into English from another language. Thus Homer and Sartre are taught in English courses by professors with Ph.D.'s in English and perhaps not more than a dan-gerously small acquaintance with the Greek and French in which the books were originally written. Scholars in the foreign languages un-derstandably resent this, for what they consider to be a nonexpert is appropriating "their" literature and teaching it. The problem becomes particularly severe when enrollment limits enter the picture; if a French course does not have the minimum number of students required by the university administration and the legislature, then the course cannot be offered at all, but across the hallway an "English" course in the same author may be offered because it met the minimum enrollment, in part by luring students away from the more difficult French class.

In the open university we minimize this problem, first by eliminating minimum enrollment quotas and then by encouraging interdisciplinary team-taught courses and recommending that faculty from different disciplines communicate frequently with each other. Most faculty are quite willing to give a five- or ten-minute impromptu lecture on a field in which they have expertise to a fellow faculty member who asks even the most basic questions. One of the ironies of the academic world is that scholars and teachers who pride themselves on having a doctorate in a specific discipline and subspecialty feel awkward about calling on the expertise of other scholars and teachers who pride themselves on having a doctorate in a different discipline and subspecialty. The call is free, and in most university extensions you need only dial four or five digits. The students deserve the benefits, after all.

81 ▾ *The Atlas and the Chronology*

In general, it would be better if books were not required reading. They should be made readily available, promoted, and encouraged. But they are best *discovered,* not assigned, and the best teachers do not require reading as much as make it irresistible. But there are two exceptions, two books that ought to be provided to every student: a world (and historical) atlas and a cross-cultural time line of history, in addition to the obvious, a good dictionary. These are browsing books, books to be returned to again and again, for a lifetime. Their value is their constant presence, a constant temptation for curiosity and understanding.

A good survey course in geography and another in world history might be a fine idea, but one need not require such courses to have every student be familiar with basic world facts. It will accomplish nothing to continue the current lament about how ignorant and illiterate our students are and to add another required course or test to the curriculum. We do not want students to learn about the world for a month or two because they are soon to be tested on that material. The campus culture should be employed to prompt this knowledge. We want students to learn it because they feel the need to, and anyone reading this book realizes how quickly a little knowledge of history or a cursory look at a globe inspires curiosity and interest to know more. Why not give them away?

On the other hand, perhaps an occasional test would do some good, not by way of administrative requirement but as just plain fun; as a source of competition between fraternities, sororities, and other student groups;

as an opportunity for the hotshots and memory freaks around campus to strut their stuff. When we were young, we all had to memorize the state capitals, a usually useless exercise. But the game had a point, and expanded it could assist in providing the kind of atmosphere the university should encourage—learning for the sake of learning, learning for fun, learning to keep up with one's peers. A noncoercive knowledge test and a couple of free books thrown in with the price of tuition might do wonders for the "knowledge gap" lamented by all those highly paid mullahs. And we could do it without further degrading the undergraduates or adding one more obstacle to the degree mill.

82 ▾ *The Role of "Pop" Studies*

Popular culture is a term invented a few decades ago to describe an increasingly large, dynamic body of modern arts that were at the time not accepted into the university for study. It is a term still thought of pejoratively in many academic circles because the body of popular art does not meet the test of time or fall easily into the traditional genre categories, and it is produced largely for monetary reward, not artistic immortality. It includes almost everything, all the products of culture that are created in our daily lives—film, television, radio, popular music, dance, novels, comic books, magazines, newspapers, toys, supermarket products, sports, fashion, automobiles, travel, food, and more—in our own culture, subcultures, and ethnic cultures.

Long before popular culture could infiltrate the university classroom, it became an academic hobby for scholars. Trained to collate, catalog, absorb, and analyze the traditional artistic corpuses, scholars found it refreshing to put Shelley and Sophocles aside for a brief period and instead study "Star Trek," rock videos, and Big Macs. It was rarely the big guns of the academy who attended a Popular Culture Association conference, but one of the things to notice there, besides the paucity of big-name university affiliations, was always the unusually high level of enjoyment on the part of the participants.

Popular culture is finally becoming part of the university curriculum. Literature courses include books written within the last few years, and there are courses on jazz, whole programs and departments of film studies and media arts. General civilization and culture survey courses now regularly include the study of film scripts, rock music, or some other aspect of popular culture. There is still a long road to march, but the more attention university faculty pay to what the students are genuinely interested in and the more they notice that one of the ways to reach the students is through the popular culture they encounter every day, the more easily they will get the average student's attention.

There are ample opportunities to observe students at leisure around the university. Sitting in a lecture hall before class, chatting in front of a vending machine, holding a beer while standing on the lawn of the fraternity house on Friday (or Thursday) afternoon, they talk. They talk about movies, MTV, travel, their cars, parties, food, and the like. They rarely read on their own, but when they do, it is most often the school paper or *USA Today* that they seem to find of interest. Since this is what they appear to be interested in outside of the university, it is through such sources of popular culture that their academic interest can quite easily be piqued.

They may not be ready to discuss in class Antigone's motives, but they certainly are ready to argue with you about Madonna's. We keep emphasizing the importance of passion in a university education, and here we find it in the flesh. Whether students love Madonna or hate her, they almost all have a strong opinion about her, and with very little guidance the discussion of Madonna can be rechanneled in whatever direction the course description requires—music, art, psychology, philosophy, theater, history, poetry, feminism, multiculturalism, religious studies, or whatever. Pop studies go wrong, however, when they become the main course instead of the hors d'oeuvre—when the "pop" eclipses the "culture." And when pop scholars argue—without a hint of humor or self-mockery—that Sting is as great as Yeats or Sappho, we know that pedagogy has given way to hucksterism.

One of the aspects that makes our popular culture so unique is its democratic omnipresence. We have at the end of the second millennium reached a point at which there is so much leisure time, so much consumer art, so much money available that the arts have spread from the aristocratic concert halls and museums into every living room and bedroom. The arts have spread from Paris to San Dimas, from the Vanderbilts to the unemployed average teenager, and they range from artistic celebrations of the aging process (*Driving Miss Daisy, On Golden Pond*) to all-morning marathons for preschool children. That just a simple idea like the Teenage Mutant Ninja Turtles affects comic book design, the toy and clothing industries, television, books, and the cinema, that hundreds of millions of dollars are spent on four imaginary turtles, bears witness to the historical uniqueness of the spread of popular art and the merging of the artistic and financial worlds. This is not to be ignored, but neither should it eclipse the study of those four old Italians for whom the turtles were so whimsically named.

Popular culture in our era reaches unheard-of numbers of people in an extremely broad spectrum of ages all over the world. To omit its study from the university curriculum is to seal the campus off from its future as well as from the rest of society. Popular culture is not really a threat to the traditional arts. In the traditional arts new painters, musicians, dancers, and authors are emerging every year. Years from now our popular culture will have become art history, and art historians may look back on our era and offer a "traditional" course on our turtle phenomenon, "Media Corporation Children's Art of the Late Twentieth Century." Some of the most exciting changes are taking place in the popular arts, and universities would be well advised to embrace their study just as they are embracing wisdom and lore students from various cultural heritages.

83 ▾ *So What Should They Read?*

The simple answer to the perennial problem of what students should read, though lost in the scuffle over requirements for multiculturalism and Western civilization, is that students should be encouraged to read *everything*. That is, we want to make them voracious, compulsive, critical readers. It does the students no service to teach them to be contemptuous of non-Western literature, and it certainly does them no service to teach them to be contemptuous of the often-difficult classics of Western literature, books that are hard going even for an eighteen-year-old who is inspired to read them.

Our job is to make our students curious and interested, and if they get their kicks from comic books and *Cosmo* and *USA Today,* that is not in itself a problem. Indeed, if they can critically think their way through the evening news or an old episode of "Star Trek," that is no problem either. What we need to do is get them to read, and to think and open their minds and look for more. If we can recommend "a good read" to them and make reading even more exciting, we won't have to worry about their reading the "right" books. They have the rest of their lives to do that.

PART XII

Culture(s) and "Correctness"

84 ▾ *What Is Culture?*

In our ideologically egalitarian society, *culture* has long been a suspect word, suggesting the pretensions of an effete and foolish leisure class, represented, for example, by the grande dame played by Margaret Dumont in the Marx brothers films. The pretensions of a self-appointed cultural elite notwithstanding, *culture* refers to nothing more objectionable than a system of shared knowledge, values, beliefs, symbols, rituals, and habits that hold a society together. Within a culture we are kindred spirits, whether or not we agree or get along, simply because we understand one another. There is nothing particularly political or polemical about this concept of culture, which was brought into prominence by anthropologists only about fifty years ago.

In academic circles the word *culture* has achieved a new moral and political significance. Because the concept of "culture" and the mix of cultures have become so confused, culture is now recognized as one of the necessities of life. Thirty years ago a Princeton psychologist argued that people deprived of their past become morbidly depressed. So, too, a people without a culture, a heritage, will find themselves at a severe psychological disadvantage. Within a culture we know who we are and where we've been. This accounts for the vigor with which ethnic groups are celebrating their cultures and, where necessary, inventing their past. This accounts for the vehemence with which competing cultures maintain the validity of their own. Accordingly, higher education has become more attentive not only to the importance of culture but to the great variety of cultures. Western "high" culture has always received its due in the university. Now the demand is to pay attention to the others as well.

85 ▾ *Multiculturalism*

"Multiculturalism" is probably the most important, the most stimulating, and at the same time, the silliest movement to hit the university since the beginnings of democratic education. It is important because it has awakened the university to the multitude of vibrant cultures of the world and mandated a new sensitivity to other cultures and literatures. It is stimulating because it has shaken up many of the tired routines of a university droned to sleep in its own restrictive self-made history. It has become silly only because academics tend to be such self-righteous enthusiasts that they can turn any good idea into nonsense, if only by converting insight into dogma and sensitivity into obligation. In this case the nonsense is "political correctness," which started as self-effacing humor among those who recognized the rigidity of their own behavior but has turned into the perverse fight for the constitutional "freedom" to be a bigot and a racist. If one were to believe the press, "political correctness" is shutting the universities down. For those of us who live there, it is just one more silly polemic whose origins are quite exciting but whose rhetorical excesses, isolated as they are, bear no relation whatever to what we do.

Multiculturalism is the catchphrase, the fashion of the day. Anthropology has moved from the margins of the university to its center, although little attention seems to have been diverted to the actual knowledge of the anthropologists. For multiculturalism is not concerned with cultures as such. It is an abstract thesis *about* cultures. According to the more modest demands of multiculturalism, every culture deserves respect, and many cultures are worthy of study. In the more radical versions of multiculturalism, cultures are also said to be incommensurable, which means that they cannot be compared and evaluated and are therefore not subject to criticism. Every culture is what it is, and we have no right to criticize, only to understand—if we can. In still more radical versions, other cultures may be worthy of respect, but our own culture, "Western" culture, is not. Indeed, "Western culture" is said not to be a culture at all. What used to be celebrated as the triumph of Western civilization is now viewed by the radical multiculturalists as the tragic victory of cultural imperialism and genocide.

One must admit that, much to its discredit, the considerable powers of Western Europe and more recently America did not always employ either respect or restraint in their approach to other civilizations, and in art and ideas as well as in religion and politics, Western civilization tended to present itself not as one culture among many but as human nature developed to its fullest. Today that pretense is rapidly being corrected, the tides have turned, and other cultures and other perspectives are represented in courses and books all over the university. No responsible history professor would think of presenting the history and mythology of the Old West today without consideration of the lives of the people who already lived there any more than one would present the antebellum South without some harsh words and anecdotes about the cruelty of slavery. Eastern and Middle Eastern art classes coexist easily with the usual Western art surveys, and African-Asian programs in language and literature are now to be found on almost every campus. To be sure, there could be more of them, and as student demand increases, there will be. But multiculturalism is a fact about university life today, not just a political polemic.

The well-publicized fights that make their way into the media, on the other hand, are the usual academic grandstanding, professors who see one more way of "frightening the philistines," lectures that say too much and programs that demand too much. The recognition of alternative perspectives is bound to encourage reactionary views. Once it is generally acknowledged that Western "culture" has functioned as an instrument of oppression, one can only expect that a few extremists will insist that it has never been anything else but an instrument of oppression. Once it is admitted that students do not know enough about other cultures and, at the same time, betray a modicum of racism themselves, it is all too tempting for one or another little academic dictator to require a "corrective" course for them.

But only a fool or a demagogue would diagnose these excesses as a disease that is killing the university. Those who see nothing of value in Western culture are soundly refuted in every quality lecture on Western art, music, literature, and philosophy on campus. And the last thing the university needs right now is another required course. Shakespeare and Plato continue to be taught, but Sappho, Borges, Mishima, and Mahfouz are now joining them. Multiculturalism is a fact, not a threat. It is the academic recognition that the world is complex and fascinating.

Western culture has indeed developed in its attitude toward other peoples so that it is now necessary to reconsider some of our traditional modes of thinking. It is time, for example, to abandon the notion that there are certain "transcendental" ideas that are manifested exclusively in Western thought or that all of civilization grew out of the Caucasian tribes of the ancient Adriatic. Even so, every culture is ethnocentric. We read that the word for *human* in Javanese is simply the word for "being Javanese," and a vigorous debate still continues in China on the question of whether non-Chinese can be properly said to be human. The history of the world before and outside of the European colonial invasions was anything but the pristine harmony envisioned by some of our more naive multiculturalists. There was an active slave trade in Africa long before Europe took on that ghastly business for itself, there were grisly mass sacrifices in South and Central America before the extermination of whole cultures at the hands of Cortés, and systematic genocide was the explicit purpose of many Asian wars.

To be banal, there is good and bad in virtually every culture and much to be learned from them all. Simply to dismiss the accomplishments of "Western" culture is as foolish as to dismiss the vitality and contributions of other cultures. The question is not one of superiority, and what is at stake is not mere "difference." The point is to learn as much as possible and to get along, to synthesize and criticize and not just "appreciate" what we all have to learn from each other.

86 ▾ *Multiculturalism and Racism*

The issue of multiculturalism has become notoriously explosive on university campuses, but multiculturalism is only a symptom of a much larger concern that is no mere academic teapot tempest. The multiculturalism debate has been trivialized and focused as a question about the curriculum and required courses, but what the multiculturalism debate is really about is the running sore of North American racism. The civil rights movement has all but collapsed, the courts that once legitimated it now chop away at its gains, the students who once supported it now feel threatened by affirmative action, and the government that once encouraged it now turns a blind eye to human rights violations and economic oppression that still cause shock and outrage even in foreign countries.

It is not multiculturalism that is at issue—as important as that may be. It is that there are more reported racial incidents on campus now than at any time in the past thirty years. It is that minority representation among students is still far from adequate and that minority representation among the faculty remains pathetic. The presumption of dominance among white students is unmistakable.[1] Accordingly, "multiculturalism" is a euphemism. It has very little to do with the understanding of cultures and everything to do with getting a fix on the problem of racism.

Many black student leaders are not at all shy about their own idea of multicultural education: Make every white student take a course on the history of slavery. Nor are they at all unclear about their political objectives: Drastically increase the presence of black faculty and students on campus to dramatically improve respect from white students. These are just and important goals, but it is not at all clear that disguising the issue behind the multicultural screen, much less pushing the addition of yet another course requirement, is the solution to racism.

For one thing, that once-descriptive word *racism* has become nothing more than a term of abuse, a way of stopping a conversation. The word *multiculturalism,* too, has become little more than a red flag and a provocation to a screaming match in which only the most extreme and nonsensical positions seem to get heard. Instead of serving as a solution, the word aggravates the problem. Mutual accusations promote not mutual understanding but mutual distrust and hostility. And the broadly stated requirement for multicultural courses comes to look like a punishment, not an education, which many students quite rightly resent.

The debate itself has been conducive to anything but mutual understanding. By presenting itself as a wholesale attack on Western civilization, the multiculturalism movement has antagonized most of its plausible supporters. When students and political outsiders chant at Stanford, "Hey, hey, ho, ho, Western civ. has got to go," what could that provoke but resentment and reaction? But on the other side, the shrill defenders of "the canon" and the self-appointed censors of American decency inspire just as much contempt and indignation. Regardless of whether they intend to do so, they activate and condone the students' most poisonous prejudices.

Both sides exaggerate and overdramatize the claims of the other, but the truth is that "multiculturalism," for all its apparent pluralism, too often overlooks most of the world's cultures. Asian-Americans feel that the debate utterly ignores their needs as well as their existence, and many students feel, like other immigrant groups, that what they mainly want out of the university is to learn how to get on well in America, not just to take courses on cultural self-appreciation. Needless to say, the multiculturalism debate gets very quiet when the Japanese enter the picture. Can they be presented as an "oppressed people," struggling against Western capitalist imperialism? Most striking of all is the general exclusion of the Arab and Persian peoples in these debates. Indeed, what other people in recent history have been more clumsily stereotyped and universally misunderstood and misrepresented?

Hispanic students, too, have legitimate cause for complaint, but multiculturalism is proving to be more of a curse than a blessing for many of them. What they want is adequate preparation for an education. What they do not want is a "special" education. True, an account of Texas or Arizona history ought to pay considerable attention to the perspectives and interests of the ethnic groups that dominated those lands, but to encourage Mexican-American students to spend their time studying the history of the Southwest or taking the easy out with a Spanish major is a way of limiting and not expanding their understanding of the university, the world, and its promises for the future.

The critical fact is, again, that the number of Hispanic students on campus is far fewer than it ought to be and the number of Hispanic professors fewer still. But to bury this problem under the rhetoric of multiculturalism and to celebrate Hispanic culture in opposition to the "dominant" American culture is to make the problem of prejudice intractable. So, too, as many students "of color" will tell you, the special attention now paid to them detracts from rather than lends credibility to their status on campus. Instead of special treatment and "understanding," they want respect, and they want an education.

87 ▾ The Most Insidious Form of Racism

A visiting Arab professor recently complained to one of our colleagues, "I don't know what they want of me." His expected role, it seems, was to inject some exoticism into the curriculum. But the exotic had nothing to do with what he taught or how he taught it. In the multicultural frenzy, what knowledge he shared with his "Western" colleagues was deemed of little interest. He was to be valued for his "difference." In fact, he was caught in what is becoming perhaps the most insidious form of racism on campus.

Many nonwhite students now complain that they are not taken seriously when they claim to be interested in any subject other than multicultural studies. It is assumed that their interests are determined by their race. Black students should want to do black studies, and Hispanics should want to do Chicano studies, and if they should express an interest in German literature or aerospace engineering, they are accused of treachery and often demeaned. The odd variation once again applies to Asian students, who are assumed to be interested only in math and science.

It is also fast becoming a matter of dogma that black studies ought to be taught by black instructors, and the fallacious conclusion is that black faculty on campus must therefore be part of the black studies program. So, too, feminism courses have to be taught by women, so all female faculty members can be assumed to be feminists. The tales of "political correctness" employed against fellow black and female colleagues are hair-raising, but what is even worse is the de facto segregation of nonwhite, nonmale faculty to the margins of academia. Of course, there is always room for one or two outspoken black nationalists and feminists on the faculty who are not only entitled but expected to excoriate the university on a regular basis. That is a role that has become ubiquitous and, accordingly, well insulated. But for most of the nonwhite faculty and students on campus, the new focus on race and culture fostered in the name of "multiculturalism" has probably been as much of a handicap as the not-so-subtle exclusionary tactics of an older last generation.

But then, it was just a generation or two before that nonwhite and female students could not be found on campus at all. The idea of a "color/gender-blind" campus has always been something of an illusion, an excuse to continue the old-boy network. There is no doubt that matters have greatly improved. On many large campuses the percentage of minority faculty has doubled in the past ten years. But the new emphasis and concentration on race and cultural differences threaten to maintain the old inequities under a new name. A fascination with other cultures must not lead us to marginalize those cultures on campus, even under the guise of giving them center stage.

To see the multiculturalism debate not as a celebration of differences but as a renewed concern about racism on campus focuses our attention. The problem of multiculturalism does not involve anthropology but a very specific racial and ethnic conflict. (Indeed, it is illuminating that the anthropology departments in the country seem to be the least affected, let alone consulted, by the multiculturalism debate.) The question is not the concept of culture as such, much less some abstract schema for the coexistence of cultures. It is a very concrete concern for the status and well-being of a particular and particularly significant proportion of our population and, accordingly, the health of our society overall. Questions about culture in general and exotic cultures in particular have their important place on campus, but they should not be confused with the straightforwardly political and social domestic questions now facing American society.

Beyond Affirmative Action:
88 ▾ What the University Can Do about Racism

The explosive issues of prejudice, affirmative action, and curriculum reform are unquestionably interrelated, but they have nevertheless been confused, one distracting from the others. And it is all too clear how the belligerent opposition, those who like the overly white complexion of the university, are already starting to play the one against the others. Curriculum reform is an issue guaranteed to keep faculty fighting for years without results, save for an occasional emergency course, usually ill thought out or badly designed, whose only aim is to alleviate political pressure.

It may be true that white students should not feel guilty for what happened in America over a century and a half ago, but they are the beneficiaries of an inequality of circumstances that survives today. Black students have no warrant to blame their fellow students for the past, but they do have a valid claim for bettered opportunities in the present. There are too few black students in the university and far too few black faculty members. There are too few fellowships for them and too little attention paid to their special problems. Black studies programs may have succeeded in fostering ethnic pride and providing black and some white students the opportunity to focus on black history and experience, but the establishment of such courses too readily allowed the faculty and administration to wash their hands of the problem, isolate black students even more than before, this time with their approval, and hire just a few black faculty members to run those few programs.

The lack of black and Hispanic representation on the faculty is the most basic problem. There is indeed a "small pool" of minority candidates, especially in such fields as physics, mathematics, classics, and philosophy. The recent move to make deans strong-arm departments is not going to change the demographics. A large state university might compete with a few Ivy League schools and some other universities that pay considerably higher salaries than most can afford, but the likelihood of acquiring one of those few candidates is exceedingly small. In a few fields there may be only one or two candidates, and they virtually have their pick of the top universities in the nation. We could lower our criteria and hire more minorities from less prestigious schools and with less promise for academic success, but this would soon establish a "second-tier" faculty that would guarantee continued resentment. The "bum's rush" demand for hiring more faculty emanating from the administration right now is only going to end in frustration and embarrassment.

What we need is a *long-term* program to develop, not just find, minority faculty who can join the university, not as token or second-class citizens but as fully competent teachers and scholars. We need to reject these short-term fixes being proposed by administration and students alike. Affirmative action, for all the heat of the debate, has created only a very small number of minority positions. It is not hard to understand why. One does not create a professor by fiat or by simply granting a credential, and the fact is that even today, with affirmative action over twenty years old, there are very few minority candidates for professorships. The future looks no better. In 1991 blacks received only 1 percent of all the Ph.D.'s awarded in the United States.

We in the fields that are so underrepresented need to go out and give lectures and teach in largely minority elementary schools. Before they are deadened by required courses and bad teachers, children readily learn to love almost anything interesting. Many of us on the faculty would gladly do this as part of our service to the community. We should expose children to academic subjects. We should show them that people actually live their lives doing this, loving it, and getting paid for it. Then the critical role of the university should be to provide scholarships so that those students can seriously study those subjects. We can encourage them to stay for graduate and postgraduate study, supported, again, by scholarships.

It is not in the present "small pool" that adequate faculty representation will be found but in generous planning for the near future. We need to take it upon ourselves to encourage and develop faculty. Multiculturalism in the university and in the curriculum will then be a natural consequence, for even if these new teachers have been primarily exposed to the same old male white pedagogy, their heritage and political interests will no doubt guarantee precisely the changes that are now being demanded. As the palette of instructors changes, so will the painting.

89 ▾ Open Cultural Horizons: Learn Other Languages

The most obvious place to start a program of "multiculturalism," although it is already fifteen years late for most students, is exposure to other languages. Texas and Arizona students and faculty may hear Spanish for the better part of their lives, but most of them know only a few words of the language. The debate over bilingual education in the schools has been remarkably one-sided. True, it gives Spanish-speaking pupils a chance to learn other material while they are learning English, thus protecting them from built-in retardation and perhaps fatal frustration with their progress in school. But little attention is given to the desirability of English-speaking students' speaking Spanish in states with a Spanish-speaking population.

So, too, "foreign" language requirements have been shrinking over the past twenty years. As always, we do not urge requirements, but we certainly encourage our students to study foreign languages, and the culture of the university should be such that a monolingual student is thought to be a deprived and second-rate student. In the midst of a loud and caustic debate over whether students should learn about the history and past experiences of various peoples, not to learn at least a little about their languages is ludicrous.

We recommend the study of foreign languages as well for students who hope to spend their lives working with foreign business. We see large numbers of students pouring into courses on international business in hopes of getting a piece of the action as Asian and European corporations confront American enterprise and as new markets open up in Latin America and Eastern Europe. But there is incredibly little encouragement to study the international languages of business—French and German, Japanese and Chinese, Spanish and Arabic. Every bit of evidence available to students should tell them that speaking a foreign language is the best possible credential for the very best jobs around.

Knowing another language is also a way of "being in" the culture rather than simply appreciating its history, rituals, or business patterns. It is not just that the culture becomes accessible in a way that it never would without the language. It is that one finds oneself already in it, from casual conversations with a waiter at a restaurant to high-level business and political negotiations overseas. We do not have to mandate the study of languages in order to make it clear that students who are monophones are educationally backward, professionally disabled, intellectually inferior, and culturally deprived. Instead of requiring politically suspect and often pointless "multicultural" courses, why is there not more clamor about language courses?

90 ▾ *History Is Not in the Past*

History, for most of its own history, has been the telling of tales, the remembering of great events, the commemoration of heroes. Indeed, in many cultures the distinction between history and mythology has been acknowledged only with considerable hesitation. In our own American culture the myths of the Founding Fathers and the open frontier have long served as the most widely known part of our early history. It is almost impossible to overestimate the importance of such grand stories in the sense of a people, and having grown up with them, it is almost as impossible to imagine not having them. How automatically, therefore, we dismiss the counterclaims of those multiculturalists who challenge the factoids and myths of history—that Columbus discovered America or that Cleopatra looked like Elizabeth Taylor.

History gets misunderstood as the study of the facts of the past. We read a fact in a book and immediately assume that it is indeed fact. Sometimes facts are facts—the Japanese bombed Pearl Harbor on December 7, 1941. Sometimes they are not—this bombing came or may not have come as a complete surprise to the American government. Even when the facts are evident, their significance is up for grabs. And when the facts themselves are in question, as they often are, history becomes a stage on which the conflict of cultures, nations, and peoples plays itself out.

Over the past twenty-five years, numerous books, television exposés, and a provocative film have suggested that one of the tragic events of our own times, the assassination of John F. Kennedy, was a conspiracy of immense proportions. In an obvious sense the cynics are right: JFK is dead and there is little we can do about it now. But aside from the gut-reaction, emotional defenses of and assaults on the Warren Commission report, a number of people have become interested in discovering the truth. A busy research center has opened up in Dallas, and thousands of people have taken up studying the JFK assassination as their avocation. Because of the conflicting and limited evidence, they have not yet reached the full truth and perhaps never will. No side will ultimately convince the other side that it is "wrong." What thousands have learned, though, is that history is in a perpetual state of flux and re-creation; there may be facts, but when the meaning of the present is at stake, there are no universally satisfactory answers.

The quincentennial debates about the meaning of Columbus's arrival will not restore the Aztec empire, but they are of the greatest significance for the descendants of peoples on both sides of the ocean. In that dialogue we are forced to get over the simplemindedness of our own mythology ("discovery" indeed!) and uncover not only the complexities of the past but the living vitality of history. And when African-Americans attempt to forge a more or less unified history that goes back not only to tribal Africa but to Egypt and the Greeks, why should we belittle that effort, and why should we be so dogmatic about what we were taught as the "facts"?

> To be sure, "that's ancient history" has often been used as a dismissal phrase, but one did not expect it to be used against Ancient History.
> —John Passmore

The university with its research library provides an opportunity to pursue such important historical questions. For ethnic, emotional, reactionary, or intellectual reasons, students turn to historical research to uncover a few thousand years of conspiracies, mythologies, and utter falsehoods. In doing so, they learn what every faculty member knows— that knowledge is unfixed and that every discovery and assumption must be periodically questioned and retested. Einstein's theory of relativity does not answer all the questions of modern physics, and the value of Milton's *Paradise Lost* undergoes careful scrutiny with each new generation of readers.

Human knowledge may have limits, but it is the endless, unrestricted pursuit of knowledge that universities encourage. Too much of a university education consists of facts and dogma, not openness and adventure. Much of what we have learned turns out to be self-serving illusion, and the multicultural historical debate has ushered in a fresh impetus to review the established historical facts and theories. If this impetus is followed up properly, if ethnic groups and scholars alike review the evidence thoroughly, then that shared activity brings us closer to a cure for both ignorance and mutual alienation. After all, it is all *our* history, once that pronoun is understood in its full global significance.

91 ▾ *Criticizing Cultures*

Cultures are not inwardly narcissistic, and that view of multiculturalism that stresses "knowledge of one's own culture" to the exclusion of knowledge of others' is killing the idea of culture, not saving it. No matter how self-contained and content a culture may be, there is always something in another that can be learned or coveted, whether it be a new way of cooking, a new way of thinking, or an appreciation for the electric guitar.

The first fact of multiculturalism is not "difference," much less "the other"—two extremely disagreeable pieces of academic jargon—but rather cross-fertilization. Whether it is curiosity or paranoia, hostile or helpful, people find themselves fascinated by other people. And with fascination comes comparison. Even as the Europeans were conquering the cultures of the Americas and Asia, they found themselves adopting their customs, copying their habits, appropriating their values as well as their goods and languages. The religions of Asia have long served as promises of redemption for jaded Europeans and now North Americans, and the environmental mentality of Native Americans has now become a paradigm for more recent inhabitants. It is a waste if not a betrayal of multiculturalism to treat it as nothing but a forum for mutual admiration and tolerance. It is in confrontation that societies are prompted to think about themselves and their values and learn something new.

What is missing from the multiculturalism debate, presumably in the name of mutual respect, is the willingness to criticize. But one respects a culture and its ideas by grappling with them, by pointing out what one takes to be their deficiencies, not by shrugging one's shoulders and chanting the "Different strokes for different folks" mantra. Criticism is not lack of respect but true respect, treating the other not as a curiosity to be viewed at a distance but as an equal who has something to teach. Of course, this process involves dialogue, not merely observation from afar, and it is in dialogue that one comes to appreciate the other. Would a multicultural course provide or encourage such a dialogue? That would be the test. If the new requirements are just another bunch of lectures, however distinguished, the distance between those who study and those who are studied will not be bridged.

One of the virtues of multiculturalism is that it forces a culture to come to terms with its own provincialism and limitations. Religious people who owe their moral allegiance to a group that transcends the culture they live in often play this role. So do intellectuals and social critics who are devoted to the search for the truth or some ideal that differs from the current state of society. Pluralistic societies inevitably experience an internal clash of cultures, and however much competition there may be between them, a mutual exchange and learning process nevertheless proceed. Cultures in confrontation inspire converts among the disaffected or rebellious, as we have seen in the recent popularity of Indian religion and in the current popularity of Latin, African, and South Asian music. These may seem like peripheral phenomena, but in fact, they reach deep into the heart of a culture. One may not understand the donor culture, but one will inevitably see one's own culture with a new and more critical eye.

One of the purposes of the university is to encourage such a critical eye and the multicultural perspective that goes along with it. It is a matter of rumination on basic values and the question, "How do I want to live?" Looking at various cultures, for instance, we may be provoked to think about how spiritually impoverished we are, how overly concerned with consumerism we are, how disconnected and indifferent our so-called communities are, how little we respect our city streets and highways, how horrendous are our crime rates and our waste of human potentialities. In the end we may accept and be able to justify ourselves, but there is all the difference between naive self-acceptance and the humbler but wiser self-assurance that comes only with an appreciation of other ways of living and a serious reexamination of one's own.

92 ▾ *The Bogey of Relativism*

If cultures are different, is it possible that different cultures will have different values and hold different beliefs? The answer is obviously "yes." But if cultures are different, is it therefore *necessary* that different cultures have different values and hold different beliefs? The answer is just as clearly "no." And yet the debate over multiculturalism often comes to blows over the issue of "relativism"—namely, the idea that what people rightly believe is relative to their culture and their times. Therefore, it is said there is no ultimate distinction between right and wrong.

This is mistaken, however it may work as a scare tactic for those who warn of anarchy in our classrooms. Theologies and mythologies may seem to differ considerably, but several scholars have argued that almost all religions have some common basis and that the practical dictates of religion—for example, the Golden Rule—seem to hold in virtually all cultures. And since all peoples of the world face the same biological facts about life—the need to eat and sleep, the need for shelter and security, the need and desire to procreate, the final fact of death—we should not be surprised to find that every culture has a system of values defined by the same critical facts. Of course, there are differences, dramatic differences, but the important point is that relativism does not mean that these differences are insurmountable or incommensurable.

The real fear, of course, is that if values are relative, then "anything goes." There is even the possibility that the values of the nazis might have been right for them even if they are evil to us. Relativism seems to relieve us of the burden of fighting or even thinking about evil. But relativism does not entail giving up the fight for what one believes in, nor does it entail giving up the notion of universal values. What relativism does require is an open ear and an open mind, a willingness to listen and learn as well as the need to discuss and argue and to stick up for what is right. Relativism is not an attack on values. It is an attack on dogmatism. The fact that there are so many dogmatic relativists in the university today shows only the need for restating what is in fact a quite sensible, even self-evident, position.

Relativism is often lumped into a family of ethical concepts that are, in fact, quite different. For example, relativism is often coupled with "historicism," which for some reason enjoys an honorific reputation, whereas relativism is damned even by some of the most articulate theorists. Historicism is essentially relativism applied through time to history and the thesis that people and events are to be understood in the context of their own epochs. Again, the aim is to counteract the dogmatism of the moment, the assumption that all people have always been essentially the same and can be judged by the standards we use now.

For example, Aristotle defended the institution of slavery twenty-five hundred years ago. The dogmatist would vilify slavery wherever and whenever it existed. The historicist would say that it must be understood in the often-harsh terms of its own times. But again, the two positions need not be placed in such stark opposition. What historicism adds to relativism is the notion of development and evolution, the idea that concepts and institutions change over time and, despite superficial appearances, may be quite different once the whole context of a culture is understood. Again, the lesson is not that "anything goes" or that slavery might be "right" for some societies but rather that glib judgments are not warranted and understanding is necessary. Historicism does not excuse slavery in ancient Athens or sexism in Victorian England. It puts them into context.

"Subjectivism" is often used as a more personalized version of relativism. If relativism insists that a phenomenon is relative to a certain culture or conceptual framework, then subjectivism charges that a judgment is based on a purely individual perspective. The charge of subjectivism is a favorite way of dismissing an argument in supposedly "objective" academic discussions, but it, too, is often misunderstood as "merely personal" or, even worse, "merely emotional." Subjectivism does not mean that subjective judgments cannot be widely shared or even that subjective judgments cannot be right. Subjectivity can also employ reasons and be articulate and persuasive. Of course, there is the "You have your opinion, and I have mine" subjectivism of some sophomores, but that is better characterized as intellectual sloth than as subjectivism.

The most ominous version of relativism goes by the name of "nihilism," invented by the Russian novelist Turgenev to describe the young rebels he knew in czarist Russia. The nihilist believes in nothing and disdains all values. The truth, though, is that there are no nihilists, not even the psychopaths who shoot passersby randomly in the street. There are some horrible things that happen in the world, but most of them come from the fanaticism that insists on seeing all human behavior through the polarized lens of good and evil rather than the magnifying glass of close contact, conversation, and understanding. Relativism is not a problem for multiculturism or for modern pluralist education. An intelligent, thoroughgoing, nondogmatic relativism is, to the contrary, what education is all about.

93 ▾ *"Political Correctness"*

In Moscow, several years before *perestroika,* the official censors were on the lookout for politically offensive language. A biologist was preparing for publication a book on the subject of colonial polyps, a primitive social organism that grows together in colonies. The censor informed him that "in the last few decades, the colonial system of imperialism has collapsed once and for all. Therefore the term *colonial* is offensive to those peoples who have been liberated from imperialist oppression. We suggest that you call your book *Developing Polyps."*

At the University of Pennsylvania last year, the trustees blithered over a proposal to change the name of the Department of Oriental Studies, for although the word *Orient* in geographical terms means "East," there were unpleasant connotations, as the proponents put it, of "Western colonialism." At Harvard Divinity School, according to a well-circulated but not fully confirmed story, a recycling bin for "colored paper" was relabeled by a student "paper of color." The administration, short on both humor and backbone, expressed its hope that no one had actually been offended.

This is the phenomenon of "political correctness," now sufficiently familiar on and off campus to be reduced to an acronym, *PC.* It is perhaps one of the most ludicrous media creations of the past few years, wholly devoid of both significance and substance. True, some professors have been humiliated for their "politically incorrect" views in recent years, and more than a few students have indeed suffered at the hands of ideologically oriented professors who have insisted on "correct" views in student papers and exams. But to think that this constitutes a crisis in higher education, much less a calamity of "McCarthyite" proportions, is total nonsense. Senator McCarthy cost thousands of people their jobs, branded innocent people for life, and caused a significant number of suicides. "Political correctness" has caused the publicized humiliation of several dozen students and professors, few of whom have suffered loss of status, much less loss of life.

"Political correctness" was originally motivated, of course, by a laudable emphasis on mutual sensitivity, especially concerning groups for whom language had long been an easy means of derogation and put-down. University women properly bristled at the designation "girls" while their male colleagues were routinely called "men." African-Americans rightly resented the multitude of outright offensive references that carried with them all the baggage of slavery and its aftermath. When in the sixties it was generally insisted that African-Americans be called "black" rather than "colored," "Negro," or worse, there were no grounds for objection.

> In the nondebate over nonissues that goes on here, the hands-down winner is the culture of euphemism. Witnesses before Congress are actually awarded points for their expensively coached lying and emollience. Meanwhile, self-defined radicals sell the past by announcing that anything is better than being "offensive." The two rivulets of drool merge softly and imperceptibly, and we end up with a public language by which almost nobody employs plain speech.
>
> ——Christopher Hitchens

The atmosphere started to change when it became apparent that the desire not to offend was becoming eclipsed by the urge to manipulate, chastise, and feel superior. Perhaps the defining moment of this shift was evident when several black leaders announced to an already confused world that the most recent designation, *Afro-American,* should be replaced by *African-American. Afro-American* had replaced *black* by way of several short-lived intermediaries, and the general public both in and outside of the universities found themselves in a position similar to that of liberal arts professors who try to keep up with current French philosophy; by the time they've grasped a concept, the movement is already passé.

Those who stayed at the front knew the latest propriety and could look down on those who did not. They could confirm their suspicions that most people, even those who claimed to be liberal and tolerant, were in fact racists and sexists. More important, they could confirm their sense of their own proper thinking, as evidenced by their politically correct language. They had become, in effect, liberal fascists.

Any group has the right to designate itself as it chooses. But when the terms change month by month, those rights turn sour and delegitimate themselves. That is surely where we are now, as a certain fringe of the women's movement insists that *womyn* is politically correct (to replace *women*), and elementary school administrators are insisting that six- and seven-year-old female students not be called "girls." *Colored people* is now back with a linguistically barbarian twist, *people of color,* to refer in general to nonwhite (but not Oriental) persons, to which one soon-berated English professor compared the phrase "jeans of blue." Some handicapped people are now insisting on *differently abled,* rightly insisting on recognition for their skills and abilities.

Whatever the language games now being played, racism continues, sexual inequality is being corrected only slowly, and life for most handicapped people remains difficult and sometimes tragic, not for lack of the right words but for lack of funds and public support.

The phenomenon of "political correctness," however, is the creation of people looking for an excuse to "crack down" on the universities. We too easily forget that the initiating cause of, and now the alternative to, political correctness on many campuses is hate speech, and the attack on political correctness is clearly condoning if not encouraging a form of free speech that one would have thought had no place in the university—or anywhere else. Some of the blame for the threatened crackdown belongs to those self-appointed, "politically correct" professors who, in the spirit of radicalism but under the safe shelter of tenure, confirm the accusations against them. Most of the blame for "political correctness" lies in the hands of all those administrators, professors, and students who for so many years have looked away from racial and sexual harassment on campus, much of it not merely verbal. Unfortunately, the "politically correct" professors use the battle against racism to promote their own political agenda, which naturally leads to a response in kind from those who make a career out of ridiculing the Left. The sad truth is that they are betraying their own cause and giving politically incorrect speech the greatest impetus it has had in years.

To be good is noble, but to teach others how to be good is no-bler——and less trouble.
——Mark Twain

---

94 ▾ *On Being Offensive*

"I was just trying to be funny." "Can't you take a joke?" These are the routine laments in lieu of an apology that often follow an insensitive or offensive comment, and to be sure, "some things are not funny" and some jokes are more offensive than amusing. But we think that anyone with both a sense of humor and an understanding of just how important a sense of humor is has to conclude that we as a society are getting ourselves into deep trouble.

Political correctness is symptomatic of a society that takes itself too seriously, entertains a naive view of the world and its tensions, has lost perspective, and puts ideology above understanding. In a society known for its "can-do" and adventurous attitudes, we now find ourselves scrambling for the victim roles, searching for forces or powers or groups or conspiracies to blame, resenting those who do not share our sense of oppression, and above all, turning on those who get amused rather than indignant at our foibles and prejudices. Our ability to be offended has been cultivated to dangerous lengths.

It has been charged that the university is not teaching values, but the fact is that it is teaching the wrong values. It is teaching that it is easy and always appropriate to be offended and that it is always wrong to be offensive. But the difference between being offended and being forced to face up to reality is not always obvious. What is offensive is often a reason to laugh, to think, to re-evaluate, and the best books and teachers are sometimes those who shock, poke fun, and promote irreverence. We will know that multiculturalism is a success when ethnic jokes become matters for mutual enjoyment rather than occasions for sectarian indignation.

PART XIII

Professors

95 ▾ *Who Killed Socrates?*

Once upon a time, there was a philosopher named Socrates. He was a terrific teacher. He was adored by his students. He had some of the best ideas in the world. He was spectacularly witty and devastatingly smart. He loved to talk and debate, and he could win any argument. He was devoted to his subject and his students. He said he would rather die than not talk philosophy. So the Athenians killed him.

Why did they kill Socrates? The glib answer, of course, is that he never published. And so he perished, thus confirming two millennia before its time the best-known warning in the academic world. It is worthwhile wondering how Socrates, the ultimate teacher (together with his near-contemporaries Confucius, the Buddha, and Lao-tzu), would fare in academia today. Would his excellent teaching count? Would he get tenure?

These are silly questions, but the truth is that not one of history's great philosophers would be hired by virtually any philosophy department in this country. They would be too odd or too controversial or too independent. They would not have the right credentials. Immanuel Kant, one of the few actual professors among the great philosophers of modern times (and a great teacher), did not publish his ideas until he was in his midfifties, too old to be hired by most pension-conscious institutions today. He would have been driving a cab in Königsberg by his midthirties. Like many other great thinkers, he found that he did not really have anything to say until he had worked it through for several decades.

In a few fields—most notably mathematics, physics, and revolutionary lyric arts—geniuses peak by their early twenties and are over the hill by thirty. But even though in most academic fields real wisdom comes much later, aspiring professors are forced to publish before their time. Their teaching is ignored and often neglected. Their real talents are snuffed out before they have time to develop.

Socrates is still being murdered, but not by the Athenian jury. He is routinely executed by a tenure system that prefers published pages to pupils, rehashed compendia to fresh ideas, and a quiet demeanor to a controversial thinker.

Socrates's student Plato avoided the dangers that were his teacher's undoing. He recorded (and richly embellished) Socrates's conversations and set up "the academy" as a way of institutionalizing the Socratic philosophy. He was perhaps the first professor, although his publications in dialogue form would not have counted as "serious" work today. His effort was doomed from the start, however. How could one reproduce the spontaneity of the street and Socrates's lifetime of experience between cloistered walls? How could one pursue the life of wisdom within a "curriculum"? But Plato thus established the structure in which intellectual life has flourished (and been confined) ever since.

Most important of all, the academy provided protection from the hoi polloi, the people. The public was not invited. Plato's student Aristotle, an accomplished scientist and a theoretician in virtually every realm of thought known to the ancient world, continued and expanded the tradition of education Plato had already established. When he was threatened with Socrates's fate (entangled as he was with the politics of young Alexander), he famously fled, commenting that Athens would not have the chance to sin twice against philosophy.

96 ▾ *"Profscam": The Attack on the Professoriat*

Today there is no single Socrates to attack, but there is in progress a wholesale attack on university professors. Illustrative is Charles J. Sykes's book *Profscam:*

> The story of the collapse of American higher education is the story of the rise of the professoriat. No understanding of the academic disease is possible without an understanding of the Academic Man, this strange mutation of 20th-century academia who has the pretensions of an ecclesiastic, the artfulness of a witch doctor, and the soul of a bureaucrat. Almost

singlehandedly, the professors have destroyed the university as a center of learning and have desolated higher education.

Professors are an easy target for public abuse. They are often eccentric, and their work is typically out of touch with the banalities of everyday life. They tend to be pretentious. They seem to have "a seven-and-a-half-hour workweek." Given the American propensity to hold up both the teacher and anyone who smacks of being an "intellectual" as objects of scorn, the attack on the university finds eager takers among the disgruntled youth of the academy and their parents, failed academics, journalists, and a few resentful professors. Everyone who has been to college has had at least one professor he or she hated. Consequently, the attack on the university is a popular theme. Enter the politicians.

Ronald Reagan took it up as governor of California in the sixties and began his populist rise to the presidency. President Bush embraced it at the start of the nineties, as part of his bid to prove himself "the education president." Ex-philosopher and Secretary of Education William Bennett confronted the professoriat with such a tough, intimidating message that he proved his qualifications to become "drug czar" and take on the cocaine barons of Latin America. Ex–Texas governor John Connally once praised a colleague, the former chairman of the Texas Board of Regents, for his "courage" in standing up to the faculty. Attacking the faculty is a time-honored tradition and convenient political practice. It also takes the courage of a hummingbird.

For all their skills at articulation and rhetoric, professors are not very good at defending themselves. When they try, their response is all too often self-righteous indignation in the name of the eternal verities and the survival of Western civilization. Such pretentious platitudes only confirm the prejudice against them.

Most of the faculty we know are thoughtful, attentive, and dedicated, and they put in considerably more than the standard forty-hour week, let alone "seven and a half." Like most dedicated employees in our self-declared entrepreneurial society, however, they are ignored. The shocking scams and failures come to public attention, but not the routine successes. The legislature focuses on the small number of hours spent in the classroom and ignores the hours spent preparing for the course; preparing for each class; making up study and exam questions and reading student responses to them; counseling students having problems in the class; giving time to interested students; attending meetings; writing up reports, recommendations, and reviews; not to mention the hours of reading, study, and library or laboratory work. The senior faculty and the dean's committee look primarily at publications and take the teaching for granted. A handful of the faculty "see through" the hypocrisy and perpetrate the scam, neglecting their teaching and ambitiously playing whatever game is in fashion to get ahead. But there is no basis for the generalizations about professorial scams and widespread irresponsibility, much less "liberality," in the university. Indeed, such books—and there are now several—only make the situation much worse.

Bad teachers should be fired as teachers. But the primary problem in the university is not the few who are incompetent or dishonest. It is the many good teachers whose efforts are undermined by those few and by an indifferent and intrusive administration.

97 ▾ Who Are the Professors? (Their "Dirty Little Secret")

Most professors are, by the nature of the profession, students themselves. They may be authorities in their field and formidable intellects. They may be authoritarian or haughty. They may appear on television and meet with the leaders of foreign countries and corporate heads. But they are still students, both in the sense that they are still learning and eager to learn and in the sense that they are still looking for more or less immediate feedback, working for grades, so to speak, for praise and recognition. It is a devastating realization, accordingly, that once they have achieved tenure, there are, for the most part, no more grades, no more promotions.

Many professors have never been out of school, except, perhaps, for a couple of years in the armed services or the Peace Corps. Since kindergarten professors have been watched over and evaluated by their elders, through high school and college, then graduate school, a job or two, and finally tenure and promotion to full professor, if not an endowed chair. And yet the identity of most professors turns on being at the top of the class, showing promise, getting the gold star. To suddenly find themselves taken for granted, ignored, ungraded! It is enough to make a good student lazy, disdainful, or rebellious, perhaps even—a deconstructionist.

To understand this is to understand why most professors, without even thinking about it, go where the recognition is. Assuming they do not neglect their duties simply in favor of some more exciting avocation, they will naturally get involved in petty publishing, politics, departmental intrigue, or for those who get bitten by the bug—university administration. If the university praises publishing, they will publish. If it encourages grant mongering, they will monger grants. If their colleagues lust after travel or making money in the stock market or getting consultantships, then they will travel, speculate, and consult. If the administration recognizes pandering and sycophantism, you can be sure there will be panderers and sycophants.

Money is the most embarrassing topic, which is why it is the subject of so much hypocrisy and the primary problem of the administration. If money is the administrative measure of recognition, you can be sure there will be faculty fights over the most meager "merit raise." But the truth is that it is the recognition, not the money, that counts. The subject was well summarized by one of our distinguished colleagues, who, when asked to write a chapter for a book we were putting together, responded that he would be delighted to do it for free, so long as everyone else was doing it for free as well. But if anyone was getting paid for his or her contribution, he insisted on being paid as well as the best of them.

That is a blunt way of putting the matter, but it is far more straightforward than all the self-defeating blabber about competitive salaries and merit. Professors do what they do because they love it, and they want to be recognized for doing it well. If they demand more and more money, it is not by way of compensation but rather competition, artificially created by administrators, who then turn around and complain about high faculty salaries.

Even the best teachers become discouraged when the only recognition they get for their efforts comes from the class, when their teaching is all but ignored by their peers and administrative superiors, when the opportunity to teach and earn a living by doing what they love may start to seem like a trap, a series of repetitive chores like the laborings of Sisyphus. They become discouraged when the security of tenure becomes sinecure, the awful realization so often felt by those who have just achieved tenure after years of wanting little else.

To be sure, one might insist that a professor *ought* to get ample satisfaction from the class, from a job well done. So, too, one might argue, everyone in every job or profession ought to get ample satisfaction from a quality product, from pleased clients, from a job well done. But that ain't the way it works, for better or worse, and perhaps it is a good thing that it does not. People always like to think that they are serving some higher purpose, doing something for the community as well as for themselves and their immediate contacts. Teachers love to teach. That is why they do it. But that does not mean they do not want and need recognition as well.

This is the professors' collective "dirty little secret." Most of them would be perfectly happy where they are, making what they make, and their happiness is maintained much more by a modicum of appreciation and camaraderie than it is by money.

98 ▾ *Peter Abelard, Superstar*

What has contributed most to the breakdown of the traditional university, perhaps, is the coming of the superstar. There have always been famous professors, of course, from Peter Abelard back in the twelfth century at the Université de Paris to the current roundup of suspects at Harvard and Berkeley. For the most part, they made a university their home. They stayed in place. They may have been handsomely compensated and fully appreciated, but just as often, they accepted comparable salaries, thought little about it, and just did what they loved— teaching, exploring, thinking, and writing. Today, too, there are Nobel Prize winners and world-famous teachers who make a university home for themselves, establish themselves as members of the community, and teach each undergraduate class as if it were the most important thing they do.

In the high-flying university, however, some of today's superstars have a different personal mission. They are entrepreneurs on the "fast track" of university life. Superstars are, to be sure, often spellbinding teachers and an inspiration to their students, even if they remain at a university only for a year or two. But superstars are for sale. Stanley Fish, currently at Duke, has been widely quoted as aspiring to be the "highest paid humanities professor in the world," a status that he has, we have been told, achieved.

Superstars have learned that they can do what they do anywhere, and when the offer is right, they call the movers and pack up the several tons of books yet again. They play an important part in university life, not only as the subjects of legend but as passing divinities. But they set a devastating precedent as well, for few of the "top of the class" students who are now distinguished (or not-so-distinguished) professors in their own right are willing to settle for less than superstar status. For every Mozart out there, there are hundreds if not thousands of Salieris, burning with envy, taking it out on their classes, and waiting with a dose of poison.

So the question that needs to be asked is, why are so many universities fighting so hard and paying so much for superstars? To be sure, there are brilliant scholars whose very presence stimulates and consolidates the talents of everyone around, colleagues and students alike, providing the one kind of leadership that makes a university flourish. But leadership is not a quick fix. It must be cultivated over time and based on trust and camaraderie as well as admiration. The high-flying superstar bought in from the outside rarely accumulates such trust or cultivates such loyalty. Indeed, the better policy would seem to be to nurture your own superstars from within the university, to cultivate emerging leadership, not buy it. But too many universities have chosen precisely the opposite course, displaying contempt for their own faculty and cultivating resentment instead. And the salaries for those high-flying few keep getting higher and higher.

99 ▾ Making It: Celebrities, Sages, Scholars, Wizards, and Entrepreneurs

How does one "make it" in academia? Unfortunately, the answer virtually never is "by teaching brilliantly." Indeed, the most famous teachers typically achieve their fame posthumously, when some articulate student finally gets around to memorializing them and their complete devotion to their vocation long after the last class bell has sounded. Nor does the answer lie in the all-pervasive imperative to publish. Not to publish may mean perishing, but publishing does not mean thriving or even surviving. Most journal articles are effectively dead before they appear in print, and most books "fall stillborn from the press."[1] And yet making it in academia is not a mystery. There are a number of well-worn tracks, some of them quite ancient, others more modern. Some of those who make it are celebrities, sages, scholars, wizards, and entrepreneurs.

We live in a celebrity culture. Celebrity differs from recognition for work done, and so it differs from fame. It may depend on a life of hard work and achievement, but it may just as likely depend on being in the right place at the right time. Today it is more important to be heard of than to produce anything of value. Academics who are known fools get invited to all sorts of international conferences, thus enhancing their reputation and their foolishness. On the other hand, some of the celebrities are scholars and scientists of great worth in their own right. Einstein was a big American celebrity in the fifties. Jacques Derrida was an accom-

---

Showing off is the idiot's version of being interesting.
——Steve Martin, *L.A. Story*

---

plished scholar before he achieved international celebrity status. By necessity the number of celebrities is small. Most of the professors in the university have to do the actual work. Celebrities rarely have the time.

Sages rarely attain celebrity status, but they do attain somewhat similar status on the local level. They rarely publish very much. They become known for their profundity and are typically a fatherly or motherly figure, full of advice and good sense, sometimes couched in indecipherable oracular language. Their main value as sages is as a source of inspiration to those around them, colleagues and students alike. Their books, though rarely comprehensible, become holy texts.

Scholars are the grunts of the humanities, the ones who unearth the bones and details with which the more high flying take off and soar. Thank goodness for them. They are the true heart of the university, if only more of them were better trained at teaching as well and if administrations knew what to do with them. Unfortunately, scholars tend to recognize only their own kind, and so they tend to emphasize scholarly credentials and virtues (e.g., being cautious and careful and thorough) to the exclusion of all others (e.g., being exciting and daring and broadly speculative), which can make for some extremely dull departments, courses, and classes.

Wizards are clever technocrats who have mastered the latest and most difficult tricks of the trade. In philosophy logicians have long held the prominent claim to being wizards. One can be a wizard in almost every specialty, but to be a true wizard, one must master one of only a very few fields, all of them more or less derived from mathematics. Semioticians pretend to be wizards, based on a trumped-up technology. Wizards, like scholars, tend to define their disciplines in their own image. This sometimes threatens to turn humanities into a technological puzzle, indigestible to most students and disagreeable at best to the rest of the faculty. And yet wizards have their invaluable place in every field. They keep alive the need for precision.

Entrepreneurs are organizers, arrangers, matchmakers. They of necessity have a great deal of energy and enjoy making contacts and meeting people. They put together conferences and colloquia, anthologies and programs. Occasionally, they build entire departments, sometimes from scratch, typically in a remarkably short period of time. Oddly enough, they do not make good administrators, primarily because the psychological storm they inevitably generate all around them, albeit exciting, gets tiresome and downright disruptive as a style of administration. The last thing one wants from a dean are a lot of new ideas energetically pursued. But as a source of constructive activity, there is nothing like a good entrepreneur. And if it looks as though the entrepreneur is about to get tiresome, never fear. He or she will be off to some new challenge before you know it.

Of course, these are pure types, and most successful academics display a mix of several of them. But such a list (though incomplete) is necessary to make the point that professors are not all the same, that the word *success* has various meanings in academia and there are various motives in pursuing it. Much of what is called "fraud" and "incompetence" in academia is simply the application of the standards for one kind of success to another. The truth is, the university is all the richer for the variety of these types of academics, even if they do not always get along.

100 ▾ *The Problem of Autonomy*

Give professors their own time, schedules, choice of courses, and administrative duties, and what do they do with this freedom? In most cases they choose to work hard, set schedules that suit the students, pick courses that really need to be taught, and with little arm-twisting accept assignments on committees and, on occasion, even agree to be chair or dean. But there are other cases that serve as a good argument against personal autonomy. Steven Cahn tells the uncharming but illustrative story of one professor who had grown accustomed to scheduling all his courses at an obviously unpopular time, on Friday afternoons. Asked by his chair if he would be willing to teach an important class on Monday afternoons, he was shocked and outraged, replying, "If you don't have Mondays off, what do you have?"[2] For a few, autonomy means irresponsibility.

It is an extreme example, but it illustrates a tendency all too familiar in America—*entitlement.* Get someone used to some advantage or privilege, no matter how extravagant or undeserved, and he or she will take it as a God-given right. But although their feelings of entitlement give professors some sense of deserving or "being owed," any reasonable perspective allows them to see beyond their own interests to a larger context, compare themselves and their situation with others, get a grasp on the larger picture, and feel the pull of other people's needs and interests. What any such thinking makes perfectly obvious is that in return for the privileges professors enjoy—doing what they love for a living and doing it pretty much according to their own schedules—they owe something in return. In academic practice this means a dedication to the students and the university.

In place of a sense of responsibility, however, what is now being widely proposed is the more politically appealing notion of *accountability.* What this implies and sometimes calls for is the imposition of discipline from the outside, an end to faculty autonomy. The result of such outside discipline will be resentment, rebellion, and the refusal to do more than what is required. Professors think of themselves as independent, devoted intellectuals. They do not, as a rule, enjoy taking orders. They resent the suggestion that they don't work hard.

The professoriat, like most of the professions, has been overly protective of its membership and has showed too little responsibility to its clients—namely, the students. It is understandable that professors should rally together to protect themselves from the hostile and often ignorant intrusions of government and the senior administration, but it is not forgivable that they do so at the expense of their students. Inadequate teachers must be reprimanded and retrained, and the faculty would be well advised to do this for themselves. Poor teachers should be fired. But before there is a need for such drastic measures, there is much the faculty can do, starting with a general consensus that teaching is the *most* important thing they do and that good teaching is to be encouraged. Bad teaching and irresponsibility must indeed be accounted for, not to those above but to those who work with and under the faculty—other faculty and students.

As of now, firing a tenured professor requires years of committee hearings, grievance procedures, lawsuits, and countersuits, during which time the even more distracted and disdainful "teacher" continues to torture undergraduates. What is important, especially where the curriculum is involved, is that the faculty must have some sense of joint responsibility. This does not take committees and mandates, and it does not require someone "in charge." It simply takes professors who have an interest in the students, who pay attention to what their colleagues are doing and make it a matter of personal obligation to see to it that all—not just their own courses—are taught well.

101 ▾ *Teaching Differences*

The idea behind faculty autonomy is surely a good one. Different faculty have different metabolisms, different habits. Some of our friends routinely stay up all night writing and teach in the afternoons. Others are up before dawn and after a fast jog are already at the word processor and ready to teach by eight. Given the variety of professorial types, the distribution of preferences usually works out quite well, and if certain time slots get more clogged than others, it takes only a slight incentive (a better classroom, for example) to shift a few flexible faculty. Given the range of faculty interests, the basic curriculum is usually covered, and it is taught much better, in that everyone has more or less chosen his or her favorite courses. The alternative—again, less autonomy and more resentment—would have a very different result.

One of the topics that is sure to get faculty and their overseers in a rage is the matter of the "teaching load," the number of courses handled by each faculty member. But again, the first question is one of differences. One faculty member, for whom teaching is like theater and each performance improves upon the last, enjoys repetition and is willing and happy to teach the same course in multiple sections. Another professor, who prepares brilliantly and exhaustively, cannot possibly handle more than two courses a term. Some people can juggle three balls at a time. Others can handle only one. And yet state legislatures and some authoritarian administrators seem to feel that setting a minimum load helps assure that everyone does his or her share. But of course, that says nothing (nor is there much that could be said) about the quality of those courses.

There are also the slackers, those who not only do the minimum but do it minimally and irresponsibly. Short of certain extremes, there are no sanctions for tenured professors who think they have better things to do with their time, who fail to show up for class, or with a bit more subtlety, regularly replace their lectures with class discussions led by a teaching assistant or cancel them altogether.

Everyone seems to grant the importance of specialization in an area, but the same respect for different styles of teaching, different pedagogical virtues, is lacking. The real question is how to keep all teachers fresh and motivated—how to place all of them in just those circumstances in which both they and their students will flourish.

102 ▾ *Beyond Expertise*

> The lover of wisdom has a passion for wisdom, not for this kind of wisdom and not that, but for every kind of wisdom.
>
> —Plato, *The Republic*

A professor is someone who professes, which is not, first of all, spreading information or pontificating but inquiring, probing, and expressing infectious enthusiasm. We do not do ourselves a service when we insist that we all be "experts" on some particular subject, much less some corner of some subspecialty of a carefully delineated aspect of some particular subject. Indeed, there are even experts on "what it is to be an expert." Mortimer Adler voiced his opposition to the current emphasis on "specialization" two decades ago in his unheeded call for "generalists." Friedrich Schiller lamented the increasing "fragmentation" of human life almost two hundred years ago, about the same time that Adam Smith was celebrating "the division of labor" as the basis of capitalism.

Twenty-three hundred years ago, Aristotle's students, unable to keep up with their master, were already becoming specialists in one or at most two facets of the philosopher's encyclopedic mastery of the world. Ever since, the direction of learning has been "more and more about less and less," until it has finally reached its inevitable conclusion. Fields of expertise have shrunk to the point of absurdity, and much of contemporary research is virtually an exercise in solipsism, the occupation of one's own little world. Witness the graduate course catalog of any major university or the dissertation topics listed in the commencement program. The insistence on expertise has produced monsters, but very tiny, ineffective, and irrelevant monsters. There are limits to how little a person can know.

Nevertheless, one would be hard put to find all that many professors who in fact fit the caricature suggested by this official portrait of the specialist. Most professors know much about many things, and if the university were more conducive to wide open, interdisciplinary discussions, they would be glad to participate. But specialization is required by the university. Undergraduates are forced into majors, which is a mistake to start with. Graduate students are encouraged to choose their fields early and, by the time they get to their dissertations, to have laid claim to a molehill with mountainous pretensions. Assistant professors are judged early on whether they are indeed experts in their field, no matter how narrow, and whether within a few short years they have made a "significant and original contribution" to it. Accordingly, most professors specialize as a matter of necessity. They will be judged by their peers based on their alleged expertise, and the joys of general learning must be prudently set aside.

Thanks to such specialization, professors are hesitant to make a statement that lies even slightly outside their realm and become ferociously indignant when someone lays claim to their turf. It suggests, right from the start, that the professor is "on top" of the field, knows more than anyone else, and is therefore beyond the stage of listening to and learning from others—hence the tendency among the professoriat to pontificate. It is expected of them as experts. Hence, too, the importance of having a position, taking a stand, instead of being open to listening and learning. All too often, instead of conversation and comprehension, what we read and hear is practiced sophistry and skilled articulation, not real learning.

In addition to the corruption of one's personality, the insistence on being "expert" has far-reaching effects on undergraduate education. It makes professors resistant to developing a new course outside their specialties, even when students are clamoring for such a course and there are overwhelming reasons for giving it. If a number of undergraduates desire such a course, the faculty ought to be willing to give it. But when we stick ourselves with the false idea of the professor as an expert rather than an explorer, a learner, the result is the impoverishment of the curriculum and the undergraduates.

A notable example of such impoverishment can be found in the area of survey courses. We have emphasized the importance of such courses, and though they alone do not make an education, the absence or inadequacy of them makes most students' years at the university something of a joke. The vision of the professor as expert militates against such courses. Even introductory courses in a particular field are too often thought to be "beneath" the established professors, who prefer to teach only their specialty. Courses that are really important—courses such as "History of the World" and "Introduction to Modern Science," the courses without which many students remain appallingly ignorant of the world around them—are generally left to temporary instructors, new assistant professors, even graduate students.

Survey courses are just the courses that ought to be shared by *all* the faculty, and preparation and teaching alike ought to be a delight. What could be more wonderful than to take advantage of a chance to think (perhaps for the first time) about how to present the *Iliad* or what to teach in an introductory biology class or how to make interesting a general-information geographical survey of the world? Saint John's College in Santa Fe and Annapolis requires that all its teachers be able to teach all its courses. Though this may be excessive for most faculties, it is only an extreme version of a great idea. Indeed, in response to the new demand for more "multicultural" courses, no professor would be harmed by spending a few months during the summer reading through once-"foreign" literature and integrating it into his or her courses.

If most professors are "experts" in one or several subjects, this is not what distinguishes them. It is not the result but the process that counts— how they got there by being fascinated, by steeping themselves in the literature of the field and related fields, by not letting any question go unanswered. They got there, one hopes, because they had the hunger— not the professional obligation—to read everything written on the subject and the creativity to formulate it all in their own way.

Most of us find, however, that our creative talents are limited, our theories and opinions ultimately derivative. Remaining familiar with the full range of a burgeoning literature in the face of all our other duties and obligations becomes more and more difficult, and for most of us there is the growing awareness that we will not, after all, be the next Einstein or Aristotle. That is an opportune time to expand our interests. Unfortunately, the temptation is to contract our expertise more.

A professor is first of all a learned person, who inspires and teaches others to learn. He or she is not distinguished by a specialty but by the love of learning, a breadth of interests, and the passionate depth to which he or she feels compelled to investigate a problem. That is the nature of what we do. We are lovers of knowledge and wisdom.

103 ▾ "Respectability," Conformity, and Cowardice

> Scholars define their problems in terms of those set for them in the literature. One cannot help but wonder whether less attention to the literature in the field and a more liberal attitude toward legitimacy might not lead more frequently to significant intellectual advances.
>
> —Lynne Sharp Paine, *The Ethics of Competition*

Quite the contrary of a "marketplace of ideas," most disciplines today are run by a cartel. In nearly any field professors and most graduate students can identify the two or three gurus or institutions that virtually control the discipline. A subject is acceptable if it is acceptable to them. An idea is correct if it is in the "mainstream" they define, however unimaginative, repetitive, and jargon-filled it may be. Indeed, the right jargon is often applauded for its own sake, but the wrong jargon can get one instantly dismissed from the conversation. Conversations end with a reprimand when incorrect terms appear. Even in scientific research, for all its praise of objectivity, there are hypotheses of the moment and no others will be heard. In AIDS research, for example, the opinion of several distinguished virologists (that the HIV virus alone did not cause AIDS) was utterly ignored, just because it violated the then-accepted framework for the research program.

The exclusivity of the professions is nowhere more obvious than among the professoriat. The myopic insistence on solving technical problems indecipherable and irrelevant to anyone outside the discipline is well documented, as is the insufferable jargon in which these questions and their solutions are to be codified. Examples of this nonsense have filled many books. At a recent conference on literary theory, a young woman stood up after five hours of labyrinthine sophistry and asked, "Does it really have to be so complicated?" She was guffawed out of the room.

But why does it "have to be so complicated"? The answer lies not in the current sophistication and progress of the profession but in its timid resistance to opening up the debate. The security of tenure, we might add, has not led to massive abuses of academic freedom, as its detractors would claim. Quite the contrary, it seems to have had a paradoxically chilling effect on academic discourse and created entrenched hierarchies that cannot tolerate questioning of their status. It is often said that academic politics is so vicious precisely because there is so little at stake, but the opposite also seems to be true: When the risks are so minimal, the tendency to take them all but disappears.

> At the logical extreme, such an inbred system would cease to innovate altogether. One can observe in certain academic fields a gradual narrowing of topics and approaches considered legitimate. Scholars define their problems in terms of those set for them in the literature. One cannot help but wonder whether less attention to the literature in the field and a more liberal attitude toward legitimacy might not lead more frequently to significant intellectual advances.
>
> —Lynne Sharp Paine

Professors insist on being "respectable," but what we really need to do is take more chances. We need to raise new questions and undermine old ones, not for the sake of notoriety but in order to open up the field. We need to reach out rather than spend our time consolidating our positions within our disciplines. We need to take advantage of our time and security to open intellectual and cultural doors, not shut them.

104 ▾ *Professors/Professionals: Curmudgeons, Cranks, and Critics*

Professionalism has two faces. On the one hand, it means dedication, and on the other, it means a kind of credentialism, exclusivity, superiority, and status. Bruce Wilshire declares this to be the crucial problem in his ominously titled book *The Moral Collapse of the University*, and indeed, the professoriat has become professionalized. It has become a hermetically sealed, self-protective, and self-perpetuating system. But then professionalism also means knowledge, skills, and wisdom, which are passed on from generation to generation, with an emphasis on the public service and the good of the society as well as one's own advancement.

Professors complain about their lack of power, but the most horrifying fact about academic life is the abuse of academic power and the contempt so often evident for one's colleagues and students. A first-term assistant professor is chosen to be a commentator on a lecture to be given by one of the authorities in her field. It is her first opportunity to appear in public, before a large audience at her new university. She is anxious to do a good job. But she has to wait two months—until the evening before the lecture itself—to obtain a copy of the lecture. She has received no preliminary version, no outline, no indication of what claims she will have to consider. Anyone who has been in academia for more than a year knows that this is not an unusual phenomenon. Leaders in the field who might reasonably be expected to be responsible leave their colleagues in the lurch on such occasions, with no thought of the difficulties they are causing. Of course, they are busy. Of course, the muse does not always arrive on schedule. But perhaps the muse should be spanked.

Professionalism entails responsibility. We teach our classes even when we are not feeling well. We teach our classes even if we have been up the night before working on a project. We teach our classes even if some of us have trouble putting on socks that match. It is the profession of professors to be models of responsibility. However "absent-minded" they may be, professionals take deadlines and responsibilities seriously. But the embarrassing truth is that our profession is filled with—almost defined by—missed deadlines and broken promises.

One of our colleagues is a professor who for twenty years has shown up for every one of his public lectures unprepared. He still gets invited because he is considered one of the "brightest" scholars around. But what he gives his audiences (for a substantial fee) is more often a lesson in professional irresponsibility than any discernible content. The sad truth is that social incompetence is not punished. It is even adored and encouraged and accordingly envied and imitated. Self-correction is, or ought to be, the essence of professionalism. A profession should not tolerate or encourage those who violate its very reason for being.

One of the lessons of intellectual life comes from putting together a timely collection of essays on a hot or neglected topic. By doing so, one learns firsthand about the peculiar nonrelationship between academics and deadlines. Give them a year, and they will take two. Give them two, and they will insist on four—but not at the beginning, of course, when arrangements might be made or it might be politely suggested that the other authors and the publication cannot wait so long. Again, perhaps one cannot count on the muse. But one should be able to count on manners and some minimal consideration rather than suffer such arrogance, cowardice, or overzealous scheduling. Our proposal: Publish the names of these deadline deadbeats in the *Chronicle of Higher Education* and make it clear that such behavior is not acceptable and shall not be the norm.

One of the more subtle violations of professionalism, too often taken as part of the profession as such, is professorial nastiness. We do not adequately distinguish between eccentricity and irresponsibility, between nastiness and critical acumen, between arrogance and sophistication. There are too many professors who pride themselves on their "steel-trap" minds, quick and tough and merciless, the academic version of the gunslinger. Remember when the stereotype of the professor was "old and kindly" instead of "smart and nasty"?

Whatever it is, I'm against it.
—Groucho Marx, as Professor Wagstaff in *Horse Feathers*

One of the groups that ought to be the beneficiaries of professorial professionalism is one's colleagues. To tell the truth, though, the level of mutual respect in academia is probably the lowest of any job or profession in America, except perhaps for professional wrestlers. Many professors despise or resent their colleagues in the same field because they disagree with their findings or their orientation. They scorn those outside their field for their poor taste in interests and the methods these engender. They despise those in other disciplines that deign to investigate similar problems with inferior methodologies. And they refuse to understand those in very different disciplines, sometimes vocally expressing dismay that they should be housed in the university at all.

Thus philologists dump on translators and logicians ridicule metaphysicians, philosophers show their open contempt for psychologists and literary theorists, and the literary theorists and psychologists return the favor to the philosophers. All of them turn a jaded eye toward the "hard" scientists, but the humanists, social scientists, and "hard" scientists join together to loathe the mere technologists and the business school. Everyone seems to think everyone else is an idiot, and this opinion only becomes stronger as the moments of actual acquaintance become rarer. And then we complain that other people don't respect or appreciate us!

From elementary school to graduate school, future professors are evaluated and ranked as individuals in competition with one another. There is very little emphasis on teamwork and cooperation. Moreover, for most professors there are no clear standards for success. The prestige of one's university may represent an achievement of sorts, but one lives one's life within the institution. The smallest slight may seem like a judgment on one's career as a whole. And so the "life of the mind" has given way to a system of compulsive competition, recognition, *ressentiment*, and rewards.

The *vita contemplativa* may still be an inward affair, but the tests and rewards of that life have become externalized. There is an exaggerated concern for credentials. One despises or at least suspects a colleague because he or she went to a different graduate school or studied with another professor or in another program. But that is the way we have been trained, and that is the game of mutual resentment that is played on us by a conscientiously divisive and competitive administration. Getting over that false sense of competition and defensive superiority must be one of the primary steps in re-creating the university.

PART XIV

The Open University

105 ▾ Socialize the Faculty: Create a Community

The university is a community, but on too many campuses the academic "community" is nothing but a joke. Professors appear for class, hold a formal office hour, and disappear. The same professors may encounter each other at department or college meetings, but this is less an opportunity for camaraderie than an invitation to mutual resentment. Gathering around visiting speakers is an excuse to collect the faculty in a more academic setting, but all too often these, too, are noncommunicative, passing affairs involving little real contact among the faculty.

The problem is that we think of our professorial responsibilities as individual duties, not shared pleasures. Instead of avoiding and despising one another, we need to arrange more seminars and discussion groups, not "meetings," to talk about matters of mutual interest. Participants should be drawn from as wide a base as possible, and topics should be serious and even "deep" matters of broad concern. We have found such occasions to be enormously rewarding and invaluable in breaking down artificial distrust and departmental barriers.

The best schools we know hold frequent seminars where faculty conduct ongoing discussions of each other's work and interests. Junior faculty in large universities often do this, prompted unfortunately by the pressure on all of them to publish but nevertheless resulting in some valuable discussions and much more mutual understanding than they expect of their senior colleagues. Indeed, one of the many hidden penalties of tenure and promotion is being cut off from one's younger colleagues and having much less chance for inspirational interchange.

Despite the productivity one enjoys as a lone scholar, we all know that intellectual life is best when shared. We are, or should be, aware of our limitations, our knowledge, our methods. On one hand, this awareness explains why so many of us are guarded and even dogmatic and dismissive of alternatives. On the other it shows why alternatives are so necessary.

> I learned the joke at the core of American self-improvement: knowledge was just so much junk to be processed one way or another at great universities. The real treasure the great universities offered was a lifelong membership in a respected artificial extended family.
>
> ——Kurt Vonnegut, Jr., *Bluebeard*

A high-powered technical discussion with a like-minded colleague can be exhilarating; but the most interesting and productive campus conversations occur between those in seemingly opposing disciplines. They correct each other's outlook and mark limitations. An economist is brought back down to earth by a businessman. A philosopher is shown the ethnocentricity of his or her generalizations by an anthropologist. A conversation between classicists and epidemiologists sheds new light on the plague of ancient Athens—a longstanding mystery unsolvable by classics or medical research alone.

Our temptation, starting in graduate school, is too often to shy away from anyone who might "show us up," thinking of ourselves, as we are trained to do, as experts. Or else we feel compelled to assert ourselves and our command of the field, viewing all others as either an audience or as misguided competitors. This makes for some ugly, one-sided conversations. The corrective is to talk with colleagues—not just colleagues around the country at conferences and symposia but with the people one lives with, in one's own department and others. The life of every university is shared knowledge. Knowledge is best spread through small discussion groups where one can come to appreciate colleagues and overcome the pretension that one is alone in the pursuit of the good, the true, and the beautiful.

106 ▾ *Teach One Another, and Open Up the University*

Too often the classroom is treated as a kind of cocoon, a wholly private place where a teacher cannot be disturbed. The very presence of another professor in a class usually freezes the discussion or the lecturing teacher. But teachers are students and learners as well as peers. They need to learn from each other, evaluate each other, and students lose no respect for a teacher whom they see as also being a learner. The classroom should not be thought of as a private reserve, nor teaching as a private performance. Professors ought to sit in on each other's classes, so that it becomes a regular part of the scene. It will improve teaching, and it will surely enrich the intellectual life of the university.

The idea is to break down the barriers between faculty as well as between faculty and students and faculty and administrators. We are all in this educational mission together, and no one should be confined to an isolated role. We have a lot to learn from each other, teachers from students and administrators from teachers. What could give an administrator more of a sense of place in the university than actually to participate in its mission rather than "watch over" its workings from above?

We should open up the faculty, expand our notion of what it is to be a university teacher. Once we accept the notion of professors as professionals in the sense of devotion and competence and reject the notion of their being professionals in the sense of exclusiveness, then one of the most formidable walls around the university comes tumbling down. Why should "full-time" professors have exclusive rights to teach in the university?

There are a great many qualified people who are great teachers, who although not academics would love to teach and share their experiences. This is most obviously the case in the business school. Why pay a hundred thousand dollars a year for a retired executive when you can have a real, live one, very likely for a fraction of the price, as a matter of goodwill? In the sciences why not an official revolving-door policy in place of the hypocritical unofficial one we have now, taking in research and development scientists for a term or two, sending out our faculty on research assignments for even a few years—at company, not university, expense?

There are thousands of qualified, interesting people around the country, not just on the celebrity speaker circuit, who would be delighted to be asked to give a course and mingle with the next generation. The resulting openness would be very healthy for the university. Indeed, the considerable talent of these nonacademics would challenge the false snobbishness of some professors and force them to really show their stuff rather than play insider politics. Perhaps that is why such outsiders are so systematically excluded from the campus now.

107 ▾ Publishing and Research Reconsidered

In Part I of this book we argued that research is often misunderstood, too often defended on the model of technological research that has ready application and a quick pay-off, and too seldom considered an asset and an adjunct to teaching. Indeed, too often the fact that professors are not producing "ground-breaking" or "original" research is conflated with the accusation that they are not even keeping up with the field. And too often the notion of research is simply identified with publication, as if publication in a proper scholarly journal in itself signifies some significant contribution to the field.

We have already insisted that research has its essential place in the university, but it does not take the place of teaching. Insofar as research is simply the expression of the faculty's interest in expanding and continuing to explore the frontiers of knowledge and contributes importantly to "keeping up with the field," it is perfectly appropriate but still secondary to teaching. Insofar as research is a profitable activity in its own right, it should be housed in a separate "institute," affiliated with the university, perhaps even under its roof, but it should not be allowed to compete with teaching either in budgetary matters or in the prestige and status of its members. Of necessity, participation in such an institute will be very selective, and many of the faculty members who now consider themselves "researchers" would not be hired for their research abilities alone.

University research institutes are, of course, extremely valuable, and they can provide funding as well as excellent teachers for the undergraduate program. But when the funding flows the other way, and when researchers are hired as "teachers" who do not teach or teach very poorly, then the idea of research is being abused, and education needs to be protected. Apart from such institutes, research may take any number of forms and may yield any number of rewards, but insofar as it deserves to be supported *by the teaching budget* and take the time of those who are paid to be teachers it cannot and should not be judged by the same criteria appropriate to a self-sustaining institute. There should be no set agendas and no official expectations of financial reward. Supporting research by good teachers should be considered part of their support *as teachers*. The enthusiasm they bring to their work and the excitement they generate in others should be the only consideration.

In the liberal arts, research rarely pays, and it is only by the most tendentious arguments that it can be said, as such, to hold promise for the future. To be sure, scholarship on the Dead Sea Scrolls, for example, is fascinating and does promise to alter some of our ideas about the formation of the Judeo-Christian tradition, but that is not the same sort of promise as is offered by research into superconductivity or nonfossil fuels. Indeed, much of what is called "research" in the liberal arts is neither research nor scholarship but rather what now parades rather indiscreetly under the banner of "theory." There are few frontiers, only fashions, and fame often turns on notoriety rather than new knowledge. Such controversies as define the latest uproar in the Modern Language Association or among the philosophers are essential to university life, and they stimulate general thinking and discussion far more than most scientific discoveries. But "research" in such areas is not an end in itself, only the atmosphere in which teaching takes on the added sense of adventure and novelty. It is of value because it stimulates the teacher and reaches the students and the community, stimulates them, and indeed gets them thinking.

It is with this in mind that we need to reconsider the traditional notion of "publication" as well. To publish something is to make it public and available. But with the proliferation of professional journals, many of which survive just to serve the desperate market of "publish-or-perish" untenured professors, to publish material is often to bury it once and for all. A professor giving a lecture to a few dozen students and colleagues reaches a larger audience than the author of many scholarly articles. But the journal market feeds on itself, as other professors manufacture their own publications by referring to and refuting these articles, regardless of the worth or interest of the literature or the subject matter. Not only is much of what is published "junk" by virtually any reasonable standards, it is, by the nature of the medium, unintelligible. And yet the bureaucrats in the dean's office still count publications and "citations" as if they alone were the measure of a person's importance.

In the push for publication, academia's support institutions have come to exercise unchecked power that is virtually unimaginable even in the largest multinational corporations. Professional journal editors, with life and death decisions in their hands, may take eight months in reviewing an assistant professor's seven-page article before saying "not suitable" or "revise and resubmit." Once a piece is accepted, publication may take years. Academic publishers take as long as a year (with an "exclusive submission") before calling in the report of an inappropriate and hostile reader for a book manuscript, and book publication takes at least a year and on occasion as long as five. What is the poor tenure candidate to do, when some university committees will now consider only published books, not accepted manuscripts, in making tenure decisions? Why do we continue this cruel and pointless system, which distracts young professors from their teaching; forces many of them to publish, as we have said, before they could possibly have anything important to say; and herds entire disciplines down the road to oblivion?

Professional communication is absolutely necessary, of course. People at the forefront of a discipline, and for that matter people just plain interested, need vehicles for sharing and expressing ideas and viewpoints that are unlikely to reach the pages of *People* magazine. But the journal as we know it is something of a dinosaur. It is inefficient and encourages corruption. There are alternative forms of publication, though, and a great many academics already use them, even if they do not count with the bureaucrats or the old-line powers that be. There are newsletters and computer networks and electronic mail. There are conferences and conventions where the most important ideas emerge not from the podium but on the floor, in the halls, and in the elevators. In the social sciences meetings often feature "poster sessions," in which one summarizes one's data or findings on a three-foot signboard and then stands around to chat and argue with whoever happens to be interested.

And then there are good old conversations, dismissed by most university authorities as simply background noise. But where do the knowledge and excitement of the learned world get better expressed or have more immediate impact? Indeed, some of the most valuable people in either of our fields are those sages who are always bursting with ideas and enthusiasm and get all of us to think and re-examine our positions, though they may publish very little or not at all. They are usually fired for being "unproductive." But why are we so hung up on "publication"?

The book is not a moribund form of publication, but the book-for-tenure ought to be. University faculty are a self-motivated lot, and most of them will continue to study and "publish" whether or not they have to. But most of them should without shame abandon the pretension that everyone in the university is doing valuable "research," not because most are not continuously at work expanding knowledge and contributing to the ongoing conversation but because the science-bound implications of the word make it sound as if each and every one of us were an Aristotle or an Einstein. It is not false humility to admit that very few of us are changing the course of knowledge, nor is that what we are supposed to be doing. We are teachers, keeping knowledge and culture alive and using it to turn on a new generation. And regardless of whether we publish a few books on the side, is that not quite enough?

108 ▾ *On "Popularization"*

Popularization is a bad word among academics. It suggests a giant step down into the midst of the hoi polloi, ordinary people who could not possibly understand what we scholars are doing. It implies an inevitable oversimplification of sophisticated and subtle work. But Einstein was brilliant at popularizing his work, as have been many of the greatest scholars and scientists. Simplification is not necessarily distortion. On the contrary, it often represents a deeper understanding of the material. Moreover, the attack on "popularization" underscores the tendency of academics to see their work as an exclusive domain, without responsibilities to the surrounding community. Indeed, a piece of work is now considered "popularization" if it is aimed even at fellow academics outside of a very small circle of like-minded scholars.

We need to reach out with our knowledge. We need to break down the walls between disciplines and between the university and the community, not fortify them with more jargon. We need more conversation and controversy between what are now distinguished as disciplines—conversation and controversy based on shared curiosity and cooperation, not battles over turf and the exclusive right to knowledge.

Most of all, we have an obligation to open up our research and our teaching to an outside audience, the audience that, after all, does pay for what we do. All academics ought to be journalists as well. True, "popularization" rounds off subtleties and makes one's ideas all the more prone to misunderstanding. But it also forces one to clarify and articulate those ideas. Professional jargon, despite its apparent precision, only disguises confusion. "Theory" is too often a pretentious mask for criticism without a bite, stated by critics who refuse to take responsibility for what they say.

For every technical paper professors write, they ought to write a popular paper as well, explaining the same subject to any intelligent person who is interested. Research does not consist of fighting with one's colleagues. It consists of opening up the world to the community and, first of all, students. Of course, this will mean a restructuring of much else in academic life, too, but none of it will be missed by those professors who really care about education.

109 ▾ The Bane of Our Existence: Why Is Campus Politics So Nasty?

Why is campus politics so famously vicious? Woodrow Wilson's comment about his stint at Princeton preparing him for the presidency is remarkable only in that Wilson actually learned something from the experience and carried it with him to a larger field of endeavor. But why in this world of free inquiry and open debate is there so much back stabbing and clandestine strategizing? Why in this almost idyllic profession, in which we can spend our time doing what we love to do and act as exemplars for students, is there so much scrambling for position and power, so much angst and anxiety?

The fact is, few social situations are so emotionally loaded. Less the use of murder, traditional Mediterranean or Appalachian feuds and vendettas and the dangerous liaisons of the decadent French aristocracy all pale in passion before the simmering hatreds of collegiate *ressentiment*. Pointless as it may be, campus politics becomes an obsession. Indeed, it is so much a part of the ritual that one condemns the futility of it all even while indulging in it full-time.

The ritual continues into the chairship and the deanship, which are strategic plateaus on which to build one's fortress and rain quiet havoc down on those with whom one has too long been battling as equals. But of course, the battle continues at that point as professors who once were enemies scramble to ally themselves with the dean, and deans battle deans and occasionally the higher powers of the administration, almost always to lose and have to face the wrath of their once-again-equal colleagues. It makes for some amusingly pathetic literature—*Who's Afraid of Virginia Woolf?* is the modern classic of the genre—and it makes for a miserable life.

The paradox embodied here is that one wants faculty involvement and faculty responsibility, but involvement and responsibility seem inevitably to lead to battles and protracted trench warfare. And once faculty get into a position of modest power, it seems that, by mutual consent, they cease to be faculty. It is as if professors feel the need to reject the very idea of power, even as it obsesses them and becomes a central concept in their discussions and analyses.

Why is academic politics so nasty? A promising analysis starts not with questions of power or even prestige but with the model of rats in a crowded cage. Pressed in against one another, perhaps for decades at a time, professors grow to despise one another. They prudently put as much distance as is available between themselves, but inevitably two tails get tangled, one steps on the other's toes, one gives a course that conflicts with another, one makes a statement at a meeting in which he or she casually ridicules another, and the battle is enjoined. And in such a small cage, the others cannot help but get involved, even if it is only by squeezing themselves against the most distant wall and avoiding the scene altogether. The aim is then to get to the top of the cage.

> "There's not much to joke about when you're Dean," he continues. "It's responsibility without power. You know, I ought to be able to order you to do it."
>
> "You can't," says Bob Busby smugly, "not without asking for nominations and holding a department meeting to discuss it first."
>
> "Why don't you ask Robyn Penrose, the most Junior member of the Department?"
>
> "Of course!"
>
> —David Lodge, *Nice Work*

How do we eliminate the cage? We do away with administrative units that are too small to allow free trade. For the students small social communities are essential, but for the faculty the very opposite is the case. Unlike the students, who arrive disoriented and in desperate need of a social order, the faculty arrive if anything too well oriented in their profession and, in decent circumstances, tend to find or create a community for themselves quite easily. But departments are not communities, usually not even communities of shared interests and understanding. Both interpersonal and professional interests transcend artificial department boundaries, and as administrative units they tend to be utterly arbitrary—or worse. They force together people whose ideological antagonisms very likely outweigh whatever professional camaraderie they share, and insofar as they do have professional camaraderie, it will most likely be employed in establishing departmental turf and opposing other departments.

What would eliminate the most vicious campus politics for most of the faculty—we are, of course, not talking about those for whom politics has become the very reason for being in the university—is simple freedom and mobility. If you do not like your colleagues, move your office. If you do not like your dean, move to another college. And if you do not like the place, hit the road. "Fast-tracking" among administrators, we suggest, is a serious problem. But "no tracking" among the professors is just as much of a problem. Where there is no mobility there is no escape, and where there is no escape there will be internecine warfare.

110 ▾ *Break Up the English Department (and That's Just a Start)*

Most of the mud and fury of recent years actually originates not in the university as a whole but in that caldron of seething resentment called the English department. This is where the vicious debates about multiculturalism and the "canon" get started—not in French or German or Slavic or Oriental languages, not in history or the history of art, and not in the sciences. It is where the most extreme and least responsible radical politics (both Right and Left) find their rhetorical home—not in government or political science or sociology. It is where the vehemence of "political correctness" originates, not in the social sciences, where political bias and outright propaganda would seem to be a natural problem. Where else would the magic of the mere *word* be systematically substituted for a political solution?

English departments teach the basic writing courses to virtually every student in the university, they teach creative writing to aspiring authors, they teach English literature, they teach literature from every other country (as long as it has been translated into English), and now they teach literary theory.

English departments often have fifty, sixty, or seventy faculty members and hundreds of graduate students, distributed among these various categories. Locked in this departmental cage with competing areas of scholarly interest, while faced at the same time with the ominous prospect of teaching thousands of students how to read and write, English professors—unappreciated, angry—turn on each other. And using their considerable rhetorical skills, they turn outward to the world, where they represent their battles as the essential contradictions of the university.

Literature, by its nature, is one of the primary sources of a culture that prides itself on its ideas, its inherited narratives, and the vitality of its language. The very idea that literature should be the impetus for sectarian battles rather than a gold mine of mutual enjoyment and understanding is therefore an affront to the very idea of the university. One of the most vicious battles during the past few decades has been over theories of reading, but this has turned reading itself into a suspect activity. Given the attractive choice of alternatives in videos and MTV, students by the millions are abandoning books and leaving the English departments to their squabbles.

What students need is not a theory of reading but good, protracted lessons in how to read and write. Literature professors do not like to engage in such low-level, usually tedious work, and so they define themselves otherwise and look down on those who do tackle this most essential chore in the university. Not surprisingly, there is mutual contempt between the two. Occasionally, there is open warfare. The widely publicized and bloody battles of the multiculturalism wars are the result of this internecine hostility.

There is no reason why "English professors" exclusively should teach English composition and reading. *Reading and writing should be taught by every professor in every department.* Indeed, "English" should not be a department at all, except to assign responsibilities and allocate facilities.

Nevertheless, the university needs literature and writing specialists. When it was simply accepted that literature professors were responsible for teaching reading and writing and the joys of literature, they typically taught the subject in the most direct and obvious way: They read with their students, often aloud in class, commenting on and discussing the passages along the way. The best professors brought the text and its characters alive, by virtue of their own thespian skills, by virtue of their sensitivity and insight into the text, or by way of their keen knowledge of the author or the period or the circumstances.

But this hardly counts as "research" in the university, and since "research" is the ticket to success, English professors had to invent something more sophisticated. They took to *interpretation,* no longer mere reading but deep analysis. Interpretation dressed itself in the heady robes of *hermeneutics* and turned into textual criticism. Criticism begat theory, and theory begat radical theory, and radical theory begat deconstruction, and soon the text threatened to disappear altogether, buried within a matrix of semiotics ("signs") and political agendas. And this, in turn, has achieved enormous status within the university as well as notoriety outside it. What has been lost, however, are the basics: reading, writing, and literature—and the students.

The English department has lost its place in the university and should be disbanded. Of course, the study of English and American literature would continue to be an important sequence of courses, and literary theory would remain as well. There would continue to be scholars specializing in Spenser, Milton, Jane Austen, and Joyce. There would still be biographers of Mark Twain and Hemingway, but they would no longer be in direct competition and confrontation with those whose job it is to teach basic composition or literary/cultural theory. Why should they be in competition and confrontation at all?

Active writers of poetry and fiction would have, as they often do, their own programs, now nominally attached to the English department. With the end of the English department that attachment would end. But indeed, apart from minimal organization and administration, why should they be a "department," when most of the time they have little to do with one another? This is not to say that they ought not to have anything to do with one another or that the university should discourage the mutual fertilization of ideas. But what is highly desirable—and perhaps even personally necessary—for the artists involved is confused by the university's mandate for organizational structure. If there is anything that will guarantee animosity and the impossibility of collaboration and mutual inspiration, it is forcing creative people to enter into politically explosive but functionally irrelevant administrative debates with one another. The same is true of visual artists, musicians, and dancers. It is a mark of bureaucratic insanity in some universities, for example, that artists, art historians, and art critics are often housed in the same department, when historically they have always hated one another.

Why do we need departments at all? Most administrators, as in a contemporary beer commercial, seem to respond "Why ask why?" But to confuse minimal organizational needs and requirements with the essential social and educational structure of the university is to beg for disaster and commotion. Which, of course, is just what most professional administrators want. It just shows how much they are needed and demonstrates beyond a doubt that faculty are incapable of governing themselves.

One of the most celebrated topics in recent years has been the importance of "interdisciplinary studies." Administrators pride themselves on it. Whole schools make their reputations on it. But the fact is that interdisciplinary studies are few and far between. Administrators despite their rhetoric make it all but impossible for professors in different departments or colleges to "team-teach" courses, and faculty tenure committees routinely dismiss interdisciplinary research as irrelevant to the field and, worse, as "dilettantish." Interdisciplinary programs pop up here and there, but even the most established of them, "Comparative Literature," tends to float on the margins of academic respectability. It remains a program, not a department, and it has to justify itself and draw its resources from the established departments, which they, of course, are loathe to relinquish.

Departments, as we have said, are cages. They contain decades of well-nurtured grudges and prejudices, simmering resentments protected and maintained by a rigid structure. The university should take interdisciplinary studies very seriously and at the same time solve the problems caused by the self-enclosing nature of departments. The answer, quite simply, is to eliminate the departments.

It is important to distinguish between administrative and academic units. The former may be necessary just for the sake of order and organization, but they should be invisible. All academic divisions, on the other hand, are arbitrary and insidious. They force false differentiation and create antagonisms. Philosophy and psychology, for example, are not two distinct disciplines, or insofar as they do differ, they are a multitude of disciplines whose boundaries are changing with every new piece of research. On the other hand, English literature, freshman composition, and creative writing are only tangentially related, and it is folly to force them into the same department. So, too, art and art history, political theory and nitty-gritty studies of the workings of government. These subjects should not be forced together, but neither should they be separated. The university, like intellectual life, should be a free-for-all. Everyone should talk to everyone. And everyone should be jointly responsible for everyone else. Insights should not be restricted by departmental boundaries, and disciplines should not be artificially limited by administrative fiat.

Eliminating departments would also eliminate department meetings, where the battles originate. These would be replaced by the interdisciplinary group meetings we described earlier. Such meetings would encourage, finally, real interdisciplinary thinking.

It would probably be a good idea to mix offices around, as is done at Smith College, for example. Important committees can be assigned to bigger units and drawn from around the faculty. An intelligent administrator ought to be able to recognize diversity and difference without departmental labels.

We can also then abandon departmental curriculum committees, which argue for two years and then regroup the next year to undo what little they have done. Is it not enough to have a dedicated bunch of teachers, in touch with the students and one another and concerned about the problems that arise? At the risk of overstatement, we would say that almost all the important knowledge lies between the so-called disciplines. Great scholarship presupposes breadth, not just narrow focus. And great teaching can never be departmentalized. A professor belongs in an all-embracing community.

111 ▾ *Academic Freedom*

Academic freedom is a personal liberty to pursue the investigation, research, teaching, and publication of any subject as a matter of professional interest without vocational jeopardy or threat of other sanction, save only adequate demonstration of an inexcusable breach of professional ethics in the exercise of that freedom. What sets it apart is its vocational claim of special and limited accountability to professional integrity.

—William van Alstyne, past president, AAUP

The university is not just any community. It is a community defined by ideas, by opinions, many of them controversial and some of them outrageous. Accordingly, academics must be free to do and say certain sorts of things, and what academics do is to talk and express their opinions about a wide variety of controversial matters—in politics and religion, for example. But every American is guaranteed freedom of speech by the Constitution. Why, then, do academics need not only a special freedom but a special name for it?

They need it primarily because of a history of unwanted restrictions and abuses by government and various university administrations. The teaching of evolution in biology classes has been outlawed in the past, and university administrators have been known to strongly discourage or even prohibit any mention of Marxism or homosexuality in courses in political or social theory.

Such restrictions are indeed intolerable, but their very intolerability throws into question the need for any legal protection or professional censure. In the nineteenth century the university was an oasis in the middle of an illiberal society. In Germany, where the concept of academic freedom (*Lehrfreiheit*) first became prominent, the professor needed some special protection to teach and explore. We do not need that special protection.

On the other hand, the university today can and does restrict what can be taught in all sorts of ways—for example, through requirements and through hiring. If faculty are hired to teach state history according to a set syllabus, it is not a violation of academic freedom to demand that they do just that. Nor does academic freedom include the freedom to undermine the purpose of such a course—for example, by presenting the history of the state and its most prominent figures as thoroughly corrupt, utter idiots. But surely a teacher does have the right, even the obligation, to be accurate in such a course and not whitewash the unflattering or brutal aspects of history. This, too, is part of the job. A university has no business expecting a chamber of commerce course on the unsullied glories of the place. Religion often demands a special sort of treatment, but, again, it is not the business of a state university to provide religious training or edification. Sectarian universities routinely specify such courses, but one is not well advised to study or teach at a religiously defined university if you find such restrictions unacceptable.

In the classroom, too, what one is permitted and obliged to do is defined in part by the course, in part by the situation. If a well-known politician is hired to teach a course in the university, one should not expect a politically unbiased class, whether the politician be a Republican, Democrat, or socialist. On the other hand, teachers in a class that has nothing to do with politics do not have the academic freedom to editorialize or pontificate about political matters.

To take advantage of that very special forum and captive (not to say receptive) audience of the classroom is indeed a violation of one's responsibilities. So, too, academic freedom does not include the freedom to make false statements (which is not the same as oversimplifying for the sake of understanding) or to invent fictitious sources. It does not include the freedom to tell pointless dirty jokes or to humiliate students in class. What academic freedom includes is just the freedom to do what one has been hired to do, and it does not mean—as too many professors suppose it to mean—that their power in the classroom is absolute and that they can say and do anything they damn well please.

Academic freedom also includes the freedom to do research as one chooses, but here again, this depends on what one means by "research" and what its goals and aims are. Not long ago, animal researchers tortured animals just to see how they would react to various sorts of suffering. Psychologists used to put captive undergraduates through such humiliating experiments that legislation was required to put a stop to this dubious use of freedom and power.[1] The University of California at Berkeley was one of several schools that fought its way through a major crisis some years ago when a faculty member published research touting the intellectual inferiority of blacks. To make matters more complicated, the professor who published this research was a physicist, not a psychologist, so his research could not be defended as part of his job. And to make matters more complicated still, the same arguments are now being put forward by a few black scholars. Is the question the same in both cases?

One part of the question surely has to do with the temper and sensitivity of the culture at the time. What is an outrageous theory or unacceptable research at one point in time may be routine in another. The theory that the earth revolved around the sun was blasphemous in the early Middle Ages but is accepted by even the most literal biblical fundamentalist today. Anatomical research based on dissection of the human body was criminal several centuries ago but is commonplace today.

There is also the question of whether there is any reason to fund research at taxpayers' or tuition payers' expense. Is the refusal to do so a violation of academic freedom? Should professors expect to be supported in whatever research and conclusions they deem relevant to their teaching position? We think the answer is no.

The matter of relevance is not always so obvious, however. Every field of research has its acceptable, marginal, and unacceptable areas of inquiry. A few years ago feminism was virtually forbidden as a research topic. Today it is almost mandatory for women in certain fields. A colleague in literature tells us that confessional poetry is considered "not appropriate" for quality research. Until very recently "urban anthropology"—the study of culture in cities—was not an accepted topic for anthropological research. But notice here that the constraints on research are not, for the most part, imposed by political or religious forces outside the university or by the powers that be in the university itself. The constraints are imposed by one's fellow professors and colleagues in the field. Are those restraints to be considered under the rubric of "academic freedom"? And if some faculty members abuse another or deny tenure to another because they do not approve of certain research, is this a violation of "academic freedom"? Or has the very concept lost its value, particularly considering that such abuses by fellow faculty, rather than the few much-publicized and usually abortive intrusions of some head-line-seeking politician, are the main obstacle to research freedom?

Academic freedom, like so many other concepts in otherwise so word-conscious academia, is treated with incredible inattention and almost promiscuous applicability. Consider the following examples:

▼ A professor is forbidden by state law to teach theory X.

▼ A professor is not allowed by her department to teach theory Y.

▼ A professor knowingly gives his students false information.

▼ A professor unknowingly gives his students false information. (He just hasn't been keeping up to date.)

▼ A professor gives her students a greatly oversimplified version of Z.

▼ A professor makes a pro-Republican speech in class.

▼ A professor makes a pro-Republican speech in class and then allows a point-by-point discussion of the speech.

▼ A professor switches his party membership from Republican to Democrat, much to the irritation of his (all-Republican) colleagues and chair.

▼ A professor joins an off-campus Ku Klux Klan rally on a Saturday afternoon.

▼ A professor joins the Ku Klux Klan.

▼ A professor makes a pro-Klan speech in class.

▼ A professor makes a pro-Klan speech in class and then allows a point-by-point discussion of the speech.

▼ A male professor tells an obscene and (by any reasonable account) sexist joke in class.

▼ A female professor tells the same obscene joke in class as an example of sexism.

- ▼ A male professor tells the same obscene joke in class as an example of sexism.
- ▼ A professor abuses his students, using intimidating (but not obscene) language.
- ▼ A black professor defends the natural superiority of blacks. Does it make any difference that across campus another (white) professor is defending the natural superiority of whites?
- ▼ An untenured professor of philosophy decides to study the philosophy of Shirley MacLaine and is denied tenure despite having published two reputable books in staid "mainstream" subjects.
- ▼ A tenured professor of philosophy decides to teach the philosophy of Shirley MacLaine, but his department refuses to allow him to do so.
- ▼ A tenured professor feels pressured not to include the subject of suicide in a course on "Contemporary Moral Problems" because two students have recently committed suicide.
- ▼ A tenured physics professor who has studied the IQ differences between whites and blacks comes to a controversial conclusion, and his courses are picketed by outraged students.
- ▼ A botany professor uses a day of class time to denounce the federal government's foreign policy.
- ▼ A politics professor uses a day of class time to denounce the federal government's foreign policy.
- ▼ A professor uses a day of class time to denounce the administration's tuition policies.

These various examples point to a wide variety of questions, not a single issue of professional rights and freedom. Moreover, the seemingly singular concept of academic freedom is almost always couched in terms of *freedom from* external restraint or threat, but the critical question is whether professors themselves, individually and as a group, can and will restrain themselves and not abuse their special forum. We believe that outside pressure and interference are almost always a mistake, not only because they chill legitimate thought and conversation but also because they make martyrs and give excessive attention to ideas that would most likely die of their own stupidity otherwise.

Given room for response and rebuttal, almost any discussion can and should be appropriate, even on the most extreme issues. In the absence of such reciprocity, the professor damn well better save his or her opinions for the weekend. But what if a professor defends extremely controversial or unpopular views out of class, on his or her own time, unsupported by taxpayers or tuition payers? Should the university have any authority to punish or fire such a person? We think the blanket answer has to be no. In most cases this seems to be just another extension of the right to freedom of speech granted to everyone in America. On the other hand, we are properly wary of "slippery slope"–type arguments that play fast and loose with "If you give them an inch, then . . ." It is one thing if a professor attacks what he or she sees as a tragic foreign policy or a self-destructive domestic plan. It is something else if a professor joins the Ku Klux Klan or becomes a spokesperson for some other hate group.

It is nonetheless a mistake for the administration to appropriate the power to legislate such differences. It is all too easy for a malign dean or provost to become offended and vindictive because of some honest protest or ordinary ideological difference. It is all too common for some thin-skinned politician to react all too brutally to some direct criticism of his or her policies. To be sure, there are important and vital differences here, but to appeal them to the power of the administration or external forces is to undermine the vitality of the university and replace healthy controversy with cynicism.[2] To ignore them under the blanket warrant of "academic freedom," on the other hand, is just as unhealthy and much more insidious.

Finally, does academic freedom apply to students? Many university administrators have denied that students have any such freedom at all. Student newspapers have been censored and student editors punished, not only for the predictable bad taste that inevitably finds its way into any student publication but for questioning and challenging administrative or government policies. This would seem to be a clear violation of their rights, and as citizens, students are entitled to the same freedom of speech as their elders. Students have the right to read and study what they want. If we make courses as well taught and attractive as they ought to be and remove the overzealous emphasis on requirements and credentials, students will have more freedom to choose their classes as well, to "vote with their feet" regarding the quality and effectiveness of their university education.

Moreover, students also have rights *against* certain freedoms of speech—notably, the right not to be indoctrinated or proselytized in class or forced into any political or religious situation in which they will be humiliated.[3] Conversely, one area in which students do not have freedom of speech is the right to shout down a professor, a visiting speaker, or for that matter a fellow student. True, when this becomes an issue, the professor or the other student was very often out of line.[4] And when it happens with a visiting speaker—the most common case—there is a legitimate question whether that speaker should have been invited at all.[5] (See "Outside the Classroom: Beyond the Celebrity Culture," in Part IX, Chapter 69.)

Nevertheless, although students have the right to respond and the right not to listen, freedom of speech cuts both ways at once. For students as for faculty, the critical question is not academic freedom but academic responsibility: what speech promotes discussion and understanding and what merely incites discord and hostility? For students as for faculty, abuse cannot be defended as academic freedom, and restraint should not be confused with repression. It is academic responsibility that we should be talking about, and that includes our willingness to respond to others' abuses as well as our readiness to both restrain and engage ourselves in the ongoing controversies that promote learning and define the university context.

"Academic freedom" refers to nothing other than the fundamental freedom of speech to which everyone is entitled. Every American is guaranteed freedom of speech by the Constitution, and singling out academic freedom of speech only creates one more artificial division between the university and the larger community, one more cause for resentment, one more image of irresponsibility. The fact is that what most professors say in or out of class would not count as controversial in any case, and those few who do hold really radical opinions can and should be protected by their colleagues as well as by the courts. Eliminating talk of academic freedom would not eliminate freedom. It would just make us look more closely at what we mean and what we do.

PART XV

Get Rid of Tenure

112 ▾ *The Horrors of Tenure*

Before we appall our colleagues and suggest the unforgivable, that tenure ought to be abolished, it is important to explain the tenure system to those who have never lived in what they falsely believe to be the wonderful world of job security. True, professors who have tenure—associate and full professors—do have lifetime job security. They cannot be fired except "for cause," which in practice means unless they are convicted of a major felony. Or what is much more controversial, they can be fired in case of extreme financial exigency in the university. Even then, however, professors whose programs or departments are eliminated are usually transferred within the university. This sounds terrific to those whose jobs depend on quarterly reports and who nervously watch their "IN" boxes for pink slips, but let us begin not with the enviable security of tenure but with the horror of the insecurity it causes. Like some ancient versions of paradise, the blessings of tenure turn out not to be fair compensation for the sacrifices and humiliation it takes to get there.

Most professors get tenure, if they get it, when they are already in their midthirties. They have been working at the profession for no less and often much more than ten years, through graduate school at pitiful if not criminally low pay and as an assistant professor on a barely subsistence salary, often while trying to raise a family. During this time they are humiliated, exploited, manipulated, and judged daily. Despite the fact that it is understood that assistant professors will be on the faculty until they "come up" for tenure after six years, they are often on one-year contracts that can be canceled with remarkably little fanfare. One political misstep or insubordinate expression can get a good young teacher with considerable promise cashiered off campus and into the local community college or, more likely, into the first year of law school. Whether or not they are "with cause," such terminations are rarely challenged.

Assuming that one does stick through the entire six years until one comes up for tenure, the pressure is unbelievable to produce original and interesting work within a few years out of graduate school while teaching a full load of new courses. Few jobs in the world require so much preparation and demand so much so soon. Inevitably, what emerges as "original research" is work that can be completed as quickly as possible, has the highest probability of acceptance by the most prestigious professional journals, and has the smallest likelihood of error or political infelicity.

Not surprisingly, most of it is nit-picking, fact mongering, and slightly glorified bibliography. Psychologists design and run dozens of experiments in a row, most of them adding up to very little except for a good number of publications and citations. Literary theorists provide one more interpretation of an American or a Russian or a Brazilian classic, careful to follow the latest trend in critical theory and not to offend anyone's delicate ideological sensibilities. Novice art historians prudently pick some third-rate Renaissance artist to study, queasily confident that their work has no conflicting antecedents because no one but a dissertation student or candidate for tenure would ever bother examining the works in question.

After struggling for anywhere from four to ten years under the yoke of graduate education, newly hired "assistant" professors get to live in the most humiliating set of circumstances imaginable. They are exploited in terms of work load, placed in the most vulnerable and awkward administrative situations in the name of a bogus equality, judged every time they open their mouth, and subjected mercilessly to the current dictates of "political correctness." First-year assistant professors are assigned to search committees to find new faculty before they have had a chance to discover what the old faculty are about and, more urgently, which political views will get them into hot water. They get assigned to dean's committees where they lack power and have the opportunity only to destroy their careers and ruin themselves. A casual comment over lunch may ultimately have more weight in a tenure decision than a published book, so no professional encounter is unthreatening. One might call this *professional hazing,* except that, unlike fraternity hazing, it goes on without respite over a period of six or seven years and not just a couple of pledge weeks.

Tenure can ruin a life or several lives. Tenure decisions typically hit about the time that a young family is established in a neighborhood, in a school, in a life, and that life can be uprooted when the decision turns out to be negative. Moreover, the frequency of divorce after negative tenure decisions is striking. But even when the tenure bid is successful, the cumulative anxiety and humiliation can take it's toll. Young scholars waste the most important years of their intellectual development pursuing short-term achievements and neglecting the long-term cultivation of more ambitious and profound projects. By the time they obtain tenure, such projects may well seem impossible or pretentious. Indeed, academic life may have already lost all joy and promise.

At the other end of tenure, there is a problem of "rotten wood." This is not to be confused with "deadwood," which is frequently lamented and ridiculed but in fact endangers the university very little. Rotten-wood professors, on the other hand, are commonly burned out on their subject and possibly on academic and intellectual life in general. They may have an articulate often-repeated set diatribe against it and against the administration, colleagues, and students. Perhaps they were overtaken by changes in the field and never caught up, or perhaps personal problems simply eclipsed whatever interest and talent were there prior to tenure. But now they devote themselves full-time to their one remaining interest—vindicating themselves and punishing those who turned against them.

One such professor can destroy an entire department and, with sufficient ingenuity or personal power, can keep it in ruins for decades. This individual may be a horrible, even sadistic, teacher, but because of tenure no one can threaten or even challenge him or her. Any change in the department—mandated by a disgusted administration, for example—will have to get around this professor, and the nature of the tenure system makes that impossible. And so, like an infected tree in the middle of a once-flourishing woods the rotten-wood professor kills everything around him or her. Is the "security" of tenure really worth the price?

113 ▾ Maximize Security: Get Rid of Tenure

Tenure should be eliminated. It has become a brutal rather than benign institution. It has resulted not in job security but in greatly increased insecurity. It has exaggerated differences in power and status and led to all sorts of abuses. It has reinforced the bias against the university and in particular against the liberal arts. It has certainly done nothing to improve undergraduate teaching. The very notion of tenure suggests a privilege shared by the professoriat that is enjoyed virtually nowhere else in society.

Few professors will tolerate the suggestion that (their) tenure be eliminated. Politicians, of course, would be delighted. Administrators, too, are quite happy with the idea, needless to say, but only a few of them dare to express it. Cutting out tenure would give them free rein to "shape" the institution, fire expensive but unproductive faculty members (that is, those who bring in no grant money), reduce costs, and (in a few cases) eliminate a constant irritant and source of interference. But for an administrator to express such an idea would inevitably betray an ulterior motive and antagonize the faculty. Nevertheless, the idea of eliminating tenure has much to recommend it.

The question is largely one of job security, but in every job, except for part-time and per-job contract labor, there is the presumption of continuance, and in these jobs a person can be fired only "for cause." The burden of proof is on the employer, and any administrator can tell you how hard it is to fire even a mediocre employee after only one year. It is simply not true that the presumption of continuance is a special privilege of academics.

Why should professors, unlike some employees and professionals, be immune to the fluctuations in their own market? If we found ourselves with a tenured professor of alchemy, should he or she be continued in the chemistry department? The example is not as farfetched as it seems, considering how fast some fields change. But neither should a mere change of fashions dictate the dismissal of a competent professor, for many fashions are just fads, no matter how important they may seem at the moment, and given how quickly they change, it would be inhuman and probably impossible to change the curriculum and the faculty fast enough to keep up.

Contemporary French philosophy, for example, which informs much of the work in literary theory as well, has a half-life of about three months. By the time it gets to Yale or Berkeley, it is dead in Paris, and by the time it makes its way to the Southwest, it has been repudiated ten times over. A professor hired for his or her knowledge of one of these fad fields who refuses to learn anything new may be stuck there, misinforming the undergraduates and undermining the graduate program, for another forty years. Of course, we can hire people who will themselves go through these changes and keep up with each new fad as it comes along, but this is a recipe for superficiality in the curriculum. Whatever else it may be, the university is not a fashion school, and truth does not change its dress nor its underwear every day.

Even in the sciences it is not always evident that the latest research is the best research, and sometimes an old approach or hypothesis turns out to be the best approach or hypothesis. But in the humanities and social sciences, even the notion of "progress" is controversial and up for grabs. The latest literature or theory is unlikely to be the best, and the battles that are now taking place between the latest hotshot theorists and those who "do not keep up in their field" are far more often battles over ideology rather than competence. But this does raise a very real, flesh-and-blood question—not about fads and fashions but about people and their livelihood. Should every university try to keep up with the latest ideas? Assuredly so. Should a university jettison professors who do not do so? Assuredly not. Nor need there be a conflict between them. But what we need is a different way of thinking about the faculty.

The most obvious solution is to have a more flexible faculty—teachers who have a broad range of interests and do not feel bound to a tiny bit of turf that they alone can call their own. Everyone doesn't have to do everything, but why should anyone do one thing only? As specialists become generalists the faculty can prove their value and worth may times over, not just by making themselves authorities in a single subject but by enlarging and enriching their own world and the undergraduate curriculum as well. As we open up the university, there will be hundreds of talented writers, critics, and journalists who will be delighted to visit for a semester or two to teach at the crest of the latest wave, without thereby being sinecured to do more of the same for the next several decades. Professors can and will remain at the same institution for years, often for a lifetime. But this should depend on their continuing dedication and competence and not on a hotly debated, perhaps hair-breadth decision made many years ago.

And yet some people lose it. They fail to achieve their promise or, especially in the case of young mathematicians, go over the hill long before it is time to retire. What does the university do with them? Having given years of service to an institution and a community, professors (and for that matter staff members) should not be thrown out like an old pair of worn shoes. If professors are learners, there is no reason why they cannot be expected to learn a new field, given sufficient time and resources. And there is much to be done in the university by way of teaching and education besides the standard classroom performance. For forty years IBM managed to figure a way to keep even its least-competent employees and put them to some good use. One would think that the university, which prides itself on its humanity, might be equally creative.

The problem of dismissal does not affect just the elderly, for whom gracious retirement or a change of careers is a reasonable alternative. There is the vulnerability of professors who step out of line or get in the way of ambitious administrators. The academic freedom argument—that tenure protects those who say something outrageous—is virtually beside the point. Professors are hardly ever threatened for what they say. They are threatened for crossing a powerful dean or challenging a pet university policy. Academic freedom is hardly ever the issue, and tenure is both unnecessary and inadequate to help such people. What is in question here are basic employment rights and fair employment practices, especially due process, and they alone can assure fair treatment of those who talk out of turn without at the same time guaranteeing them employment for life. But the most palpable threat to most faculty comes from the internecine rivalry and bitterly intense prejudices that define departmental politics. It is always shocking to realize that (quite the contrary of "team spirit") most of the faculty of a great many departments would happily fire most of their colleagues. But once we get rid of departments, genuine collegiality might have a chance, and hire and fire decisions will no longer be a matter of intimate animosities. When it comes to job security, the real need is not protection from dismissal for cause but protection from the sometimes psychotic, intolerant, and narrow prejudices of one's fellow academics.

114 ▾ *Alternatives to Tenure*

Our suggestion for an alternative to tenure is hardly original. It has been around for years. We recommend five-year renewable contracts after an initial one- or two-year contract. Given the current chaos of the hiring process, it is easy to make a mistake. Assistant professors are typically hired on the basis of three letters from their supervisors and a fifty-minute interview with a few of the faculty at a convention hotel. The faculty should not have to live long with its inevitable mistakes.

Nor should the students. Student evaluations should play a primary role in the move from the initial contract to the first five-year contract, and they should play a central role in every renewal. The present assumption that the faculty should be the sole judge of a young scholar's work is simply wrong. An outstanding teacher's main service to the university may not be obvious—indeed, may even be threatening—to them. But to stimulate the students to think in new ways and to shake up a faculty that is stuck in the past is hardly cause for dismissal, as it now often is in the present tenure system.

Between the initial contract and the first five-year contract, a supportive university might also consider a paid year for research. The first two years of teaching are typically overwhelmed with preparation and learning to deal with the students. A year of research leave is both a good reward and an opportunity to begin one's research career in earnest—or at least try it out. Vassar College, for example, routinely gives such a reward for good teaching, and young teachers can throw themselves into their classes with some confidence that they will have a full year to do research later on.

Of course, if we had our way, this year would not be under the brutal pressure of "publish or perish" or the utterly unreasonable demand to make "an original contribution to the field" before one has even had time to get one's feet wet. Indeed, publishing as such should be all but irrelevant to university employment except insofar as publishing is evidence that a professor has something to say. But how about a year just to read, to get one's thoughts together, to plan new courses and make a few basic decisions about the course of one's teaching career?

If we eliminate tenure, won't teachers be dreadfully insecure, and won't academic freedom go out the window? The legal presumption of job security and the availability of due process, especially in state-supported institutions, is such that the elimination of tenure will have little or no effect on the sense of security of most faculty, excepting only those who now *ought* to feel insecure—who enjoy unchecked freedom to teach poorly and have not read, much less written, a book or an article in their field for years. Due process provides substantial protection (witness that it is now much, much harder to fire a secretary than it is to get rid of an assistant professor). In making the senior professors slightly more vulnerable, we aim to give security to those who really need it.

Won't a contract system encourage "sucking up" to authorities and a return to more traditional, less risky teaching? Assistant professors are already forced to prostitute themselves for six or seven years, and most of them have trouble getting rid of the habit once they get tenure. Won't it intensify already bitter academic politics? With more or less equal vulnerability, academic politics might even become more civilized, with more emphasis on rights and responsibilities and less nonsense about matters of mere status and privilege. In short, no one on a university campus should be so vulnerable that he or she can be fired without good cause.

At the same time, no one should be invulnerable. This is not just a matter of justice. It is also the prerequisite for an accountable faculty and a civilized community. Tenure now protects those who should not be there and makes it impossible for many others to know whether they should be there or not. But if the elimination of tenure is in part an attempt to equalize the vulnerability of the faculty, it is equally necessary to spread that vulnerability and accountability to the administration. If we cut tenure, we must eliminate the power of the administration. We do not intend to leave outspoken faculty as "sitting ducks" for vindictive administrators. Administrators must be answerable to the faculty and students, and politicians will just have to learn to keep their hands off the university. Hiring and firing should be done by the faculty, but by special committees, not departments. Continuation should be a matter of merit and not of politics or ideology. And enough of this "colleagues do not fire colleagues" mentality. We do not need a mandate of "accountability" from above to insist that our profession perform responsibly, competently, and enthusiastically. Those who violate their position and do not appreciate or contribute to the benefits of academic life have no right to remain there. Enough of the grumblers and slackers, and enough of those who abuse the security of tenure. We want professors who are in for life, or in for just as long as they want to be in, not because their place is secured but because there is no place else they would rather be.

115 ▾ *End Competitive Salaries*

"Equal work for equal pay." That would seem to be the basic principle of our concept of fairness. Of course, it is no easy matter to compare the requisite skills and difficulty of two very different jobs—say, nursing and truck driving. But when the two jobs are identical—for example, two professorships at a state university—we have no such problems of commensuration.

The teaching abilities of the two professors in question may go in different directions—one may be a master with graduate students and sophisticated undergraduates in a small seminar, the other a knockout as a lecturer in large introductory courses—but in an obvious sense their responsibilities are the same. Why, then, should one be making twenty-five or thirty thousand dollars a year and the other more than one hundred thousand?

The present system creates inequities between departments and between colleges. The inequities depend in part on "the market" and in part on the perception of what different specialties are "worth"—usually in inverse proportion to their traditional stature on university campuses. Thus accounting, which was taught in no university until very recently, is deemed more worthy than German literature. Why? Because everyone knows that accountants make more than German literature professors.

There are inequities between universities as well. A small liberal arts college cannot possibly pay what a large research institution pays its faculty, and a "flagship" state university will pay its faculty considerably more than the local community college. But it is worth noting that large state schools now tend to pay considerably more than the most prestigious private institutions, which is how California, Michigan, and Texas manage to steal away all those professors from Harvard.

Such differences wreak havoc with morale and spur resentment among the faculty. Professors do not like to think of themselves as civil servants, but they are, and that is a good thing. The free-market cowboy economics that has preoccupied academics only in the past few years, in which a few superstars have been able to command huge salaries, has been a disaster. The very idea that being a professor means entering into a free market in which one's worth is to be bargained for is antithetical to the very idea of professorial life. (That, of course, explains the antipathy to faculty labor unions, no matter what the expected benefits.) And the idea that two professors who do almost exactly the same thing—teach—

should be paid wildly different salaries for doing so corrupts the system and, at the same time, is extremely expensive. For as one salary grows by leaps and bounds, the demand for at least incremental raises for everyone else becomes overwhelming.

Teaching in the university is a joy, and although it deserves and demands sufficient financial compensation to support a family life free from financial desperation, it should not be a way of getting wealthy. Nor should the fact that a professor happens to teach a subject that commands a large income outside the university be any argument for a larger income within the university. If surgeons can make half a million dollars in their part-time practice (and could make another half million if they were not teaching), that is no argument for their making any more than a professor of French, who might otherwise earn only a subsistence wage as a translator. If a professor of accounting can make much more as a full-time accountant with a large firm, that is his or her choice. But it is not a choice that the university or the taxpayers should have to pay for. The money could be much better spent on hiring more teachers for more course offerings, or for assisting impoverished students.

It might be argued that the lack of competitive salaries will kill any incentive for the best people to go into university teaching. This is nonsense. People do not go into university teaching to maximize their incomes but because they love teaching and university life. Teaching is and should be its own reward, so long as everyone receives a decent living wage. That means more for the younger professors, less for overpaid senior professors and superstars, not to mention the coaches of the sports teams. In today's financially strapped university, there is no excuse for anyone's making close to a hundred thousand dollars a year on a university salary, whether he or she has a Nobel Prize, a winning basketball season, or the presidency.

116 ▾ Teaching: "A Full-Time Job"?

Faculty members are supposedly hired "full-time," but if you asked professors to recount their weekly schedules, it would be only the rare compulsives who measured out their academic workweek in forty-hour blocks. There are many gray areas—e.g., the time spent walking to and from the library, stopping to chat with a student or colleague on the way; reading the morning paper and pondering its implications for one's lecture later that day. But if there is no easy way to identify hours spent for the university, it makes very little sense to talk about a "full-time job." Besides, professors routinely do work for outside pay. They read and review manuscripts for publishers for a nominal honorarium (often paid in books instead of cash). They give lunchtime lectures for a neighboring university or the local Kiwanis club for a modest fee. Others make considerably more money consulting for the manufacturing outfit across town or even working part-time for a research team, perhaps one that they themselves head.

If a professor wants to add to his or her experience and salary with outside activities, we see no reasonable argument against this. Of course, there are obvious abuses of this freedom to pursue outside interests. When consulting causes canceled classes and leaves the professor unprepared, then we have a clear breach of contract, a conflict of interest.

The question is not what else do professors do outside of their university teaching responsibilities but how well they do what they are paid to do. Is it so obvious that working thirty hours a week on a scholarly book that has nothing to do with teaching is "part of one's job," whereas consulting with a corporation or writing a textbook with expectations of a substantial income are not? We are all, in this sense, part-timers.

Our status and respect in our fields often depend on "outside work." Surgeons making $250,000 university salaries not only can but must have patients "on the side." In fact, the time spent with patients will undoubtedly occupy the bulk of their workweek. How can business professors keep up or show that they are keeping up with the field without getting involved in corporations? What would it mean to be an engineering or architecture professor and not be involved in actual building? The idea that such outside interests pollute or corrupt the university is nonsense and encourages precisely the ideal of the isolated ivory tower university that we reject.

To use a personal example, students come to respect a subject such as business ethics when a professor actually spends some time talking to corporations about that subject and then shares some of those insights with the students. It gives the subject, which is otherwise an academic exercise having "nothing to do with business," both legitimacy and relevance, not to mention practical content. Engaged and successful professors make the university lively and relevant. Increasingly, what we want is more engagement and more "outsiders" coming into the university to share their knowledge and experience.

What must be avoided, however, is a two-tier salary system based on outside income. Today business and engineering professors will find a ready demand for their services in the fastest-growing industries, whereas liberal arts professors, for the most part, can augment their income with a few outside lectures and perhaps a book designed as a text or aimed at the public. The inequalities, accordingly, are inevitable. But this does not mean that these same inequalities should be duplicated within the university. Professors are professors, and since they do pretty much the same teaching, they deserve pretty much the same salary. But what they make on the outside, so long as it does not interfere or conflict with their duties in the universities, should be no one's business but their own (and the IRS's).

117 ▾ *Academic Welfare: "Deadwood"*

What do we do with an incompetent, "deadwood" professor who is kept on for years, teaches badly, and wrecks the morale of the faculty? The truth is, there are few such problems in the university. Most older professors develop in style what they lose in energy, and mellowness provides a not unwelcome substitute for ambitious motivation. At a recent honors program "favorite professor" dinner, it was not surprising to note that the majority of the professors invited were near retirement age—fifty-five, sixty, or older.

There are indeed some "old-fashioned" professors who stand in the way of the smooth advancement of bright young theoreticians, but given the hyped-up nature of so much theory these days, these conservative voices are an essential part of the intellectual checks and balances of the community. Many older professors tend to spend more time with students. If young professors provide the university with energy, older professors endow it with gentility.

There are, however, problematic cases. Some professors do not mellow. They teach poorly and become petty politicized tyrants. They make life miserable for others, so they should indeed be pushed up and out. Who has the power to do the pushing? Well here, of course, we hit the hardest problem in the university, but the answer has to be some version of "the other faculty."

Emeritus professors need not actually quit the field, of course. One of our most delightful colleagues is ninety-four. He still publishes a book every year or so, attends lectures and colloquia regularly, and can often be seen participating at a variety of international conferences.

For those who are really tired, there is retirement. Unfortunately, this suggestion is not always taken gracefully by professors who now enjoy the luxury of tenure. "Why don't you retire at two-thirds pay?" one chairman recently asked a member of his department well past his prime. "Because I am already retired at full pay," came the unanswerable reply. In such cases, retirement should be mandatory.

University retirement programs are more generous than ever. Professors can retire earlier than ever, and quite frankly, younger professors can use the space. And encouraging early retirement, at reasonable pay, makes good economic sense, for under current conditions there will be a considerable difference in salary between the retiring faculty member and the just-hired younger faculty.

There is also partial retirement, available now in many universities, which allows a modest amount of teaching and continued professional involvement on a voluntary basis. Other alternatives are available as well. Professors who cannot stand being in the classroom may nevertheless be good with individual students. They may provide valuable help in the library. Indeed, they could even learn some new skills. It is remarkable how tired professors perk up when the position they are complaining about is suddenly no longer secure. But there should be more options for older professors. There is a lot to do around the university and elsewhere and a lot of different ways to help education. The best thing to do with deadwood is to give it life again.

PART XVI

"Leave Government to Clerks and Desks"

—Ralph Waldo Emerson

118 ▾ Who Runs the University? Who Should?

As public universities are presently constituted, neither students nor faculty are able to effect significant change. Organizations of student bodies, run by an elected student president, usually have to concern themselves primarily with well-calculated annual threats or implementations of tuition hikes, and the university only offers them token representation at meetings of the faculty or the board of regents. In addition, the presidents of the student bodies at large public institutions, most typically young people who aim for careers in politics or law, serve in that capacity because it improves their résumé. The last item on their agenda would be to present themselves as revolutionaries who advocate drastically changing the balance of power in the university.

Similarly, over the last thirty years university faculty members, increasingly detached from the involvement of the sixties and early seventies, have watched their political influence wane. At public institutions they still have the opportunity to serve as dean, although this position is now less often held by active teachers and scholars, but they virtually never have the opportunity to serve as provost, vice-president, or president. To do so, they need to cease being a faculty member, and therefore they no longer represent the faculty or even think like a faculty member.

Representative faculty groups, faculty senates, have no authorized constitutional power to effect change, nor do faculty troubleshooting committees. On the contrary, at some institutions the disenfranchising of the faculty has reached the point where a department's own chairperson is a "head" appointed by the dean, who is appointed by the provost, who is appointed by the president, who is appointed by the board of regents, which is appointed by the governor. Who along this chain of command is an active teacher or scholar? Who has even stood in front of a classroom filled with students, let alone been in charge of a class, within the last five, fifteen, or twenty-five years or, in the case of the board of regents, ever?

The answer to the first question posed in the title of this chapter, "Who Runs the University?," is presently "administrators." These are the appointees referred to in the previous paragraph, and in the early 1990s they find themselves in complete control of public institutions of higher learning. They claim that they welcome the opinions of faculty and students, but this is a political ploy; in reality they have relegated faculty and student opinion to merely an advisory capacity. The more administration runs the university, the less opportunity and desire the faculty and students have to salvage any remnant of administrative authority and involvement.

The answer to the second question, "Who Should?," is "faculty," who will focus on educational goals that are in tune with the needs of the students. But in the running of the university the students should not be passive recipients, victims, pawns, or consumers. It is their voice as well as their needs that guide the faculty.

Recently across the country there has been some movement to change the arrangement, to return some of the decision-making power to faculty organizations. Administrators fight back by declaring the security of their own power through self-reference. In a recent address one university president said to his faculty senate:

> I want to warn the faculty about avoiding unfulfillable expectations. Given that it is the president of the University who is personally accountable to the Regents and to the Legislature for how things run at this insti-

tution, it would be an error to assume that governance arrangements ever can place the faculty in the position of deciding everything rather than advising on significant issues. To think otherwise would be a delusion that can lead only to frustration. In my view, the faculty would be best advised to focus on improved arrangements for consultation and advising, and to recognize that the president, as the accountable individual, must remain free to decide whether to accept that advice or otherwise, as appropriate.[1]

119 ▾ *The Administration*

The existence of almost absolute power in the hands of noneducating administrators and the lack of power among faculty and their students is one of the most elemental problems facing contemporary American education in institutions of higher learning. Because the present administrative power structure itself will interfere with the changes in student and faculty attitudes that we have outlined in this book, it is crucial that any change or improvement be accompanied by significant restructuring of how power is wielded by university administrators.

As these public institutions of higher learning have increasingly modeled themselves after big business over the past few decades, the power superstructure has simultaneously been transformed from faculty serving temporarily as deans and provosts to corporate-model executives whose careers become "administration." They are paid six-figure salaries and have large, plush office suites filled with abundant staff, first-rate office equipment, and shelves devoid of learned books. They "do lunch" with other administrators; spend much of their day meeting with a number of finely suited, nonuniversity individuals; and address—i.e., command—the faculty through memorandums. None of this has anything to do with higher education as we envision it, except to misplace decision-making power, waste or misallocate appallingly large sums of money, and demoralize faculty and students alike.

Some of today's administrators, we gladly hasten to admit, have become vocal champions of education—that is, good teaching. But too often they have become so in the face of enormous public and parental pressures, not because they believe in or understand education. In truth, the new wave among administrators moves in precisely the opposite direction—toward more research and prestige, toward acquiring more grant money and expanding limitlessly, the students and teaching faculty be damned. If there must be cuts, we know where those cuts will be.

Administrators today have little contact with students, and some even have little or no educational background. ("If you can manage well, you can manage anything.") The high salaries and "perks" are conscientiously competitive and intended to attract executive types from within and outside the university. Ambitious teachers, retired military, city managers, and "outplaced" corporate executives are popular these days. Some of them "fast-track" to a better job, just when they are settling in. While there, they are neither loyal nor particularly sympathetic to the school they are running, and when they depart, they leave the university in chaos. Thus our argument is that we need fewer, more academically oriented, and more knowledgeable administrators who are primarily concerned with students and loyal to the school.

Who ultimately hires these administrators and decides the agenda of the university? The regents or trustees of the university, who are most often successful local businessmen (less often businesswomen and successful businessmen's wives). Not surprisingly, they tend to view the university as a business, a corporation, with students as raw material and graduates as products. The idea is to run this business as efficiently as possible while presenting a glamorous image to the "outside," especially the legislature and the taxpayers.

Education is, unfortunately, invisible, so ample physical construction becomes essential, together, of course, with winning football and basketball teams. Detached from the university themselves, administrators seek out professional managers, with whose values they wholeheartedly agree. Again, they often have little educational background, typically none in the liberal arts. (One chairman of the Texas regents famously queried, "I don't see why we need both an English department and a linguistics department." It was not the defense of interdisciplinary studies he had in mind.)

In public universities regents or trustees are usually appointed by the governor and/or the legislature. They view their administrative responsibility as a matter of control. The same regent stated, "We don't fund what we don't control." It is in the public interest to pressure for the appointment of educated and proeducation administrators in place of the politicians and business types who now reign.

Caution must be exercised, though. We have amply expressed our own dismay with the irresponsibility that distorts education in many if not most public schools, but this does not mean that governors and legislators should "do something" and take the wayward universities "in hand." Some of the changes we are suggesting can only come "from the top," but "the top" cannot have absolute and unchallenged power, nor can it be ignorant of the virtues and purposes of the institution it is changing. The taxpaying public deserves more competent, better-informed boards of regents, men and women who are devoted to something more than the abstraction "the university."

120 ▾ *The* Cursus Honorum *(Up the Corporate Ladder)*

The ideal career of the university administrator follows a *cursus honorum,* a series of offices held, each one with larger responsibilities and a higher salary than the last. As one's administrative career proceeds, the goal is to climb the *cursus honorum* until achieving a university provostship or, ultimately, a university presidency. At that pinnacle there is no one to answer to except the board of regents (and in certain respects the legislature).

The power of the office is consummate. The salary approaches or even exceeds the $200,000 range, usually with a house or a liberal housing allowance,[2] a car allowance, and an entertainment allowance, not to mention the huge office staff housed in a plush, upper-floor suite and a number of additional perks. There is plenty of travel at university expense; ample opportunity for appointing lesser administrators, who then owe allegiance to you alone; and awarding arbitrary favors requested by favorite faculty members, who inevitably have the greatest respect for the *auctoritas* of the office of president, whether or not they have any respect whatsoever for the person who holds that office.

Granted, this is the pinnacle, but it is a goal that can be (and has been) achieved relatively rapidly by the most ambitious people, "fast trackers." After an initial, low-level appointment as an associate dean or some such, there will soon be an appointment as dean or assistant vice-president for something or other or associate something or other, and then another appointment as assistant vice-president for something else or associate something else, and so on until the appointment as provost. Thereafter, one hopes, a presidency is not far behind.

We both know several young men who advanced from faculty member to university president in less than ten years. In the process of climbing the ladder, the university president inevitably loses any active memories of being a member of the faculty. The president has left teaching and scholarship far behind. The job now is administration. The presidency is a loftier position than a professorship. In fact, in the case of the most extreme fast trackers who abandon their teaching and scholarly responsibilities early on to concentrate on an administrative career, when they are hired as an administrator, they are automatically given a full professorship without a rigorous examination of their qualifications.

The pattern is analogous to that of a political career or the corporate ladder, but with significant differences. A political career eventually requires approval of the voting public, whereas a career in academic administration requires less and less general approval with each successive stage. Students and faculty never get a chance to vote on such important appointments, and their inclusion in search committees, which is accomplished through appointment by an administrator, is at best advisory, more often mere tokenism.

Climbing the corporate ladder, although likewise potentially rapid and extremely lucrative, demands tangible results. Incompetence and lack of vision are not rewarded in a cutthroat, bottom-line-oriented commercial enterprise, and the abilities of ladder-climbing officers are constantly monitored by rivals and fiscal accountings. Academic administrators, on the other hand, are rarely subjected to a "bottom-line" evaluation after their appointment to a position. The appointed person is often subject to a full review only after five years, at which time he or she has already moved on to a better position or become so entrenched and powerful that the review becomes a simple rubber-stamping.

In the meantime the only real monitoring that exists for that administrator takes the form of an annual evaluation, normally written by the very administrator who appointed him or her in the first place. Such an evaluation is prepared by the more senior administrator and filed by the same person. It is shared only with the person being evaluated and perhaps the next higher administrator, and then it goes into a file that no one ever has the right to obtain. Because the person appointing an administrator is most often the one who evaluates that administrator, that administrator's sole chance for approval and advancement is to please the person who appointed him or her. Chances are, the more senior administrator is going to give a positive evaluation for the person he or she hand-selected, because to do otherwise would reflect badly on his or her ability to select quality personnel.

First and foremost academic administrators do not want to cause any problems. They owe allegiance to the chief administrator and want to show above all that they are team players, organization men/women who are enlightened and current with what university administrators across the country are thinking at the moment. Above all, they cannot afford to be thought of as "loose cannons" or independent thinkers. The penalty for not performing as expected by the system is considerable, if one had hoped for an administrative career.

If these individuals fail as low-level administrators (top-level administrators never fail; they just mysteriously resign "for personal reasons" and are usually given high-salaried consultantships elsewhere), they no longer have an office job or wear business clothes or command a large salary or have a sizable office staff. If they started their career as a professor, they have to go back to squeezing into a 12-foot by 12-foot office, sharing the office staff with one or two dozen other professors, paying for their own lunch, grading papers, searching for a parking space, and having only three hundred dollars' worth of travel reimbursed in a normal year. And they will have to *teach*, face students one-to-one. How horrible to contemplate! So, fast trackers always look ahead, not behind. They crave the power and money and prestige that accompany the *cursus honorum*, and along the way they learn how to play the game.

121 ▾ *Hiring the Administration*

One of the most damaging aspects of the present system is the rapidity of the administrator's rise, for it inevitably leaves the university in confusion. The fast tracker rarely stays at any post for more than four years. Some, particularly much-sought-after women and minority administrators, have been known to advance from one post to another in a matter of months. Because the best vertical advancements are almost always found at other institutions, the fast tracker keeps a stereoscopic gaze, and abandoning the present university in favor of a more prestigious and better-paying one is common and seemingly guilt-free.

Time and time again, the administrator who hired the younger fast tracker makes a public statement of how great a loss this resignation is to the university; appoints someone else—either an internal fast tracker who has been targeted for advancement or a harmless do-nothing, both of whom will do as the administrator pleases—as acting associate vice-president of that same something or other; and then appoints a hand-picked search committee to find a new, external fast tracker as a permanent replacement. Meanwhile, whatever programs, procedures, or budgets were under the departing administrator's charge are orphaned. University efficiency suffers even more than usual, and faculty and students alike find their institution abandoned and cannot even keep track of who is in charge of what. The process itself is not put into question.

Because the search for a permanent replacement is nationwide, the offer extended to the candidate must often be quite generous. A survey of administrative salaries and perks published recently by the *Daily Texan,*[3] *Fort Worth Star-Telegram,* and *Houston Chronicle* revealed such astonishing sums as the $178,500 annual salary of the executive vice-chancellor for academic affairs of the University of Texas system and the $130,000 annual salary of the executive vice-chancellor for asset management.

These figures alone dwarf the salaries of even regents professors or other endowed chairs in the humanities, and they triple or quadruple the average salary of full professors systemwide. But to make matters worse, these administrators are given in addition a house allowance, a car allowance, and $3516 in club memberships in the case of the former and an annual $9996 house allowance, an annual $8400 car allowance, and $4560 in club memberships in the case of the latter. When queried about these unconscionable sums, one administrator was quoted as saying, "It is common practice throughout universities and higher education systems to offer compensation packages." Although this is true, it should not be, and we doubt that many taxpayers would disagree with us.

We know of nothing like this ever offered to a teaching faculty member. We do know of professors hired in California who have been offered low-interest loans to help defray the huge cost of real estate there. But these monies are loans, and their purpose is to help a professor, who is being paid some $50,000, afford a "starter," two-bedroom house costing some $250,000. In contrast, the justification voiced for the exorbitant administrative salaries and perks is that they are customary and therefore needed to attract top candidates.

The same argument is made for paying professional athletes five-million-dollar annual salaries, but these individuals, at least ideally, attract that much revenue or more by their mere appearance, and there is the hope also that by acquiring such an athlete, the franchise will be able to win a championship. In academic institutions, however, there is no "gate" to attract, and there is no championship to win, despite administrative hopes of increasing national rankings and taking in more grants and gifts. Nor is there any evidence whatever that the quality of a university is measured—much less improved—by the high pay or prestige of its administrators.

When salaries and perks of this magnitude have been offered to recently hired administrators, it is only natural for the administrators already in place at any given institution to feel underpaid. They immediately begin searching for a better position elsewhere. When they ultimately find it, there is more orphaning of programs, procedures, and budgets, and then someone new must be hired to replace them, so the ante spirals up one more inflationary notch. Such a self-induced inflationary spiral is unconscionable when university salaries for faculty, graduate assistants, and staff chronically remain relatively frozen; when university budgets are inadequate to cover even elementary survey classes and required courses for graduating seniors; and when tuition at even public universities is increasing by hundreds of dollars per year and now moving beyond affordability for single parents, returning adults, and low-income families.

Most students, parents, and other taxpayers are unaware of such salaries and perks, but alert faculty are repeatedly outraged not only by the cost of hiring such "top-notch" administrators, many of whom the faculty consider to be less intelligent or competent than themselves, but by the ease with which such hirings are made and such monies spent. For a history department, for example, to replace a teacher/scholar who is retiring after fifteen years at the institution, it often takes two years of planning, negotiating, and pleading with the administration, and more often than not the administration will allow the department to replace even the most outstanding teacher/scholar with only a wet-behind-the-ears assistant professor who has just received a Ph.D. The reason is economic: A full professor might cost $75,000, an assistant professor only $32,000. But the need to fill an administrative position often goes without question. If money is a measure of one's value, those whose job it is to educate are not nearly as valuable as those whose job it is to tell those educators what they can and cannot do.

122 ▾ *Replace the Professional Administrator*

Perhaps the greatest irony in paying administrators huge sums of money is their claim that they deserve high salaries because of the heavy responsibilities they shoulder. The truth is, it does not matter whether they make the right decisions or not; the only "responsibility" they shoulder is the need to withstand what little objection their decisions might bring from students and faculty. And their decision making can cost the university as much money as several hundred students pay annually in tuition.

Take, for example, a state university's search for an administrator. In advertising, interviewing, and travel, the search can cost some $10,000 (six in-state tuitions). The university eventually hires the administrator at an annual salary of $100,000. This administrator's previous salary— when he was a mere professor—was approximately half that, so the university wastes another $50,000 (thirty-three tuitions) just by using an administrative salary bracket. The new administrator wants to improve things, of course, so the hiring package includes two assistants, one associate, and a handful of receptionists and secretaries. The university has now spent another $125,000 or so (eighty-three tuitions).

After being moved across several states (three or four more tuitions) and taking office, the administrator will next set about removing a few politically threatening department heads and/or deans by buying them out—giving them a semester at full pay with no teaching responsibilities. Their combined one-semester salaries add up to approximately $90,000 (sixty tuitions). Thus far the university administration has spent approximately a quarter of a million dollars only to reduce the teaching load of two faculty members.

Very often these administrators consider it essential to search outside the university for other administrators—ones the new administrator can control because they will owe their jobs to him. These searches will each cost another $5,000, and the new administrators will be brought in at a salary of some $70,000, about $30,000 more than their salaries for the previous year (not to mention their moving expenses [$5,000] and equipment expenses [$4,000]). Teaching assignments for the first semester? None! The new administrators must "adjust."

The administration has now spent well over a third of a million dollars and, as a direct result, a half-dozen fewer courses are being taught. Several hundred students' tuition will be needed to fund the new administrative expansion and manipulation, and there are now fewer courses for the students to choose from.

All the while, the state government is annually reporting shrinking tax revenues. It repeatedly pinches small percentages out of the state university budget. The university administration, which pays many bean counters to keep track of such things, knows full well of the impending budget cutbacks. It keeps on hiring and expanding the administration, though, and when some year there is, say, a 5 percent budget reduction, there is no room in the budget to take in the 5 percent. And this year, in many states, the cuts are 10 to 20 percent.

You cannot cancel a contract, and the administrators all have contracts, as do the associates, assistants, secretaries, and receptionists. There might be some student help not obligated by contract, so they can be let go. (That will save *hundreds* of dollars!) All other faculty are under contract, so the funds have to come from unobligated monies, and most often unobligated monies are used to pay graduate students and part-time teachers who teach basic language courses, basic writing courses, basic humanities sections, and basic math courses. Many of these courses will be canceled. Also keep in mind that the third of a million dollars added to the budget caused another 5 percent ($17,000—another eleven tuitions) to be cut. And in return for this enormous cost and sacrifice, what do we get that we could not have simply done without?

Ultimately, the highly paid administrators do not shoulder great responsibilities but actually cost the university millions of dollars per year. The hypothetical episodes described here involve only one senior administrator out of a dozen. The damage the administrators do is unfathomable, difficult to prove in an official hearing, and forever denied and explained away. But as long as the administrators continue to run the university, the university will fail to accomplish its mission.

> At a time when both the young and the mature are flocking to the humanities, universities are badly thought of only by politicians and those bureaucrats who have always resented their relative independence.
> ——John Passmore

123 ▾ Reorganize University Administration

We do not claim that the entire blame for the state of contemporary American public universities can be placed in the well-carpeted suites of administration, nor do we advocate in any way a nihilistic dismissal of every present administrator or a revolutionary overthrow of university bureaucracies. What we ask primarily is for the elimination of that ultimate and sole responsibility that administrators claim for themselves and the upper-class prestige that accompanies it. The administrative posts themselves should be stripped of their huge salaries and ostentatious trappings, trimmed in number by two-thirds, limited in power, and filled by having active faculty, who appreciate the most essential needs of students and faculty, serve for three-year terms. There should be sufficient checks and balances in the system so that no administrator can operate in a prestigiously guarded vacuum.

Administrators commonly counter such suggestions with the seemingly persuasive but ultimately sneaky argument that the university is "understaffed" as it is. Budget-minded defenders of the powers that be will point out that few top universities spend more than 10 percent of their budget for administration, and many of them spend closer to only 5 percent or 6 percent. But in a half-billion-dollar budget this is a hefty amount indeed, and the real trick lies in the weasel word *understaffed*. True, most universities could use more people taking care of the students' needs and the organizational details, but "staff" is not the same as "administrator." The average college staff person earns considerably less than twenty thousand dollars a year, barely a living wage. We could use a good number more such people, and we should treat them better. But the idea that we need more administrators just won't pass scrutiny. Staffing administrators just produces more administrators.

The present hierarchy can be leveled not only eventually by gradually eliminating unnecessary vice-presidencies but immediately by equipping faculty senates, faculty watchdog committees, and faculty planning committees and task forces with real decision-making power and, in some instances, veto power. The few remaining administrators, who should be hired by faculty committees, should also be subject immediately to regular faculty reviews, something that in some institutions happens now only after five years or in quite extraordinary circumstances. To compensate the faculty who do serve as administrators, an ample salary supplement should be provided, but by no means should "a move into administration" be encouraged for financial gain or as a fast-track career change.

Human nature, as Aristotle observed, is political, and business relationships between two people will always necessitate the various means of persuasion, dominance, and conciliation. Our concern is that scholars and teachers should replace "professional" administrators. As is done in many European universities and in some of our Ivy League schools, deanships and provostships should be held by distinguished teacher/scholars for brief—for example, three-year—periods. At the conclusion of that term, the teacher/scholar will be anxious to return to teaching and scholarship. We would like to think that that person's accomplishments as teacher and scholar will generate the respect and authority needed to run the office, as opposed to the present system, in which the money connected with and the authority of the office itself intimidate others into obedience and obsequiousness.

At no time will our new administrator be more than a year and a half away from being in the classroom. Besides, it may be that with genuine, active teacher/scholars serving in administrative capacities, the amount of administrative central planning and bureaucratic paperwork will be so drastically reduced and the number of administrative offices will therefore be so drastically reduced as well that he or she will have time to teach classes even while serving the three-year administrative term.

The result of all this should be a relatively slimmed-down, self-correcting, intelligent, and responsible administration that automatically "prioritizes"—puts education first (and actually *means* it)—and serves the needs of faculty and students. Noncareer administrators will no longer consider institutional prestige to be a priority, particularly at the expense of education. The university can then re-evaluate how it apportions its budget, new laboratory buildings will have classrooms, and services and benefits will be provided to students instead of amply funded technocrats.

If responsible people have been hired in the faculty, along the lines we suggested in earlier chapters, then we will be responsible enough to assist in running a responsible university. Prostituting one's educational and societal goals to grant, gift, and legislated monies will no longer be so rampant or so celebrated, and the new administration will understand that money given to the university from such sources can lead to less education rather than more. It will know how to look at the real costs of research. It will understand that, compared to sophisticated research, undergraduate education is quite inexpensive and that any monies given for research should include a small proportion ("overhead") for undergraduate education.

124 ▾ Faculty (and Student) Governance

What we propose—and again, it is certainly not new—is real faculty governance. Not just advisory committees. Not just a faculty "senate." Not just a forum for ambitious faculty members toying with the idea of administration or already making their way to the top. And by "governance" we do not mean the daily red tape, meaningless meetings, and paper pushing that we all do anyway. We mean genuine governing boards, made up of a small number of randomly chosen draftees, whose business it is, for at most a few years at a time, to make what decisions have to be made by the central administration of the university. But the central administration should be making fewer and fewer decisions, and similar autonomous and equally arbitrarily constituted boards should decide the more local issues as well.

Of course, there should be students on these boards, not the politically ambitious student association type but, again, students tapped during their senior year—when many of them have the blues anyway—when they can contribute their considerable wisdom and experience from the numbered-seating side of the classroom. Students also have a remarkably calming effect on faculty behavior, if not on faculty egos. A group of faculty left to their own devices will tend to grandstand, but a few disrespectful student voices have a way of bringing things back down to earth. For that matter, it will be beneficial to have a nondegree, older student from the community sit in, too, as an antidote to professorial self-righteousness. It is often thought that including students in crucial decision making means inviting in the most radical contrarious voices. These should not be excluded, of course, but neither are they the norm. The point is simply that experienced students know better than anyone the needs of their peers and the faults of the school. We should listen to them.

But what of the administration—that is, the actual nuts and bolts of finances and record keeping as well as buildings and grounds and parking? The university would continue to be staffed as always, with a few professionals who know how to run things and lots of students who are earning their way and learning at the same time and actually participating in the work of the community of which they are such an essential part. There will still be an accountant and a registrar, janitors, and campus cops. And of course, there will be the governing boards, mainly to equitably distribute funds, supervise the rather considerable coming and going of part-time faculty, and resolve what should be minimal disciplinary problems among faculty and students. What there will not be is an administration.

125 ▾ *The President*

The president, however, has a very special role to play. The president may now appear to run things, but in most universities the president is in fact a figurehead who draws political fire and represents the institution in its various political and fund-raising activities. The president is the face of the university, pointed out to the world. But as currently structured, the real power of the university lies elsewhere, even when the president is a person of apparently indomitable personality. Students tend to blame all their troubles on the president, but the truth is that attacking or eliminating the president leaves the power of the administration untouched and unchecked.

Of course, there are good presidents and bad presidents, on occasion even great presidents, but the usual university presidents are measured not by what good they do but by the image they project for the university and how little damage gets done under their auspices. The worst presidents may be national heroes and activists of the most successful sort. Almost inevitably, they sell out the university and its mission to powerful interest groups, accompanied by great media and chamber of commerce fanfare. The best presidents may be almost invisible, or at least very quiet, touting and encouraging the virtues of their institution while leaving the faculty and students mercifully alone. The ideal president, however, is not just a spokesperson but an actual representation of what is best about the university, an enthusiast for education, who sees the essence of the university through all the inevitable distractions and political and financial pressures.

We need a president. We need a leader, not to control and run things but to represent what is best in the university and speak with a single voice that contains within it a plurality of voices. But the president must also be a faculty member, not a professional administrator, an insider always, not hired from the outside. The job should be temporary. (In fact, it almost always is. Nationally, a president's term averages three years.) And he or she should *remain* a faculty member and, most important, a teacher. The president is not and should not be an administrator, much less a corporate manager, CEO, or highly paid consultant. He or she is one of us.

Indeed, if the university were to return to its original mission, decentralized and dedicated solely to the continuing education of the students and the faculty, cut free from the now-extravagant expectations for external funds and the entanglements in which it should have no business, perhaps being the university president would once again become a pleasant and genteel art, an educational role instead of a political target.

126 ▾ *Stop Screwing the Staff*

We will close this portion of the book by paying hard-earned tribute to some of the most valuable members of the university community, who are all too often treated as part of the furniture—the staff, the people who actually run the university. No department can adequately function without them, and all the students are more beholden to them than they will ever know. The staff is underpaid, underappreciated. Every faculty member knows that when some important university matter is at stake, the first avenue of recourse and information is the head secretary or administrative assistant.

When our arguments for cutting the administration are met with the reply, "But we are understaffed as it is," we insist in turn that there is a difference between staff (hands-on workers who often get less than fifteen or twenty thousand dollars a year) and administrators (who make ten times that amount and rarely see a student or an ordinary faculty member). The university does indeed need more and better-paid staff—and many of these can and should be drawn from the student population. Everyone knows administrative assistants who are far better attuned to the real workings of the university and far better able to help students and faculty through administrative mazes than the administrators themselves. Let's draw the obvious conclusion, give credit and compensation where they are due, and eliminate the mazes. As Ralph Waldo said, "Leave government to clerks and desks." With a talented staff and faculty student help, the university will run itself.

PART XVII

Doing More with Less

127 ▾ Cutting Costs: Lean but Not Mean

Across the country colleges and universities are cutting costs, eliminating programs, restructuring, facing deficits, and in some cases, considering closing their doors. We are not financial wizards, and we have no sage advice for those at Columbia University who are coping with a ninety-million-dollar deficit or all those schools now trying to decide how to cut ten, twenty, and even fifty million out of next year's budget. But we would be irresponsible if in the midst of our many proposals we left the impression that what we are ultimately asking is for more money, that our book is a subtle plea to the legislature to reward us richly for our dedication and our love of teaching.

One does not have to have a hand on the purse strings of the university to know just how much waste there is, how many unneeded luxuries, how many monuments that are only for show. And when one considers the largest single expenditure of any university—salaries for its employees, from staff to faculty to administration—one need not be a Marxist to recognize the enormous inequities and waste to be found there. Our reason for suggesting the equalization of salaries, an end to superstar and corporate-style salaries, was to eliminate envy and destructive competition within the university community, but obviously this move would have important and budgetary consequences as well. Staff, beginning faculty, graduate assistant, and football player salaries should go up, but those reasonable raises will be many times compensated by the slashing of higher faculty and especially administration salaries. A living wage to do what we love. Should that not be enough for anyone?

So, too, our reason for arguing for cooperation among various institutions of higher learning was to embrace a larger academic community and eliminate the sometimes hostile competition and duplication between universities. But this cooperation will also have a beneficial impact on the budget. How many great departments of Sanskrit do we need in this country? How many Sanskritists does a great department need? Why should five universities within a hundred-mile radius have the most expensive laboratory equipment available when a single lab might serve all of them? Of course, every college and university should generally cover the whole of the intellectual and cultural terrain, but as professors become generalists instead of narrow specialists, the infamous problem of "gaps" in the departments will all but disappear. And as departments disappear as well, the idea that every university needs a sociology department, for example, will also go away.

Education is not an expensive process. It requires a good teacher, an eager student, and not much else. The fact that we demand so much more suggests that we are losing sight of that basic, original mission. Give us a decent place to talk, a good library, an adequate lab, a piece of chalk and a chalkboard. All the rest, ultimately, is perks and luxuries.

128 ▾ *Control Growth*

> Big universities have become growth enterprises that seek to maximize revenues. . . . It's the wrong attitude.
> —Robert J. Samuelson, *Newsweek* (April 1, 1991)

Those who are most successful in university administration, the fast-tracking movers and shakers, have been a major cause of a complete and undesirable change of direction in American universities. They have so expanded the functions of the public university, become so competitive for money and prestige, fallen into such grandiose, nonacademic life-styles, and moved so far away from working in the classroom that their goals have drifted far away from good teaching and sound scholarship. By and large they tend to think in terms of the *business* of higher education, and businesses thrive only when they grow.

How are these corporate-style administrators evaluated? How do they make their résumés shine and stand out from the crowd so that they can advance up the corporate university ladder and fast-track from one organization to another? Simply maintaining the status quo—ensuring quality education for undergraduate students, proper training for graduate students, and an inspired, intellectually stimulating environment for a satisfied faculty—does not show up on a résumé. Saving money by budgeting wisely and efficiently does not show up on a résumé either, but growth looks great. Erecting a new, state-of-the-art laboratory building, adding to and subdividing the administrative organization of the institution, participating in a multi-institutional consortium, making a trial visit to a Pacific rim country, acquiring a large gift from a local business, and other newsworthy activities are the stuff that fills administrators' résumés and their departure eulogies.

At first glance, one can be quite impressed when examining a university's areas of growth. We both regularly visit university campuses all over the country to make scholarly presentations, and we see firsthand the laboratory and administrative buildings springing up and the magnificent football and basketball stadia and sports complexes. We read as well the lists of the many, many gifts and donations. It is all quite overwhelming. And some of it is even useful.

To be so, such projects must be well planned and carefully incorporated into the campus, but this rarely happens. Hundreds of tuition-paying students are crammed into lecture halls devoid of an adequate sound system while well-paid engineers and scientists with limited teaching requirements and all sorts of outside interests and entanglements work with costly equipment in brand-new, state-of-the-art buildings. English and history faculty share box-shaped, Spartan offices with obsolete correcting typewriters or, at best, limited-capacity computer equipment while administrators entertain their appointments in wood-paneled, carpeted offices surrounded by a suite of staff and automated office equipment. Dozens of students stand in line waiting to obtain reserve books from the library or to purchase supplies from the student stores or to check on their transcripts or to discuss their grades with a teaching assistant, while the football team is toughened up on its custom-fitted Nautilus equipment in a spacious weight room beneath the multimillion-dollar stadium.

The problem is a matter of what administrators call "prioritization" or, in real English, deciding which is more important—the teaching humanist or the laboratory engineer, the average student or the NFL-caliber running back, using money to assist troubled students or using it to raise more money and increase prestige (to raise more money and increase prestige to raise more money . . .). University administrators repeatedly opt for the latter choice in each of these decisions because their priorities ultimately have so little to do with education. Their priority is, in a phrase, "bigger is better." If not more students then more buildings; if not more buildings then more money and prestige—or at least more administrators.

129 ▾ Spend Grant, Gift, and Tax Dollars on Education

The president of Iowa State was quoted recently as referring to "our aspirations and commitment to be the preeminent land-grant university in the nation."[1] We wondered why this was an important commitment, what the prize would be for being declared "the preeminent land-grant university in the nation," who would determine what criteria would be used to judge "the preeminent land-grant university in the nation," and what the state of Iowa or administration of one of its public universities would do to become "the preeminent land-grant university in the nation." Is a university that has top-rated engineering, medical, and philosophy departments preeminent over a university that has top-rated business, legal, and history departments? We could continue probing with questions, but the point is clear: To be the "preeminent land-grant university in the nation" is an absurd objective, a marvelous example of fine-sounding, dangerously expensive, and misguided administrative rhetoric.[2]

Because administrators in general have become focused on increasing prestige and therefore implementing growth, and because they handle annual budgets of hundreds of millions of dollars, they have become accustomed to a big-money mentality. They develop visions of grandeur, and the concept of expansion, which they call "much-needed improvement," becomes paramount. The most obvious and costly result of such thinking is the typical university's building program, and it will be instructive to examine in a general way how such a program benefits education.

The central administration might begin such an expansion program by hiring development people to court local businesses and large national corporations. Oil corporations might then donate monies to the earth sciences (geology) department, and soon there is a need to expand into its new state-of-the-art laboratory building; huge computer corporations might then donate monies to the computer science department, and soon there is a need to expand into its new state-of-the-art computer research building; electronics corporations might then donate monies to the electrical engineering department, and soon there is a need to expand into its new state-of-the-art research laboratory; and the defense-contracting corporations and the federal Department of Defense might then donate monies to the optical sciences (i.e., lasers and SDI) program, and soon there is a need to expand into its new state-of-the-art research laboratory.

All of this expansion is designated for research. In these buildings there may be one or two classrooms, but to make room for these new buildings, old ones, which had many classrooms, had to be torn down. Barriers surround the building site and deafening noise interrupts classes and conversations during construction, which takes two or three years—that is, more than half the undergraduate experience for many students. Like the business traveler who never sees an airport not under construction, today's undergraduate has become accustomed to attending classes in makeshift rooms in ill-equipped buildings because the prioritization of the administration is to build laboratory buildings or add to the sports complex or renovate one of the administration buildings, and the students, who see the campus as a wreck already, have not bothered to pick up after themselves.

To acquire all the monies needed to expand the university's physical campus, the central administration must hire more people. These are not, of course, learned professors of linguistics or theoretical physicists. They are "development people"—professional salespersons whose job it is to promote the university and raise money for it. They probably do not understand the research being carried out, and may not have been inside a classroom since they barely squeaked by in their own undergraduate career. They simply raise money, so they have lunch meetings with corporate people, they prepare glorious color brochures with plenty of photographs of scientists peering over a complex of equipment that would have made Henry Frankenstein envious, they fly here and there, they telephone here and there, they bring visitors to their finely appointed office in the brand new, state-of-the-art foundation or alumni or development building—some campuses have all three kinds of buildings—and when they finally obtain the donation, their picture appears in the annual alumni or foundation or development booklet, which is also finely produced with multicolor images and plenty of photographs of development administrators, central administrators, corporate and small-business representatives and owners, and local private donors. Thousands, if not tens of thousands, of these booklets are distributed to the faculty and administration and to local VIPs, and it again all looks extremely impressive. Such booklets often include a bar or pie chart of monies raised by the university, which range, of course, in the tens and hundreds of millions of dollars, depending on the time frame. No one knows what the actual costs are, or if they do, they are not saying.

Meanwhile, the English professor still sits in his shared office with its old IBM Selectric typewriter, types his handout for class, takes it to the main office, runs it off on the ten-year-old mimeograph machine, and distributes forty bled-through-blue copies to his students, who sit packed in a classroom that is too small and ill equipped. Discarded candy wrappers, empty Big Gulp cups, and multiple copies of the daily newspaper lie scattered on the floor because the university has cut back on its custodial staff to save money for the new buildings.

The waste that pervades university construction projects is typical of large bureaucracies. The contract goes out on bid, and any reader familiar with business or the government knows what that leads to. For those readers who are not familiar with the bidding process, suffice it to say that it is largely by virtue of that process that defense contractors charge the federal government eight hundred dollars for a screwdriver.

After the building is completed, it needs a custodial staff and a maintenance crew. It needs to be heated and cooled and ventilated. State-of-the-art equipment requires state-of-the-art specialists. The rule of thumb is that for every new building on campus, approximately 10 percent of its cost will be required annually for maintenance, much more if special equipment and security concerns are involved.

The money for maintenance comes directly out of the university budget. The university then asks the legislature for more money in its annual or biennial funding request, and the legislature balks at the several-million-dollar increase. Since the maintenance money is a necessary expense of the highest priority, funds are realloted for the new building. The administration does not feel similarly compelled to hire a new Spanish instructor to relieve an overcrowded class, the price tag for which is in the neighborhood of four thousand dollars.

We fully appreciate the need for scientific and technical research, and we do not at all complain that such research is being carried out on university campuses. What we want changed are the priorities. Wouldn't you think that of the thirty or forty million dollars that were "developed" for erecting just one new state-of-the-art fully equipped laboratory building, one or two million dollars could have been raised or set aside for undergraduate education? Ask that question of a university administrator or even a state legislator or member of the board of regents and the answer you will most often hear will be, "That has to come from a different part of the budget."

University construction projects too rarely make use of local talent. To landscape one of the buildings at the University of Arizona, the company of one building contractor we talked to hired a landscape architect from New England. The sketches for the landscaping were gorgeous, the only problem being that the deciduous trees the New England architect called for would, if they could survive even one 110-degree Arizona summer, require thousands of gallons of precious, costly desert water each year. (The building was to be erected no more than three blocks from the same university's Arid Lands Management unit, one of the great research labs of its type in the world!)

We do not know what the New England architect was paid. We do know, however, as does everyone in Tucson, that when the university wished to redesign its official logo, it bypassed hundreds of fine arts majors, fine arts graduates, and fine arts/design faculty; ignored local people in the design business; and awarded the design contract to a firm in Baltimore for thirty thousand dollars, about a fourth of which sum was needed for travel to and from Arizona! Could not the same job have been done by awarding a one-hundred-dollar prize to the local artist who designed the best "A"?

130 ▾ Bureaucratic Waste

Within the walls of public universities exists an isolated economy. The goods of this economy consist mostly of supplies (chalk, paper, pencils, and pens), small office equipment (typewriters, copiers, and computers), and small office furniture (desks, chairs, and bookshelves). Remarkably, despite the bulk in which such goods are purchased by the university as a whole, each department, program, or unit that purchases them pays an inflated price, and this directly affects undergraduate education. The more supplies cost, the less the individual department, program, or unit can purchase; and the less they can purchase, the less they can employ them for pedagogical purposes. We have all had the experience of walking into a classroom to find only a single inch-long piece of chalk at the chalkboard, being unable to distribute adequate numbers of a handout because there is a paper shortage, distributing tests typed on a typewriter in disrepair. The teacher may claim that the university is broke and that such basic supplies are not amply funded, but the problem, again, is misplaced priorities and systemic malpractice.

Over the last few decades public bureaucracies, including universities, have partitioned off their office stores and maintenance services into separately governed, separately budgeted units. Such internally generated cell divisions are characteristic of bureaucratic organisms, as is the independence that the progeny have. It is beyond our area of expertise to judge the fiscal wisdom of such independence insofar as the university as a whole is concerned, but we know quite well the problems this causes for teaching departments. Maintenance units regularly demand a deposit from each academic unit, and then the amounts they charge for services rendered are the same as, if not more than, what would be charged if the department were to hire local, nonuniversity businesses. Their service is rarely prompt, and often individual departmental needs get lost on a waiting list. We have seen two men, a dolly, and a supervisor show up a few days late to move one filing cabinet fifty feet from one office to another and charge a hundred dollars.

Consequently, a department may opt to hire a needy student or two to help with such a move. In 1992, though, governmental regulations are so strict that this is discouraged. If the student is not already on the payroll, then a mound of paperwork has to be filled out, approved, signed in sequence, and filed before a five-dollar paycheck can be issued. This is a very silly procedure as well, so it is better for the faculty members whose filing cabinets need to be moved to do it themselves, ask someone to do it for them, or pay a reasonable amount out of personal cash to have it done.

In the era of the eight-hundred-dollar screwdriver, one would think that people with Ph.D.'s would be a bit more inclined to scrutinize how money was being wasted in academic bureaucracies, but no one seems concerned. At one university, for instance, the departmental budget for paper listed a price of approximately thirty dollars for a carton of five thousand sheets. When one of us pointed out that the same amount of paper of equal quality could be purchased at any local discount store (Price Club, BizMart, etc.) for under twenty dollars, chapters and verses from the university store's operating manual were recited until we realized that the bureaucracy was not programmed for and had no interest in saving 33 percent—the same as paying 50 percent too much—on paper. And these are retail prices. Imagine if you represented the university and negotiated a price for, say, thirty thousand reams of paper with a paper manufacturer or distributor. Would not any business purchasing that kind of volume insist on paying fifteen dollars per carton? Instead, the department had to pay thirty dollars and wait for the delayed delivery.

We often wonder what the service, maintenance, and other nonteaching units in the university do with this money, but we are sure it never reaches a classroom or an undergraduate. Instead, teaching departments within a university find themselves perennially short of funds because of such price gouging and budget wasting. The same kind of gouging occurs when a humanistic department requests audiovisual assistance. Renting a VCR for one hour can cost a department thirty dollars, and usually the equipment is three or four years old, much abused, and in scarce supply. As of the late 1980s the University of Arizona owned three portable VCRs for classroom use, one for every five thousand students.

State-legislated funds are tricky to spend. To avert waste and abuse, so it is said, some universities insist that no state-legislated funds be used to purchase food or drink. A visiting scholar comes to campus to offer a public lecture, after which the host department wishes to hold a simple reception. Time was when responsibilities would be delegated—A would bring the punch bowl, B would bring the punch, C would bring the crackers, D would bring the cheese, E would bring the cups and napkins. No one paid more than five dollars, and a simple reception was easily produced. In some state bureaucracies now, though, this is improper procedure for insurance reasons: If someone should become ill from the food, the university's insurance would not cover it. So at some campuses all receptions must be catered. If the department uses the campus food services, of course, the food and drink will be of poor quality and overpriced; if a nonuniversity vendor is used, then the bid process must be employed to determine the best vendor for the job—for crackers and punch!

131 ▾ *Who Pays for Research?*

Who pays for research? It is important to emphasize, first of all, just how much research that goes on in the university is, in fact, done for free. The research project of a philosopher or a literary theorist may require only a pencil, some paper, and a big pile of books (purchased by the professor or borrowed from the library). The field biologist or descriptive linguist may require only a bus or an airline ticket. What the university needs to provide for such research, mainly, is time. We have already argued that we should not think that the university is "paying us to do research," although this seems to be the opinion of many of our colleagues. The university is paying us to teach, and doing research is, in part, something we must do to master our subjects and thus become better teachers. The luxury of research time is one of the perks of our profession, not the substance of it. It is fair to assume that if professors are fascinated by their subject, they will want to do research for its own sake. Sending them off to a conference or two will keep that interest percolating.

Some research costs a fortune and requires elaborate facilities. The new supercollider being built in Texas (Arizona came in second in the competition) will provide thousands of jobs and require millions—eventually billions—of dollars. This is a big business, even if the results are by no means predictable. How much should the university be involved in such business? On the one hand, it is perfectly natural and desirable for university professors of physics and related disciplines to be attracted to and employed to work on such a project. Indeed, there is a good reason for them to want to work full-time on such a possibly breakthrough project. But should they do this on the university payroll? Indeed, should the university have any hand in the financing and building of such a project? We believe that the answer is no, although the university can and should allow and encourage its faculty to contribute to the project and profit from the experience. That the physics faculty and sufficiently capable graduate students should become more deeply involved in some of the most exciting science of our time is essential to the educational interests of the university. That it should pay for a project that has no direct connection to the education of the students is quite another matter.

Research is essential to the mission of the university, not only the self-proclaimed "research university" but higher education in general, where every teacher should be expected to be involved in his or her field. But to expand the notion of research so broadly is clearly to make an important statement about the purpose of research as well, which is not just to expand the frontiers of knowledge, etc., but to give substance and excitement to the business of education.[3] What we want to question is the usually unchallenged argument that research pays for itself. Research can be very, very expensive. Even leaving aside the "big science" projects, when one adds the cost of new laboratories, technical personnel, and added overhead—even deducting the much-debated "indirect charges" added to every research grant—the resulting cost is often staggering. Most of the researchers hired for these projects are too busy if not "too important" to do any teaching, so there is not even an "indirect" benefit to the undergraduates. The benefits of the research are quickly snapped up by private enterprise, who may contribute—in the larger scheme of things—only a pittance to the research itself, and the costs remain hidden in the general university budget. But if you were to ask any university administrator why all of these funds are being spent equipping a research laboratory which ought to be supported by private industry, the response is almost always, "This laboratory brings in more money in grants than it costs us to fund it."

We very much doubt this claim, and though we do not have either the accounting skills or access to the numbers, we think that the university should open and explain its books to the public, not the already public "A" budget, embellished with colored pie charts and elaborate testimonials, but the real "B" budget that actually explains what comes in and where the money goes. Instead, we hear the same argument for almost every program in the university except the Humanities: "We bring in more money than it costs us." Medicine, Nursing, Electrical and Chemical Engineering, Earth Sciences, Computer Sciences, and the Business College all make the same claim. It would seem that if we added up the ledger sheet the university would run at a surplus! Let's be honest and critical about research costs, and let's get clear about who benefits and who should be paying.

132 ▾ *How Education Loses Out*

One of us was contacted by members of our local, nonuniversity community to initiate an educational program for nonuniversity people. The classes offered in this program consisted of three-hour seminars on humanistic subjects conducted by highly regarded teaching faculty. It was agreed that the program was to be funded by tuition paid by the community participants and that the tuition money would compensate the faculty members for their time. The community participants were nondegree students taking classes only in this modest program, so there was no need for them to matriculate in the university.

Registration in the program could be accomplished by simply giving us their name, address, phone number, and a check for ninety-five dollars. Once a week the participants and faculty member would meet in a classroom, and participants from both university and community were satisfied with this symbiotic relationship, which produced goodwill, intellectual stimulation, and a little bit of extra cash. This, at least, was the arrangement set up by faculty and community members.

Then the university administration became involved. Of course, because this was a goodwill arrangement between nondegree students and faculty willing to teach a bit of overload, the university had no precedent either for the program or for determining the office through which it could be administered. First, the program was placed under the jurisdiction of the "Extended University," which immediately insisted on collecting 7 percent of the tuition as its fee. In return, that office sent to the first class a staff member who wrote down the names of the participants, collected their checks, and weeks later, processed the check for the faculty member.

Since it did not make sense to us to pay that office the 7 percent for the little service that was rendered, we moved the program instead to the University Foundation. It charged us nothing, but when some of the community participants became so enamored of the program and its faculty that they raised a modest endowment for a teaching award, the University Foundation then scooped up the annual interest earned from this endowment. In the meantime, the shortage of classrooms on campus prevented us from holding classes anywhere but in the library and the student union, both of which charged us fees, and the lack of parking spaces on campus forced us to charge extra for parking permits.

The program became a pedagogical success, nonetheless, and we offered as many as four classes per semester. But success made us a target for administrators anxious to "market" programs. Before we knew what had happened, there was a 34 percent increase in tuition; letters were being mailed out claiming that the program was in desperate financial straits and asking for additional gifts, despite a ten-thousand-dollar surplus in the foundation account; a directorship and an administrative assistantship were established, costing some six thousand dollars per year, and the central administration of the university tried to grab the teaching endowment as well. Of course, many faculty and community members lost interest in the project now that it was being professionally marketed, but somehow it ended up in a color brochure demonstrating how the university is growing and how well it is serving the community.

Suppose that the entire university were run as a straightforward educational enterprise, a bond of agreements between teachers and students with minimal marketing and no attempt to make more money? No frills, no hype about prestige or status, just quality teaching and students eager to learn. Our bet is that not only would the education be better, the budget would be much smaller as well.

Conclusion

133 ▾ *Mission Aborted.*
Who's to Blame?

> For those who end up in the corporate world, or in the world of
> work, it is a liberating experience to learn to think, to write well,
> to speak well. A liberal arts education opens rather than closes,
> and I'm concerned that with corporate leaders, and our govern-
> ment and even some of our educators increasingly calling for
> these well-trained people, . . . we may not get well-educated
> people.
> —Johnnetta Cole, president, Spelman College, Atlanta

University tuition has gone up twice the rate of inflation
over the past decade, and state expenditures have gone up, too. The majority of students cannot graduate in four years, and a majority of them
complain about the quality of the courses they have been forced to take
and the unavailability of courses that they want to take. The faculty is
disgruntled and feels mistreated in spite of considerable raises. A book a
month announces to the public that our universities have failed. Scandals
in our best universities fuel the resentment, and the politicans move in
like sharks to the kill. Who is to blame?

Well, first of all, we have to blame ourselves. We have allowed ourselves
to be distracted from our calling and the mission of the university. We
do not deny the natural desire for status and success, nor do we demean
the research and writing that are currently the basis for measuring faculty
status and success. But we have collectively made local contribution to
our students and community far less important than what is called status
in the discipline, which is mostly measured by what one does *other than*
teaching. And what is called "professional work" is often gauged precisely
by its incomprehensibility and irrelevance to the larger community—in-

deed, even the larger community of scholars within the university. It is one of the obvious limitations of a teaching career that one's excellence is known primarily only to one's students (and unfortunately, awful teaching also remains cloistered and protected within the classroom). The result is that students are too often perceived as an annoying distraction. One's powerful colleagues and a few journal editors become one's only significant audience, and teaching becomes a "necessary evil" in an otherwise rewarding career.

But the university is also to blame for the attitude that only professional status and not teaching success is worthy of being measured. In faculty evaluations teaching does not count for much. Indeed, being a "popular" teacher is often said to subtract from one's professional respectability. Good teachers are rarely tenured or rewarded on the basis of their teaching, and terrible teachers are routinely tenured if their research is adequate. Raises are based on research and "cooperation" with the administration, not on teaching. The occasional teaching award only makes clear the unintended message, which is, "By the way, we have a few good teachers here, too." The structure of the profession is such that teaching cannot be taken seriously, except at the detriment of one's career. The university itself enforces this distorted set of values, and the university— that is, all of us—could readily correct those values.

Insofar as the current model of administration is management, one has to say that the universities, even the best of them, are mismanaged. We have replaced educational thinking with corporate thinking and executive self-aggrandizement, with too many six-figure salaries and perks. Personally, an administrator may be modest and affable, but it is the very nature of the university administration today to tend to self-aggrandizement and see the university only through a manager's eyes.[1] Accordingly, we now find an emphasis on growth without limits, innovation without purpose, national attention rather than a well-earned reputation for doing good for the students. And that only encourages professors in their single-minded pursuit of professional fame to the exclusion of dedication to teaching and community service. In turn, administrators have become or have been forced to become money hungry in a never-ending cycle of higher finances and more complexities and more administrators to take care of them. But they are just as much the products as the inventors of this disastrous frame of mind, and they alone are not to blame.

134 ▾ A Plea to Parents (Students, Too)

Parents are not innocent where the distortion of education is concerned, and it is the parents as well as students, administrators, and our fellow faculty whom we are addressing in this book. Too many parents blindly demand careers for their children and view the university as a trade school and their children's education as an investment. Every semester we talk to business students, for example, who hate their studies and are not doing at all well in them but whose parents "won't let them major in anything except business because it leads directly to a job and a career." We teach too many students who should not be in school at all but feel coerced into being there because their parents are sure that sending their kids to college is the right thing to do. We readily understand the parents' anxiety and concern, but they are ill serving their children as well as the university as a whole by insisting that their kids follow a poorly written social scenario rather than their own better interests. Students who do mediocre work in a not very interesting and possibly high-pressure career-oriented program will not do well later on and will probably discover that they are without alternatives. Students who do well at almost any subject because they have made it their own and devoted themselves to it will very likely do well in anything else they choose to do, too. In the words of one recent book, "Do what you love, the money will follow." There is no better career advice for anyone.

Let your children be undergraduates. Let them study everything and anything, follow their heads and their hearts, not parental dictates or the wisdom of the latest wave of the market. Most of the professions prefer or require a liberal arts background, and the smartest corporations are now looking there, rather than to the business schools, for the best candidates for the most promising jobs. Business school is not and should not be the "fallback" for incoming students who do not have a clear idea of what to do with the rest of their lives. In fact, very few incoming students have any clear idea of what they might do with the rest of their lives. It does no favors for the business school, which becomes a day-care center for the disoriented, and it certainly does no favors for the students—or their parents—to limit the scope of their vision before they have had a real chance to open their eyes.

First-generation college students, for whom the university is an unheard-of luxury to their parents and extended family, will perhaps be subject to the greatest pressures of this sort, for college looks so much like a ticket to a better life. But that ticket entitles the bearer to pass through some wonderful scenery and allows the possibility of some fascinating stopovers. In the university we can only hope for understanding parents and do our damnedest to prepare their sons and daughters for the life they will be pursuing when they leave us. It is shocking how many liberally educated parents send their progeny down a stark and limited path through what could otherwise be a garden of delights. We might lament that their own education was less than it could have been, but why should the next generation make the same mistake?

The students themselves are also to blame for the distortion of the university mission, even if they are its ultimate victims. Too many students see college as an extension of high school ("higher" education) but without the tight controls on their time and behavior. Accordingly, many of them enjoy a dubious "freedom," oblivious to the opportunities. Insofar as they take school seriously, they see courses in terms of grades and the curriculum in terms of credentials and tickets to the future. But "tough" teachers and the defense of "standards" as well as now-institutionalized careerism encourage them in this folly. Of course, our students have their own pressures. Many work as much as twenty hours a week outside the university—a necessity largely ignored by unsympathetic professors—and others come from broken homes or have other personal or financial problems, all of which add to the predictable postadolescent traumas of their age. But the main mission of the university must surely be to teach students to enjoy that freedom of thought and intellectual self-development that, for better or worse, universities alone can now provide. Fortunately, students can easily be converted to learning enthusiasts. Often it takes just one good teacher. But the students, given the size of today's university, must take the initiative and look for one. A good education no longer comes gift wrapped on an ivy-covered platter.

And then there is the problem with the ex-students, the loving alumni. The problem is not that the alumni are interested in their old alma mater and want to remain involved. That is all well and good and essential to the health of the university. The problem is that the university feels compelled to cater to some of those alumni who contributed least while they were students and, consequently, do not understand what a real contribution to the university would be. Thus, instead of much-needed scholarship money, we get illegal under-the-table contributions to the football team. Instead of books for the library, we get bronze statues devoid of aesthetic merit. We get names on buildings that in some cases should not have been built in the first place and in most cases could have been much more modest and useful than they are. However generous the alumni may be, we can only afford to appeal to the best in them, as we should appeal to the best in them while they are still here as students.

135 ▾ The Corporation and the University

Given the corporate ties (not to mention the corporate climate) of most universities today, the business world as well is in part responsible for the state of higher education. Despite their frequent generosity, corporations too often display the same old fears and prejudices—fear of students who think for themselves and may be a bit eccentric in college, prejudice against those who have not already displayed ambition or interest in a career. But few corporate positions involve such routine and uniform work that prior education will have prepared the student job candidate in advance. And those students who show that they think for themselves in college are usually those who will make a real difference later on.

It is the corporate training program or on-the-job learning that counts, and then the question is, who is more likely to learn the requisite tasks and techniques more quickly and efficiently—a student with an open, flexible mind who is used to thinking through a wide variety of problems or a careerist who has been educated in the right area but the wrong techniques? And who is more likely to have a healthier perspective on people and their problems—a student who has lived through the various cultures, history, and literatures of the world or a student whose idea of business is mainly limited to organizational structures and number crunching?

Perhaps this is overstating the case, but it is one way of raising the question about the intelligibility of most campus recruiting programs. In his best-selling business book *Up the Organization,* Robert Townsend suggests that corporations fire their personnel department and instead send the best executives to campus as examples, not recruiters. We are suggesting the complement of that suggestion—that they should then look for the best students in the university, not those who have seen their college career as nothing more than a preparation for this job interview. Corporations have often been generous sponsors of higher education in

America. Now they can do themselves a favor in return by hiring the best students, those who are flexible and morally sensitive, can think for themselves, and have proved that they appreciate a real opportunity when it presents itself—the opportunity to get an education.

Corporations get more benefit from the university today than any other segment of our society. The university is not only a training facility but a top-notch personnel office and a recruitment center that very few corporations could afford to maintain for themselves. The university provides research results as well as research faculty and facilities that are worth billions to the corporations that utilize them, often at remarkably little cost to themselves. Accordingly, it is not asking too much to suggest that these same corporations should support the university, not by an occasional gift alone but on a regular basis, considerably easing the load on the hard-pressed taxpayer. Corporations should help pay for the education of the people they hire, and they should be more than mere "partners" in the research that as often as not distracts rather than benefits the university. For better or worse, our corporations are now the dominant institutions in our society, and by way of *noblesse oblige* if not straightforward obligation, it is up to them to make sure that we have a society that is civilized and educated as well as well trained.

This is not to say, however, that the corporations should now begin to run the university or that the already overly corporate concept of management should become further entrenched by "running the university like a business." The "corporation" of the university is now being presented as a false alternative to troubled public support, but the "either/or" argument, again, is fallacious. The corporations may have a social responsibility to support the institutions from which they benefit so handsomely, but they have no such responsibility, much less a mandate, to govern them or determine what they should be or what they should teach.

136 ▾ The University and the State: A Final Suggestion

And speaking of "hands off," finally, it is not from any lack of respect that we would urge our state officials, against their own better judgment, to keep their hands off the university as well. True, we need and solicit their continued support and that of the taxpayers, whose money they so willingly spend and withhold as it suits them. But in our experience every effort made by the governor or the state legislature to "shape up" the university, make it more efficient or the students better educated, or ensure "accountability" among the professoriat has had the primary effect of interfering with the students' education; adding miles of red tape and hours of meetings, which take the place of both research and teaching time, confusing the students and the administration and infuriating the professoriat; not to mention the time wasted in the legislature itself and the ill will created among the electorate, who pay for the consequences.

State-mandated minimum teaching loads, for example, add to the teaching time of only the most junior professors but multiply the paperwork (and the administrative ingenuity) of those above them. State-mandated courses are typically the most poorly planned, poorly taught, and perhaps surprisingly, poorly funded courses in the university.

"Accountability" has become simply a code word for more paperwork. And yet the trend to increased state interference is unmistakable, and the result will surely be disastrous. On the perverse side, it may well help some of the struggling private colleges and universities, to which the best professors and students will once again return in retreat from the worsening morale and more cumbersome education of the public universities. But the overall effect on higher education will be to lower it to the level of our public high schools, which are clearly showing the symptoms of "improvements" wrought by governmental interference and continuous public wrangling.

This is not to say, however, that the presence of state officials on the university campus is unwanted or unwelcome. As the university opens up, we would hope that those with an interest in education will actually take advantage of the educational opportunities available to them and take a course or two. Indeed, those with governmental experience and electable oratorical skills might well teach a course or two. There is no reason why there should be antagonism between government and public education, so long as they take seriously their shared role in an enlarged community rather than the merely combative and political roles of sponsor and fundee. We need more involvement from the legislature, not less, but that means putting their brains in the classroom and keeping their hands off. If we don't need anyone running the university on the inside, we certainly don't need a puppeteer pulling our strings on the outside. What we do need are educated leaders and legislators, and what is a better place to find them but in the university.

> By believing themselves to be what they are not, institutions fall short of being what they could be.
> —Ernest Lynton and Sandra Elman

Notes

Preface

1. Quoted by Robert Zemsky (Professor of Education and Director of the Institute for Research on Higher Education at the University of Pennsylvania) in the *Pennsylvania Gazette* (1989).

2. Throughout this book, we will refer to "the university" as if it were a single entity, as if we were, each of us, speaking of our own institution. We may seem to be ignoring the importance of colleges and other, smaller centers of higher education. This is not the case. True, the word is a bit ennobling, but that, of course, is our intention. The university has indeed become an institution of nearly mythic proportions. It is our intention as well to emphasize the institutional uniformity and shared problems of colleges and universities, and "the university" is a convenient designation for doing so without denying their many differences.

So, too, we will often use the first person plural to refer (without specification) to ideas and experiences, whether or not these were actually shared. This will allow us to avoid an unnecessarily cumbersome system of personal specifications and references and subsequent discontinuity in the text. The point is that we agree with each other on their significance, and so whether a particular incident happened in Texas or Arizona or Princeton or Chapel Hill, in a philosophy class or a classics lecture, is of little or no importance. And if an anecdote here or there is obviously the experience of either one of us (an incident at a philosophy convention, a conversation on a Greek archaeological site), there is no need to burden the syntax of the discussion with superfluous pronouns and references.

3. In 1990, 59.9% of high school graduates went on to college (Department of Education figures). In central Texas, a state not renowned for its education priorities, a recent poll yielded that 94% of its citizens believe it is important for their young people to go to college. Furthermore, 71% thought a college education helpful in leading an enriched and happier life, and 64% thought it helpful in becoming a better citizen (Harte-Hanks Communications and

Texas A&M University Faculty Association Poll, 1990; the usual margin of error applies).

4. Allan Bloom partially subtitles his book *How Higher Education Has Failed Democracy,* but democracy is nowhere to be found in its pages. How a book could so deeply insult and glibly dismiss the intelligence or importance of the very people who bought and praised it (whether or not they read it) will remain something of a sociological mystery, but the one message of the book that is absolutely clear is that democratic values—public education for the millions and the opening up of the university—are the very antithesis of Bloom's proposal for educating "those who are most likely to have the greatest moral and intellectual effect on the nation." See, for a sampling of critical reviews, Benjamin Barber in *Harper's* magazine (Jan. 1988) and Martha Nussbaum, *New York Review of Books* (Nov. 5, 1987).

5. E.D. Hirsch, *Cultural Literacy* (Boston: Houghton-Mifflin, 1987). In Hirsch's defense, however, his book is in fact a serious technical study of education in America. It is his readers and reviewers who have shifted the focus to his easily lampooned appendix and turned his larger concern into mere "bric-a-brac" of an academic mind.

6. Henry Rosovsky, *The University: A User's Manual* (New York: Norton, 1990).

7. Most of the current debates about the university and the most often cited examples of academic absurdity and subversion are not about the university at all, but rather about the English department. There is a good reason for this. "English" is not a natural subject, but a dangerous amalgam of functional service courses (teaching two of the basic "three Rs"), an arbitrarily truncated literature program (which seems to include only writing that does not require knowledge of a foreign language), and an often arrogant collection of literary theorists, who are typically at war with each other as well as with their more down-to-earth colleagues. They make their reputation attacking and alienating everyone else in the department. There is a very real question why and whether the university should continue to have an English department at all, but for now, we want to make a much more modest claim—that the university is not the English department, and the embarrassments and anecdotes of a few notorious departments should not be taken as the nature of the university itself.

8. It is truly remarkable how out of proportion the fear of "Marxists" and "radicals" in the university has been compared to the actual number (and effectiveness) of those so self-proclaimed on campus. But if it is subversion you are looking for, look rather to those who quote Matthew Arnold and celebrate "the best that has been thought and written," which Arnold explicitly intended as a diatribe against democracy.

9. The invitation to outside authority was only a hint in Bloom, whose

book was more of an expression of disgust and despair than a call to arms, but the hope that "help is on its way" has been openly advocated by Charles Sykes, Dinesh d'Souza, and Roger Kimball. (The phrase comes from Sykes's *Profscam*, 264.) Nothing could be more destructive of the university, or more favorable to the subversive forces that they most oppose. Thus "radical" students have always baited the authorities to call in the police, and the most foolish professors have always had their loudest say when the university is under fire. And there is nothing like a mere movement in the legislature to derail the normal business of education.

10. Cardinal J. Newman, *The Idea of the University* (New York: Doubleday, 1959); Robert Paul Wolff, *The Ideal of the University* (Boston: Beacon Press, 1969).

Introduction

1. Cardinal J. Newman, "Why are the problems of business ethics insoluble?" in *Proceedings of the First National Conference on Business Ethics* (1977), 99.

2. The first problem, perhaps, lies in the very word *undergraduate* as if it is graduation and not the learning itself that defines a student's status and there is something inferior about those who are still in the process of studying rather than finished with it, presumably once and for all. And as more and more older students come back to the university, many of them after retirement, the word becomes all the more inappropriate. Indeed, except for the classificatory fanaticism of the registrar, why should it matter whether a student has graduated or not, or for that matter, even intends to do so?

PART I: The Mission of the University

1. In a society that is supposedly devoid of "class," the university defines a social hierarchy almost as rigid as a caste system. As Paul Fussell has argued at length, the university now determines our social structure, and the significance of a Harvard, Purdue, or Valparaiso Community College degree has become as definitive as being born into the aristocracy or into serfdom in late medieval France or England. This, above all, has to change.

2. Unfortunately, a great many of them are not so much impressed by the academic freedom they may (or may not) enjoy as they are indelibly impressed by the bigotry, intolerance, and xenophobia that are to be found on every American campus. Reading the biographies of any number of anti-American tyrants, one is impressed by how embittered they were at Harvard or Yale or Chicago.

3. This is not to deny the effect of Vietnam and the draft, of course, nor the trauma and sense of betrayal following Kennedy's assassination in 1963, but accounts of the sixties' rebellion that look only to the larger political picture and ignore the specific protests at the university are displacing much of the blame that ought to fall on the universities themselves. For an excellent insider's analysis of the course of events, see John Searle's account of administrative stupidity at Berkeley, *The Campus War* (1965).

4. Peter Flawn, in his *President's Manual,* cynically suggests that "a heavy course load will keep them from protesting."

5. Courtney Leatherman, "Definition of faculty scholarship must be expanded to include teaching, Carnegie Foundation says," *CHE* 37 (Dec. 5, 1990): A1, A16; and Michele N.-K. Collison, "Big universities seek smaller classes, more contact with professors," *CHE* 37 (Jan. 9, 1991): A39.

6. Jason Eaton, "Learning is students' job, officials say," *Arizona Daily Wildcat* 84 (Dec. 5, 1990): 1, 7.

7. Allan Bloom, *The Closing of the American Mind* (New York: Simon and Schuster, 1987).

8. John Searle, *The Campus War* (New York: World, 1965).

9. "[T]hose third rate colleges and 'universities,' where you can expire trying to find someone who's read anything but a best-seller, who has an iota of historical imagination, or who manifests curiosity about anything but money, sports, 'entertainment' or hobbies." *BAD: Or, The Dumbing of America,* by Paul Fussell (New York: Summit, 1991).

PART II: "The Marketplace of Ideas"

1. The S/T ratio is, however, a very tricky number. There are many ways of fudging the calculation. But although a low S/T ratio is good for public relations—an indication of "quality"—a high S/T ratio indicates efficiency in production. At the University of Texas, extra teaching credits as well as grading assistance and discussion leaders are given to teachers who have larger classes. An assistant professor who teaches thirty students does his or her own grading, teaches an hour more a week per class, and will have to teach an extra class as well because of the deficiency in credits. Meanwhile, the administration explains and defends its dubiously derived S/T ratio of 20 and proclaims its intention of making it lower. As is so often the test, do we believe the intention or the policy?

2. See, for example, Tom Peters, *Thriving On Chaos* (New York: Harper & Row, 1988).

3. For example, see Edward Teller, *New York Times Book Review* (Feb. 23, 1992).

4. Banesh Hoffman, *The Tyranny of Testing* (Westport, Conn.: Greenwood, 1962).

5. In various polls, approximately three quarters of those interviewed in Texas declared that they did think that the university made a positive contribution to the economy of the community and the lives of the students. On the other hand, more than one state has gone through the awkward battle between the university and the prison system, with local populations predictably preferring to build a new prison. (For example, Kansas and Montana.)

PART III: The University as a Community

1. In one of the most thoughtless feature essays it has ever published, *Lingua Franca* ran on for pages denouncing the campus high-rise, its alienation, and in many cases, catapulting crime rate. True, perhaps, as in any urban community. But what else does one do, say, at a school like UCLA, where the surrounding neighborhoods of Belair and Westwood have some of the highest property values in the nation and students would otherwise commute from twenty to thirty miles away?

2. Barbara Ehrenreich compares faculty disdain with corporate loyalty. See her *Fear of Falling*. (New York: Pantheon, 1989).

3. "Why are the problems of business ethics insoluble?," in *Proceedings of the First National Conference on Business Ethics* (1977), 99.

4. One person seems primarily responsible for this shift in publishing—Steven Cahn, who has published *Saints and Scamps*, the collection *Morality, Responsibility and the University*, and is preparing a forthcoming series of books on specific topics and problems for Rowman & Littlefield.

5. We are thinking, of course, of muckraking books like *Profscam*, by Charles Sykes, but also more ideologically loaded criticism such as Russell Jacoby's *The Last Intellectual* and Roger Kimball's *Tenured Radicals*, both of which make good points against the current culture in academia regardless of whether you share their "left-" or "right-wing" perspectives (respectively).

6. For example, Michael Lewis, *Liar's Poker* (New York: Norton, 1989); Bryan Barraglia, *Barbarians at the Gate* (New York: Harper & Row, 1990); James B. Stewart, *Den of Thieves* (New York: Simon and Schuster, 1991).

7. Robert J. Samuelson, in *Newsweek*, rightly points out the disastrous effects of high-level "sleaze" on the undergraduates and the reputation of the university in his "Sleaze knows no class," *Newsweek*, (Apr. 1, 1991). He speaks of "a loose morality found all too often among the elite. That attitude is that 'what we do must be right because of who we are'" (45).

8. In contemporary ethics, there has been more than a little nostalgia for the age of feudalism, when everyone knew his or her place, when there was,

supposedly, a general consensus about values and goals. See, for example, Alasdair MacIntyre, *After Virtue* (Notre Dame, Ind.: University of Notre Dame Press, 1981).

9. Thanks to Professor Tony Coady at the University of Melbourne.

10. The "social responsibility" argument reminds us of a curious argument that greeted the call for "corporate social responsibility" back in the sixties and seventies, when Milton Friedman, at his most excessive, retorted that "the [only] social responsibility of business is to increase its profits." Friedman seems to think—or at least sometimes he writes as if—the only legitimate mission of the publicly held corporation is to make money for the stockholders.

PART V: Students in the Open University

1. This chapter adapted from Robert Solomon, *Entertaining Ideas: Popular Philosophical Essays, 1970–1990* (Buffalo: Prometheus Books, 1992).

2. This chapter adapted from *Entertaining Ideas*.

3. For a good, sensitive discussion of the fate of *in loco parentis* and the responsibility of students, see David Hoekema's "Beyond in Loco Parentis?" In *Morality, Responsibility and the University*, edited by S. Cahn (Philadelphia: Temple, 1990).

PART VII: Teach as If Education Counts

1. One of our students had already flunked out of school at the end of his freshman year, a year of dates and parties but very little intellectual effort. He had stayed out of school for another year, but when he saw Oliver Stone's controversial movie, *JFK,* he was moved to actually pick up a book (Jim Garrison's original exposé) and then to start studying the period and the political entanglements. It was not that he was a "conspiracy buff." Nor was he a particular fan of a president who died several years before he was born. But he had been "turned on." And as he read more he became more and more interested, and when he came back to school last year he had already established himself as a potential "A" student. He has given up his once obsessive interest in the Kennedy assassination, but he has cultivated in its place a real love of learning. As the kids of the Kennedy era used to say, "whatever turns you on."

2. For example, *Profscam,* pages 48–50.

PART IX: The Open Classroom

1. One of the best cooperative arrangements in the country—the "five-college" system created by the University of Massachusetts, Amherst, Smith, Mount Holyoke, and Hampshire colleges—allows the students at any one institution to take courses at all of them, providing a range of advanced courses and programs as well as a choice of spectacular teachers in more basic classes. The five schools even provide free transportation between campuses.

2. Robert Paul Wolff, *The Ideal of the University.*

PART X: Teaching Values

1. For example see Peter Markie, "Professors, Students and Friendship." In *Morality, Responsibility and the University,* edited by S. Cahn (Philadelphia: Temple, 1990).

PART XII: Culture(s) and "Correctness"

1. The emphasis on dominance rather than racial hostility itself is essential to understand the current climate of racial tension. Many white students have no hostility toward nonwhite students, but nevertheless the presumption of what Larry Blum calls a "dominance attitude" creates a sense of racial superiority/inferiority. It also explains why it is that racial insults from blacks to whites are not treated as seriously as racial insults from whites to blacks. Racism is always bad, but it is the asymmetry of the races, their very different preexisting positions in terms of power and social advantages, that makes the difference. (Blum, *Teaching Philosophy* [June 1991].)

PART XIII: Professors

1. David Hume's melancholy description of the apparently immediate failure of his *Treatise of Human Nature* (1738), now one of the most widely read books in philosophy.

2. Steven Cahn, *Saints and Scamps,* 3.

PART XIV: The Open University

1. Stanley Milgram at Yale University conducted a famous series of experiments in which students were instructed to give apparently painful shocks

to other students. However shocking and valuable the results of such an experiment, it would certainly not be allowed today. The refusal to permit such experimentation is not a violation of academic freedom. (See Stanley Milgram, *Obedience to Authority* [New York: Harper & Row, 1969].)

2. It is worth reminding ourselves that the one time in recent American history when academic freedom really was put on the line, in the McCarthy era, it blew down like a straw fence. As a legal principle academic freedom has proved to have at most marginal significance.

3. Again, this depends on context. There are classroom discussions in which a student's vulnerability becomes a valuable instrument for self-realization, and there are uncomfortable circumstances in which a student's prejudices can be laid on the line and gotten through. And there are classes, of course, in which the whole point is to confront the student with a difficult or alien set of ideas. A course in Marxism, for example, should be expected to be a course in which Marxism will be presented in as polemical and attractive a light as possible, inviting the students to disagree but making no pretense of neutrality. Indeed, we would argue that courses in such subjects that are not taught in this way—that are, in effect, "Refutations of Marxism 322"—are very likely misleading and antieducational.

4. This is an area often highlighted in discussions of "political correctness"—e.g., in Dinesh d'Souza's recent polemic *Illiberal Education* (New York: Free Press, 1991). Most of the cases in d'Souza's book, in fact, do not stand up to scrutiny, and there are relatively few (though egregious) cases of a merely naive professor being persecuted by offended students. More often than not, it turns out to be a case of mutual misunderstanding turned into a media circus. (See Jon Weiner, *Nation* [Jan. 1992].)

5. The usual argument here on behalf of the students, that the person is a political celebrity who has ample time to express his or her opinions, only underscores this suspicion. Nevertheless, once a speaker is invited, the rules of courtesy and controversy apply, which means that the sponsors of such an event had damn well better allow room for discussion and argument. Otherwise, it has no place on a university campus. Pressing for the "uninviting" of controversial political guests, on the other hand, is no violation of freedom of speech but rather an exercise of it.

PART XVI: "Leave Government to Clerks and Desks"

1. Minutes of the meeting of the faculty senate of the University of Arizona (May 6, 1991), 3.

2. *The Chronicle of Higher Education* 37 (Nov. 21, 1990), A13, reported in

the same issue that the University of Akron's presidential house contained two pools, seven and a half baths, and an elevator and that Trenton State College, despite budget cutbacks, was about to provide a house for each of three vice-presidents!

3. Tini Tran, "System Officials Defend Expenses," *The Daily Texan* (August 2, 1991). For a devastating attack on some of the problems we are pointing out here see representative Pat Schroeder's congressional report on bureaucratic waste in the university, September 1992.

PART XVII: Doing More with Less

1. "We're not all alone in this," *Lo Que Pasa* (Sept. 16, 1991): 1.

2. Derek Bok, outgoing president of Harvard, said in an interview (*CHE* 37 [Nov. 14, 1990]: A20), "We're lacking powerful models of excellence, which forces a lot of institutions to adopt the only model they see, which is the prestigious research university, and therefore try to push their institutions to do things that are not likely to be successful at the expense of other kinds of missions that would be much more valuable."

3. See Ernest L. Boyer, *The Carnegie Report: Scholarship Reconsidered* (Carnegie Foundation, 1990).

Conclusion

1. For two very different examples, see Henry Rosovsky, former dean of Harvard, in his *The University: A User's Manual,* and John Silber, president of Boston University, *Straight Shooting,* Chapter 7.

Selected Bibliography

We have tried to write a book that is as free from academic jargon and scholarly apparatus as possible, resisting the temptation to comment on authors with whom we disagree and avoiding appeals to the authority of other authors with whom we agree. Nevertheless, quite a few books and articles have influenced our opinions, one way or another, and we mention a few of them, as suggestions for further reading, without endorsement or comment.

Albee, Edward. *Who's Afraid of Virginia Woolf?* New York: Atheneum, 1962.

Amis, Kingsley. *Lucky Jim.* Harmondsworth: Penguin, 1954.

Asante, Molefi Kete. *The Afrocentric Idea.* Philadelphia: Temple University Press, 1990.

Auden, W. H. *Academic Graffiti.* New York: Random House, 1971.

Barzun, Jacques. *The American University, How It Runs, Where It Is Going.* New York: Harper & Row, 1968.

———. *House of Intellect.* New York: Harper & Row, 1959.

———. "On Testing." *New York Times,* 11 October 1988.

Berman, Paul. *Debating PC.* New York: Dell, 1992.

Bernal, Martin. *Black Athena.* New Brunswick, N.J.: Rutgers University Press, 1987.

Bloom, Allan. *The Closing of the American Mind.* New York: Simon & Schuster, 1987.

Boyer, Ernest L. *College: The Undergraduate Experience in America.* New York: Harper & Row, 1987.

———. *Scholarship Reconsidered: Priorities of the Professoriat.* Princeton: The Carnegie Foundation, 1990.

Cahn, Stephen. *Saints and Scamps.* Lanham, Md.: Rowman & Littlefield, 1986.

———. *Morality, Responsibility and the University.* Philadelphia: Temple University Press, 1990.

Cheney, Lynne V. *Humanities in America.* Washington, D.C.: National Endowment for the Humanities, 1988.

D'Souza, Dinesh. *Illiberal Education.* New York: Free Press, 1991.

Dugger, Ronnie. *Our Invaded Universities.* New York: Norton, 1974.

Epstein, Leon D. *Governing the University: The Campus and the Public Interest.* San Francisco: Jossey-Fass Publishers, 1974.

Fish, Stanley. *Is There a Text in This Class?* Cambridge, Mass.: Harvard University Press, 1980.

Flawn, Peter T. *A Primer for University Presidents.* Austin: University of Texas Press, 1990.

Galinsky, Karl. *Classical and Modern Interactions.* Austin: University of Texas Press, 1992.

Gardner, John W. *Excellence.* New York: Harper & Row, 1961.

Gates, Henry Louis, Jr., ed. *Race, Writing and Difference.* Chicago: University of Chicago Press, 1986.

Giroux, Henry A. *Schooling and the Struggle for Democracy.* Minneapolis: University of Minnesota Press, 1988.

Harte-Hanks Communications. Texas A&M/University of Texas Faculty Association Poll, 1990.

Hirsch, E. D., Jr. *Cultural Literacy.* Boston: Houghton-Mifflin, 1987.

———. "The Primal Scene of Education." *New York Review of Books,* 2 March 1989.

Hoffman, Banesh. *The Tyranny of Testing.* Westport, Conn.: Greenwood, 1962.

Jacoby, Russell. *The Last Intellectuals: American Culture in the Age of Academe.* New York: Basic Books, 1987.

Kaplowitz, Richard A. *Selecting Academic Administrators.* Washington, D.C.: American Council on Education, 1973.

Kimball, Roger. *Tenured Radicals: How Politics Has Corrupted Our Higher Education.* New York: Harper & Row, 1990.

Lederer, Richard. *Anguished English.* Charleston, S.C.: Wyrick, 1988.

Levine, George, et al. "Speaking for the Humanities." New York: American Council of Learned Societies, 1989. ACLS Occasional Paper No. 7.

Lodge, David. *Changing Places.* Harmondsworth: Penguin, 1978.

———. *Nice Work.* New York: Viking Press, 1989.

———. *Small World.* New York: Warner, 1984.

Lurie, Alison. *The War between the Tates.* New York: Random House, 1974.

Moulton, Janice, and Robinson, George M. *Ethical Problems in Higher Education.* Englewood Cliffs, N.J.: Prentice-Hall, 1985.

Newman, J. Cardinal. *The Idea of a University.* New York: Doubleday, 1959.

Nietzsche, Friedrich. *Beyond Good and Evil.* New York: Random House, 1967.

Nisbet, Robert. *The Degradation of the Academic Dogma.* New York: Basic Books, 1971.

Nussbaum, Martha, "Undemocratic Virtues." *New York Review of Books,* 5 November 1987.

Oakeshott, Michael. *The Voice of Liberal Learning.* New Haven, Conn.: Yale University Press, 1989.

Ogilvy, James. *Three Scenarios for Higher Education.* Washington, D.C.: National Education Association, 1992.

Pincoffs, Edmund. *The Concept of Academic Freedom.* Austin: University of Texas Press, 1975.

Rosovsky, Henry. *The University: An Owner's Manual.* New York: Norton, 1990.

Salman, Stanley. *Duties of Administrators in Higher Education.* New York: Macmillan, 1971.

Searle, John. *The Campus War.* New York: World Publishing Co., 1965.

———. "The Storm over the University." *New York Review of Books,* 6 December 1990.

———. Interview by Bill Moyers. In *The World of Ideas,* edited by Betty Sue Flowers. New York: Doubleday, 1990; Videocassette. Alexandria, Va.: Public Broadcasting System, 1988.

Shattuck, Roger. "How to Rescue Literature." *New York Review of Books,* April 17, 1980.

———. *Perplexing Dreams: Is There a Core Tradition in the Humanities.* Washington, D.C.: American Council of Learned Society, 1987.

———. "Who Needs the Great Works?" in *Harper's,* September 1989.

Silber, John. *Straight Shooting.* New York: Harper & Row, 1989.

Smith, Barbara Herrnstein. *Contingencies of Value.* Cambridge, England: Cambridge University Press, 1988.

Smith, Page. *Killing the Spirit.* New York: Viking Press, 1990.

Sykes, Charles. *Profscam.* New York: St. Martin's Press, 1988.

Wilshire, Bruce. *The Moral Collapse of the University.* Albany: State University of New York Press, 1990.

Wolff, Robert Paul. *The Ideal of the University.* Boston: Beacon Press, 1969.

Index

About the Authors

Robert C. Solomon is the Quincy Lee Centennial Professor at the University of Texas. He has also taught at the University of Michigan; Princeton University; the University of Pittsburgh; C.U.N.Y.; the University of California; the University of Pennsylvania; Mount Holyoke; and Smith College; the University of Auckland, New Zealand; La Trobe University and the University of Melbourne in Australia; and the University of British Columbia and Simon Fraser University in Canada. His main interests are in European philosophy, ethics, and philosophical psychology. He is the author of *From Rationalism to Existentialism: The Passions; History and Human Nature; Love: Emotion, Myth and Metaphor; In the Spirit of Hegel; From Hegel to Existentialism; About Love; A Passion for Justice; Ethics and Excellence;* a dozen textbooks and edited editions; more than a hundred articles in scholarly journals; several songs; and a weekly newspaper column. Among his various awards are the Standard Oil Outstanding Teaching Award and a President's Associates Teaching Award.

Jon Solomon is Associate Professor of Classics at the University of Arizona. He has also taught at the University of Colorado and the University of Minnesota, and has won teaching awards at all three universities. His main interests are ancient Greek music, mythology, and poetry as well as the classical tradition, particularly in opera and film. He is the author of *The Ancient World in the Cinema,* several translations, and numerous technical articles on various aspects of Greco-Roman antiquity, including ancient Roman cookery. He has served in an administrative capacity both as a program director and department head.